WITHDRAWN

THE RUSSIAN MODERATES AND THE
CRISIS OF TSARISM 1914–1917

By the same author
REVOLUTION IN RUSSIA

THE RUSSIAN MODERATES AND THE CRISIS OF TSARISM 1914 – 1917

Raymond Pearson

BARNES & NOBLE BOOKS
10 East 53d St., New York 10022
(a division of Harper & Row Publishers, Inc.)

First published 1977 by
THE MACMILLAN PRESS LTD
London and Basingstoke

ISBN 0–06–495483–8

Published in the U.S.A. 1977 by
HARPER AND ROW PUBLISHERS. INC.
BARNES AND NOBLE IMPORT DIVISION

Printed in Great Britain

For Margaret

We represent His Majesty's Opposition,
not the opposition to His Majesty.

PAUL MILYUKOV
London, 1909

Contents

List of Plates

Preface

First of all I must express my gratitude to the many individuals and institutions who have in their various ways contributed over the years to the emergence of this study. At the personal level, my particular thanks must go to Professor W.V. Wallace, now of the new University of Ulster, who was my research supervisor at the University of Durham, and to Professor E.D. Chermensky of Moscow State University, who advised me during my academic sojourn in the Soviet Union. I am grateful to the University of Durham for financing my postgraduate research; to the Reading Room and Newspaper Section of the British Library; to the library of the School of Slavonic and East European Studies, University of London; to the British Council for making possible my spending the academic year 1966–7 in the Soviet Union; to the Chief Archive Administration of the Soviet Union for granting access to the historical archives of Moscow and Leningrad; to the Central State Archive of the October Revolution and the Lenin Library (particularly its manuscript department and newspaper hall) in Moscow; to the Central State Historical Archive and the Saltykov-Shchedrin Library in Leningrad; to the new University of Ulster for granting the study leave and the extra funds to spend two months in Helsinki in 1973; and to that most civilised of havens of research, Helsinki University Library. I must also acknowledge a less tangible debt to my immediate circumstances since 1968: added insight into the stresses of the moderate position in a polarised political context has been fostered by residence in Northern Ireland for the entire period of the most recent 'troubles'.

Unless specifically indicated, all dates cited are Old Style, that is to say thirteen days behind the European calendar. Russian proper names are rendered in the form most comprehensible to readers in English rather than by the strict application of a conventional transliteration system. To smooth the reader's progress, leading personalities are identified by their first names and minor individuals only by initials: thus at first acquaintance it is clear that Paul Milyukov will figure more prominently than P.A. Buryshkin. The Tsar and Tsaritsa are referred to familiarly as Nicholas and Alexandra, partly in deference to popular usage, partly to differentiate them conveniently from other leading personages.

Two final and indispensable points: the customary *caveat* that the academic shortcomings of this study are exclusively my own responsibility; and my formal but none the less genuine thanks to my wife Margaret, who deserves more than conventional acknowledgement for her moral support throughout my protracted research.

January 1977   R.P.

1 Introduction

On 5 March 1917 the newspapers of the capital of the Russian Empire published their first issues for seven days. So news-hungry was the population of Petrograd after this unprecedented period of silence that a profitable lottery was held for the first copy off the presses. The eager reading public was not disappointed in the first editions: the headline news featured the abdication of the Tsar Nicholas II, the renunciation of the crown by his brother Grand Duke Michael and the announcement that Russia now had a 'Provisional Government'. The official statement on the creation and identity of the new government was terse to the point of being uninformative:[1]

> The Provisional Committee of members of the Duma, with the help and support of the army and inhabitants of the capital, has now secured such a large measure of success over the dark forces of the old regime that it is possible for the Committee to undertake the organisation of a more stable executive power.
>
> With this aim in mind, the Provisional Committee of the State Duma has appointed the following persons as ministers of the first cabinet representing the public; their past political and public activities assure them the confidence of the country:

Minister-President and Minister of Interior	Prince G.E. Lvov
Minister of Foreign Affairs	P.N. Milyukov
Minister of Justice	A.F. Kerensky
Minister of Transport	N.V. Nekrasov
Minister of Trade and Industry	A.I. Konovalov
Minister of Education	A.A. Manuilov
Minister of War and Navy	A.I. Guchkov
Minister of Agriculture	A.I. Shingarev
Minister of Finance	M.I. Tereshchenko
State Controller	I.V. Godnev
Procurator of the Holy Synod	V.N. Lvov
Minister for Finland	F.I. Rodichev

Confronted by such momentous news, the questions taxing the bemused Russian public in early March 1917 are not difficult to guess. Notwithstanding the *dramatis personae* of a ministerial list, who were the nation's new masters? It was explicit that the initiative in the creation of the new government had been taken by members of the State Duma, the Russian parliament granted by the Tsar by the October Manifesto of 1905, which had eked out an increasingly precarious constitutional existence over the intervening years. Eight of the twelve ministers were deputies to the current Duma, the Fourth Duma elected in 1912, and two of the remainder were ex-deputies from earlier convocations.[2] Moreover, all the ministers bar one – the volatile Alexander Kerensky – were affiliated to what were commonly termed 'moderate' parties. Despite the official claim that their 'past political and public activities assure them the confidence of the country', few ministers were widely recognised even by name. The exceptions were led, appropriately, by the head of the government Prince George Lvov, who was celebrated for organising society support for the Russian war efforts both in 1904 and 1914. Alexander Konovalov was known as a textile millionaire and captain of industry, and therefore attached to the Progressist party, which was largely (though not exclusively) the mouthpiece of Russian industrial and commercial capital. The most charismatic personality was Alexander Guchkov, leader of the numerically landowner-dominated and conservative Union of 17 October (or Octobrists), who currently also managed to combine the presidencies of the Russian Red Cross and War Industries Committees. A fervent but temperamental monarchist, Guchkov has invited comparisons with Winston Churchill (whom incidentally he encountered while fighting against the British in the Boer War). But dominating the cabinet was Paul Milyukov, the leader of the political embodiment of the liberal professions, the Constitutional Democratic Party (always referred to as Kadet from the Russian pronunciation of its initials). Playing the Russian Woodrow Wilson to Guchkov's Teddy Roosevelt, Milyukov was an academic turned politician who had acquired unrivalled parliamentary expertise and prestige over the previous ten years to bring his party to the forefront of the Provisional Government.

Of the majority of ministers, little or nothing was known. Even of those readily recognised, such information as could be casually acquired on the streets of Petrograd and Moscow could not satisfy the curiosity of the nation. What was the record of the parliamentary moderates and of the Duma itself over the years previous to their assumption of power? What was the political and ideological platform from which the new ministers had stepped into government? Most importantly, what were the chances of the Provisional Government performing any better in the wartime crisis in which Russia found herself in 1917 than the tsarist regime which it had replaced?

The questions which were so pertinent in early 1917 have proved only a little easier to answer with the passing of time. The historiographical and bibliographical barriers confronting the historian of the Russian moderates have proved a formidable challenge. Throughout the decades since the October Revolution, the Soviet government has been consistently sensitive about the morality of its power, its ideological right to rule. One result has been the close supervision of the historical discipline, descending in the Stalinist period to an insistence on a strict party line which left no scope for alternative or individual interpretations. Clio was conscripted into the Communist Party of the Soviet Union to testify to its infallibility. Soviet history, descending on occasions to the level of state propaganda, became diffident about admitting, let alone publicising, any alternative to tsarism other than Bolshevism. With the natural repository of Russian historical evidence jealously guarded by an establishment ideologically and politically antagonistic to the moderates and the constitutional alternative they represented, Western historians of Russia encountered an historiographical Iron Curtain as impenetrable as its better-known political counterpart.

More mundane historical problems have been taxing enough. The national position of the various moderate parties which had emerged in the aftermath of the 1905 Revolution was always vulnerable, for only parties whose programmes were in strict accord with the Fundamental Laws of the Russian Empire were granted full legal status. The Kadets, on the left wing of the moderate camp, were always accused by the government of flirting with socialism (if not revolution) and never received any recognisable legal acceptance. After the election of the Fourth Duma in 1912, with the government shifting confidently to the Right and the country drifting steadily towards the Left, the moderate parties adopted a more militant stance which encouraged the government to bracket the Kadets, Progressists and some Octobrists indiscriminately together as the 'Opposition'. The application of the newly-formed Progressist Party for legal status in 1912 was promptly refused. Even the Octobrists, representing a movement pledged to the reconciliation of tsarism and society, which had attempted real collaboration with the government over the Third Duma from 1907 to 1912, fell under suspicion and were denied permission to hold a party congress in 1913. As a result of the government drawing the line between legality and illegality further and further towards the Right of the party spectrum, confidentiality to the point of conspiratorial secrecy was deliberately promoted by the moderates to lend a measure of security against official harassment or persecution. Though the moderates never had recourse to the precautions practised by the revolutionaries – like invisible writing, cabbalistic codes and Byzantine security procedures – the Kadets especially consciously kept party documentation to a minimum. The moderates' policy of security for survival has inevitably meant a shortage of primary evidence for the historian.

Inside the State Duma, elected deputies enjoyed a fair measure of privilege, with the result that the parliamentary groupings which they formed (termed 'fractions') acquired a respectability and practical security impossible elsewhere. Unfortunately the relative safety of the Tauride Palace, where the Duma had its permanent location, was only occasionally reflected in proceedings very informative to the historian. Open debates were usually employed for speechifying to the public gallery or for the parade of entrenched positions, and even the more valuable committee discussions only offer intermittent and incomplete glimpses of the workings of the Russian parliament. The official records of the Duma, which were in any case subject to discreet censorship by its President, are rarely revealing about the party and lobby politics at the heart of parliamentary life.[3] .But as the only scholarly alternative to sweeping general surveys, even rather circumscribed studies of the public operations of the Duma have been welcomed as making valuable advances on a necessarily narrow front. Nevertheless, most recently, the limited horizons of the view from the Tauride Palace have increasingly offended historians to whom a more panoramic Russian perspective seems essential to a genuine updating of our understanding of the last years of tsarism.

A final more insidious barrier to an appreciation of the Russian moderates is what may be termed 'Kadet history'. From shortly after the turn of the century, the Kadets went to great lengths to cultivate contacts with the West, attracting the attention and very often the support of foreign statesmen and scholars. With the February Revolution of 1917, Kadet relations with constitutional Europe and America became intimate. After the October Revolution, the extensive emigration of Kadet leaders to the West made readily available a substantial corpus of personal testimony. The high educational and cultural level of the party soon expressed itself in a steady flow of memoirs, apologias and even polemics through the declining years of the Kadet leaders. The voluminous publications of Milyukov and his running battle with his leading party critic Vasilii Maklakov over policy in the Dumas were just the highlights of the literary activities of Kadet members with the time to ponder their past mistakes. Whether condemned for precipitating the revolution or commiserated with over the failure of Russian constitutionalism, the Kadets have always claimed and been accorded the limelight.[4]

The Octobrists and Progressists made little effort to contradict or even qualify the growing Kadet legend. Despite their importance over the pre-revolutionary era, the Octobrist leaders were embarrassed by their close association with the now-defunct tsarist regime into uncharacteristic reticence: Michael Rodzyanko published a series of largely repetitive apologias for his performance as President of the Fourth Duma but rarely mentioned the party political element; Guchkov retired into self-imposed retreat from which he released only occasional guarded statements. The same was true of the Progressists: neither Ivan Efremov nor Konovalov wrote anything resembling complete memoirs; and the industrial cliques which had supported the Progressist party, notably that led by Paul Ryabushinsky, apparently rested content that their patronage be forgotten. L. Menashe has rightly remarked that 'the role of business groups in the united front of liberal opposition is generally overlooked in Western analysis for perhaps the simplest of historiographical reasons ... one is tempted to conclude that if Guchkov and Konovalov had written as much as Miliukov and Maklakov, our whole understanding of Russian liberalism might be entirely different.'[5] By default alone, Kadet literature swamped primary material published on the last years of tsarist Russia in the West.

While the dearth of rival testimony served to cast the Kadet party alone in the role of democratic martyr of the Russian Revolution, the Kadets themselves made conscious efforts to produce a corpus of Kadet history. The American historian W.G. Rosenberg has recently, with admirable restraint, drawn attention to the 'tendentious quality' of Kadet writing and its proclivity 'to mislead through omission'.[6] It is even possible to draw comparisons between Kadet history and the better-known historical revisionism of the Bolsheviks. In opposition, both parties hoped and believed that History was on their side: the Bolshevik creed of Marx's inevitable revolution was matched by the Kadet's almost Whig trust in the irresistible progress of international parliamentarism. In their fleeting tenure of power after March 1917, the Kadets (like the Bolsheviks a little later) resorted to the dubious technique of perverting history into party propaganda. The party which had acquired its preponderance among the moderates over the last years of tsarism (arguably at the cost of many of its liberal principles) had a close interest in imposing its own brand of retrospective history on a period which was in many ways politically embarrassing. Chronologically, the Kadet record was made to jump from 1906 to 1917 to emphasise the continuity of revolutionary commitment, grossly neglecting the complaisant intervening years. In final defeat after October 1917, the Kadets continued to impose their own loaded interpretation retrospectively on the history of the Duma and Provisional Government. The principal features are only too familiar to readers of Kadet memoirs. With the inevitability of Kadet leadership of the moderates never questioned, political rivals are reduced to mendacious caricatures or (most commonly) undermined and trivialised by calculated omission. In this respect it is arguable that Kadet historiographical treatment of the Octobrists and Progressists is quite as unhistorical as Bolshevik treatment of the Mensheviks and Social Revolutionaries. Kadet virtues of idealism, selflessness and almost other-wordliness are consistently stressed, while Kadet vices – like obsessive care for their own skins and cynical political expertise – receive no mention. Blessed with total recall about events to Kadet credit, the memoirs are plagued by absent-mindedness and amnesia when less edifying episodes are concerned. It was no accident that the Kadet leader was an eminent historian. If Soviet history has approximated to the 'propaganda of the victors', in the West the history of the revolutionary period has proved the 'propaganda of the vanquished'. Forcibly prevented from determining the future of Russia, Milyukov and his fellow Kadets made a determined bid for its past.[7]

At the heart of the difficulty of penetrating revisionist history is the availability of alternative evidence. With the bulk of such alternative primary testimony in the archives and repositories of the Soviet Union, a satisfactory response to the challenge was only possible by courtesy of the Soviet historical establishment. Since the critical year 1956, as part of the political process usually dubbed 'de-Stalinisation', historical enquiry has been actively promoted and the facilities and outlets for research extended. Historical areas hitherto regarded as too sensitive for examination have been thrown open (although many remain). By the 1960s a more open, less dogmatic attitude towards the discussion of the tsarist and early revolutionary eras had evolved. Soviet historians like Chermensky, Dyakin, Laverychev and Burdzhalov have published re-evaluations of the late tsarist period based on thorough investigations of archival holdings.[8] The academic Iron Curtain has been raised to the point that foreign researchers have been permitted unprecedented (though still far from free) access to materials in Soviet historical archives. The present study of the Russian moderates and the crisis of tsarism from 1914 to 1917 has only been made possible by the Soviet Chief Archive Administration (*Glavnoe Arkhivnoe Upravlenie* or GAU) granting me permission to spend six months researching in the Central State Archive of the October Revolution (*Tsentralnii Gosudarstvennii Arkhiv Oktyabrskoi Revolyutsii* or TsGAOR) and the Lenin Library in Moscow, and the Central State Historical Archive (*Tsentralnii Gosudarstvennii Istoricheskii Arkhiv* or TsGIA) in Leningrad.

Amongst the varied historical 'funds' to which I was permitted access, ranging from the valuable papers of party leaders like Milyukov and Guchkov to the records of official institutions, three categories stood out by their historical significance and novelty.[9] The first was the complete run of communications between the tsarist cabinet and the Duma for the wartime period July 1914 to 26 February 1917. This collection from the 'Chancellery of the Council of Ministers for the Affairs of the State Duma', incorporating a variety of material previously unknown or unpublished, amounts to an unrivalled documentation of official and informal government – Duma relations for the thirty months before the February Revolution.[10]

The second category comprised the holdings of the three moderate parties. While providing valuable detail on the working operations of the moderates, the party documents made available to me proved less enlightening than might have been expected. Octobrist records were most ordered and businesslike but almost petered out after the party crisis of late 1913 and therefore reveal little of the Octobrists in wartime. Kadet records were most irregular and evasive, with only the most formal occasions completely minuted and all other meetings, even important party conferences, either indifferently recorded or passing without written record. Little Progressist material was available, the TsGAOR staff assuring me that the paucity of its holdings did not even justify establishing a separate fund for the Progressist Party. The explanation for this shortage of party documentation is impossible to judge with any certainty. Possibilities include the deliberate security policy of the moderates (as discussed above), GAU reluctance to disgorge all (and particularly its most significant) material, and the success of individual politicians in destroying their papers or removing them abroad. None the less, much material which was forthcoming was valuable: the most spectacular example was the complete minutes of the 'missing' Sixth Kadet Congress of February 1916, the only party congress held from 1907 until after the Revolution in 1917.

Where party documentation was disappointing overall, the deficiency was amply compensated for by the meticulous files of the tsarist political police, the Okhrana (literally 'protection'), which provide a chronologically complete account of the moderates, frequently at variance with that offered in published memoirs. Although it is well outside the scope of this study to defend the reputation of the tsarist 'secret' police, the Okhrana has suffered such a bad press that some justification for the historical employment of its records seems called for. The legend of Okhrana incompetence has been extraordinarily slow to die, with the memoirs of revolutionaries, often uncritically repeated by standard works on Russian history, perpetuating the myth of an unsavoury organisation whose only practical achievement was to raise the morale of the revolutionary movement by providing living proof of tsarist fallibility. With the archives of the foreign Paris-based section of the Okhrana transferred to America after the Revolution, the evidence is available to demonstrate that the performance of the Okhrana outside its native Russian environment was surprisingly high, with the effectiveness of its operations inducing the neurotic émigré communities grossly to overestimate the scope and resources of the *zagranichnaya agentura*.[11]

Even so, the Okhrana's performance in alien western Europe should not be taken as typical of its record within the borders of the Russian Empire. A large number of historians have fallen into the trap of assuming that because tsarism indisputably fell, then the tsarist political police must have been incompetent.[12] This conclusion is far from proven. With its officials legally entitled to attend all party and public gatherings, its undercover agents infiltrated into most parties, the backing of a nationwide organisation and the ample funds of the Ministry of Interior, the Okhrana experienced little difficulty in accurately monitoring Russian social and political life. Okhrana infiltration of the Russian revolutionary movement was outstandingly successful; one need mention only Azev among the Social Revolutionaries and Malinovsky among the Bolsheviks. More sophisticated techniques were steadily added to the Okhrana's nefarious repertoire, including regular mail interception and perlustration by means of 'black cabinets' in the major cities in the 1900s, the installation of a photographic laboratory in 1909, and the introduction of phone-tapping in the 1910s. Individuals of considerable if perverse talents were regularly recruited into the Okhrana, often expanding its sphere of operations into entirely new areas. Examples would include the professional cryptographer Zybin, the ingenious Zubatov (inventor of 'police socialism') and the machiavellian Rachkovsky (whose 'dirty tricks department' had its most far-reaching success in the sponsorship of the anti-semitic Protocols of the Elders of Zion).[13]

So far as it is possible to make comparisons with other contemporary police organisations, the record of the Okhrana as a political intelligence agency seems more than creditable. In a passing remark, Alexander Solzhenitsyn recently marvelled at the tiny labour-force of the Okhrana compared with its Soviet successors, and it is difficult not to conclude that the Okhrana did remarkably well for its size and budget.[14] In no area is this more striking than its coverage of the Russian moderates. Agents covering the revolutionary and labour movements, always tempted to cry wolf and maintain a note of emergency to justify their continued employment (and remuneration), have with some point been accused of sensationalism. The Social Revolutionary leader V.M. Chernov was quite justified in finding many of the Okhrana reports on the revolutionaries published after March 1917 'extremely one-sided'.[15] By contrast, the Okhrana agents covering the moderates appear to have been highly-organised, well-educated (the better to understand their intellectual quarries) and consistently shrewd. With the confidentiality of their identities guaranteed and their opinions free from the constraints of future publication, the Okhrana agents attending the moderates produced a corpus of evidence and comment admirably suitable as an alternative source. It may well be, at least on the evidence of its treatment of the moderates, that a re-evaluation if not a rehabilitation of the Okhrana is long overdue.

The newly-available archival material has at last made it feasible both to surmount the natural historical obstacles and to penetrate the revisionist smokescreens put up by the Bolsheviks and the Kadets. Integrated with the existing body of historical evidence, the new material makes practical an attempt at a methodologically balanced and historically three-dimensional treatment of the Russian moderates during what was to emerge as the apprenticeship for their assumption of power as the Provisional Government in March 1917.

2 Union Sacrée

In physical and even psychological terms, the Russia which entered the Great War in July 1914 had substantially recovered from the turmoil which marked the turn of the century. The Russian economic record since the ruinous war of 1904–5 against the Japanese had been remarkable, particularly in the years immediately preceding 1914. Thanks in large part to the conscientious if unenterprising stewardship of the Minister of Finance (and premier from September 1911 to January 1914) V.N. Kokovtsov, the material damage to the economy had been repaired and state finances put on a healthy footing. Foreign and, most significantly, domestic investment was soaring and by 1914 the annual growth rate of the Russian economy had reached 14 per cent (if admittedly from a low economic base). Though the humiliation of the Japanese War could not be expunged, its salutary effect was to force ahead much-needed and long-delayed military reform. From 1908 a campaign of overhaul and expansion was launched, culminating in June 1914 in the four-year 'Great Programme' designed to bring Russia's military capability into line with her international reputation as a Great Power. The morale of the Russian nation had risen to new heights. Shame at Russia's performance against Japan and later indignation at the 'diplomatic Tsushima' of the Bosnian crisis of 1908–9 injected a fresh nationalistic element into public life. Comforted by thoughts of the Triple Entente with Great Britain and France but excited by the continuing Balkan Wars after 1912, Russia reached a peak of chauvinistic ebullience and elemental pan-Slavism which found their natural outlet and release on the outbreak of war.

Tsarism too had regained its composure after the trauma of the 1905 Revolution. The principal architect of recovery was P.A. Stolypin, the last tsarist minister of outstanding stature, whose premiership from July 1906 until September 1911 was conspicuous for its constructive response to the lessons of 1905. An unswerving devotion to the reintroduction of law and order was summed up in his much-quoted dictum 'first pacification and then, and only then, reforms'. A major programme of fundamental agrarian reconstruction was undertaken to remedy the past state neglect of the agricultural sector and permanently to 'de-revolutionise' the Russian peasantry. Stolypin's readiness to accept the political changes of 1905 without rancour was reflected in his allegiance to the constitutional system of legislation introduced by the new Fundamental Laws of 1906. However, as memories of 1905 faded and court circles were increasingly tempted to revert to traditional autocracy, Stolypin found his moderate pragmatic course almost impossible to sustain. The Tsar Nicholas II had always disliked the institution of the Council of Ministers forced upon him in late 1905, by which the Council Chairman enjoyed the monopoly of liaison between the ministers and the Sovereign. During Stolypin's term of office, Nicholas increasingly resented the system which effectively converted the premier into a 'Grand Vizier' figure, overshadowing the Tsar and isolating him from his ministers. Nicholas became convinced not only of the unsuitability of Stolypin personally but the desirability of returning to the pre-1905 institution of a Committee of Ministers who were collectively and individually responsible to the Tsar.

The sensational assassination of Stolypin in 1911 fortuitously offered Nicholas the opportunity to intervene more authoritatively in government. Stolypin had performed the functions of Council Chairman and Minister of Interior (as well as keeping a very close eye on the Ministries of Agriculture and Foreign Affairs). On his death, Nicholas distributed the ministries among various individuals, notably the Chairmanship to Kokovtsov and the Ministry of Interior (*Ministerstvo Vnutrennikh Del* or MVD) to A.A. Makarov. In January 1914, Nicholas took the process of dismantling the 'superministership' a stage further: the recent convention of combining the office of Chairman of the Council of Ministers with a ministerial portfolio was abandoned. In his rescript of dismissal to Kokovtsov, Nicholas emphasised that 'the experience of the last eight years has thoroughly convinced me that the union in one person of the posts of Chairman of the Council of Ministers and Minister of Finance, or Minister of Interior, is incorrect and inappropriate in a country like Russia.' Nicholas now deliberately recruited a complete outsider into the premiership, the almost anachronistic reactionary Ivan Goremykin, so that he could not combine the office of Chairman with any existing ministerial portfolio. By what Nicholas himself contentedly called his 'coup d'etat of January 1914', Goremykin was introduced as the unpretentious figurehead of a cabinet in which individuals were so balanced as to preclude the emergence of any single minister to encroach upon the authority and prestige of the Tsar.[1]

Perversely, Nicholas's scheme to forestall the rise of another superminister was frustrated by his over-estimation of the authority of the Chairmanship and under-estimation of the power of the Ministry of Interior. By severing all links between the Chairmanship and ministerial reinforcement, Nicholas so drastically pruned the effective authority of the office as to sponsor inter-ministerial intrigue within the government and, most significantly, remove another obstacle to the ambitions of the Ministry of Interior. In the six months preceding the outbreak of war, the Tsar's campaign to retrieve and redistribute delegated powers had the effect of throwing the highest echelons of government into a state of disarray and flux in which the official Chairman Goremykin was being overtaken as pacesetter of policy by the unscrupulous Minister of Interior (and brother of the leading Kadet), Nikolai Maklakov.

After Germany formally declared war on Russia on 19 July 1914, the first rational thought to surface from the patriotic euphoria of Russian society was concern for the State Duma. With no war during the eight years of the Duma's existence, the present hostilities raised for the first time the question of the Duma in wartime. The moderates were afraid that the government would decide that the Duma had no role at all. Ever since the October Manifesto of 1905, the government had contrived ways to cut back the concessions which the Tsar considered had been granted under duress. By new electoral laws announced on 3 June 1907, the government had concocted an electoral system which favoured the political Right and penalised the Left, thereby fabricating an unrepresentative if amenable Third Duma. With the election of the universally unsatisfactory Fourth Duma in 1912, official circles began to discuss the possibility of either abolishing the Duma altogether and setting the constitutional clock back to the pre-1905 autocracy or, less provocatively, depriving the Duma of its legislative functions. On two separate occasions, in October 1913 and June 1914, with the blessing of the Tsar, Maklakov introduced into the Council of Ministers the subject of the reduction of the Duma from legislative to consultative status. Over the course of early 1914, Maklakov had launched a sustained campaign against the privileges of the Duma, ranging from attacks on parliamentary freedom of expression through assaults on deputies' personal immunity to the undermining of the Duma's right to initiate legislation.[2] With the fear growing that the government would consider war too good a chance to miss to abolish or emasculate the Duma, leaders of the whole party spectrum were unanimous in demanding at very least the retention of the Duma. The influential Nationalist P.N. Balashev suggested to Goremykin on the eve of war that 'it would be useful from all points of view to call the State Duma, if only for a single day, to underline the complete solidarity of all levels of the populace at this moment of crisis, and their preparedness to serve the Throne and the country with all their strength.' The Council of Ministers readily agreed on the propaganda value of a Duma sitting. The cabinet recommendation was fully approved by the Tsar, who welcomed the opportunity 'to be at one with my people' through a one-day 'historic sitting' of the Duma announced for 26 July.[3]

The granting of this extraordinary sitting did not of course resolve the issue of the rights of the Duma in wartime. Following the line that recourse to formal constitutional revolution would be unnecessary if the wartime emergency provided the pretext for the Duma's effective loss of legislative status, Maklakov informed Rodzyanko that the Duma was unlikely to be recalled until November 1915. Far from protesting, Rodzyanko argued that 'we shall only hinder you, therefore it is better to dismiss us altogether until the end of hostilities.' The other Duma leaders were outraged that Rodzyanko should so forget his responsibilities as Duma President as to welcome and encourage Maklakov's design. The notion to shelve the Duma for sixteen months was not only an insult to the national assembly but, in that the Duma had to be convened to pass the State Budget, a direct violation of the Fundamental Laws. Though unwilling to be too critical, the Duma *senioren konvent* (comprising the leaders of the major fractions) regretted government obtuseness in rejecting close identification of the state and the nation at a time of national crisis and sent a collective rebuke to Goremykin, who characteristically declined to answer. Refusing to accept this official snub, the *konvent* resorted to more indirect petition. Following the official Kadet account, 'with surprising unanimity the deputies condemned the decision of the government as unrepresentative of the mood of the Duma and country and a deputation of seven visited Krivoshein.'[4] At first sight this would seem an odd choice, for the Minister of Agriculture could not be expected to reverse or even influence the decisions of his cabinet head. In practice, the action proved judicious. Alexander Krivoshein, a political disciple of Stolypin, had for some time been the most sympathetic minister to the Duma and in a well-publicised speech in July 1913 had dedicated himself to the reconciliation of what he called 'Us and Them', tsarist government and Russian society. Just as important as his moderate opinions was the fact that Krivoshein was currently the 'coming man' in the government, high in the favour of the Tsar and Tsaritsa, and challenging the reactionary primacy of Maklakov. It is a measure of the confusion of ministerial authority caused by the Tsar that the cabinet in July 1914 could encompass two pacemakers of such divergent political views, neither of whom was the premier.[5]

With the outbreak of war, Krivoshein grew in ministerial stature to the point that his apologists have termed the full calendar year afterwards his 'effective premiership'. Krivoshein argued in the Council of Ministers that a Duma convocation earlier than November 1915 was necessary to preserve the present salutary atmosphere of cooperation and goodwill. Under strong pressure from Krivoshein, Goremykin reported to the Tsar that 'there has grown up a unanimous wish to approximate to the customary duration of Duma session following the current recess in its activities; the most prominent representatives of all political persuasions in the Duma say the same.'[6] At a cabinet meeting on 25 July a compromise was reached between the reactionary wing (led by Maklakov), who disapproved of any Duma session in wartime beyond the strictly ceremonial, and the moderate wing (led by Krivoshein and the Foreign Minister S.D. Sazonov), who envisaged a Duma wartime role resembling that of peacetime. As reported by the Kadets, 'the result of these negotiations was that the time question was resolved – not as favourably as the date pressed for by the deputation, i.e. 15 October 1914 – but all the same much earlier than originally envisaged by the government. The new date: "not later than 1 February 1915".' The concession naturally carried a government escape clause: the new date was set 'always permitting, if circumstances make it inevitable, a postponement to a later date'. By the compromise of 25 July, ratified by Nicholas the next day, the Duma occupied a median position between full peacetime rights and the excessively cramped function preached by the reactionary wing of the cabinet. The constitutional issue was far from settled and future political advantage rested squarely with the government.[7]

Krivoshein was only able to intercede for the Duma with any success because of the patriotic sentiments expressed by the great majority of its membership. The Fourth Duma, elected in autumn 1912 for a maximum duration of five years, was a multi-party assembly with a political spectrum of ten parliamentary fractions by July 1914 *(see diagram)*. The parliamentary representation of the Left, moderates and Right (or to employ Russian colour conventions, the Red, the Yellow and the Black) was not of course an accurate reflection of the political complexion of the Empire as a whole. The reapplication of the electoral laws of June 1907 had ensured that the representation of the extreme left and socialist parties in the Duma was unnaturally low: six Bolsheviks, seven Mensheviks and ten Trudoviks (or Social Revolutionaries) added up to a total of twenty-three deputies, a paltry 6 per cent of the Duma complement of 442. The suspect patriotism of the Duma Left therefore meant little to the government except as possible nuisance value. The representation of the political Right, favoured by the electoral laws, was artificially inflated: the 64 Rights, 88 Nationalists and 33 'Centre' deputies added up to 185, or over 40 per cent of the Duma total. Though tantalisingly short of an absolute majority, the uncritical patriotism and unqualified support for the Tsar voiced by the Duma Right disposed the government to look indulgently on the Duma. But the deciding factor could only be the attitude of the moderates in the centre, grouped in the Kadet, Octobrist and Progressist fractions. The crucial importance of the moderates in the Duma lay not only in their considerable combined strength – some two hundred deputies – but in the pivotal position

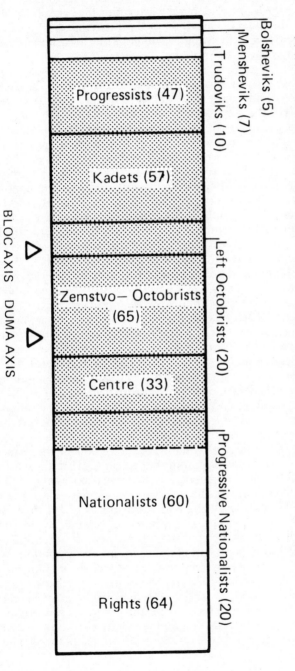

PARTY SPECTRUM OF THE FOURTH DUMA, JULY 1914 TO FEBRUARY 1917

Bolsheviks (5)

Mensheviks (7)

Trudoviks (10)

Progressists (47)

Kadets (57)

Left Octobrists (20)

Zemstvo— Octobrists (65)

Centre (33)

Progressive Nationalists (20)

Nationalists (60)

Rights (64)

BLOC AXIS   DUMA AXIS

which lent them the power to tilt the parliamentary balance either to the Left or the Right, and thereby determine the overall character and policy of the Duma. The views of the moderates in July 1914 were consequently vital to the government's decision about the whole future of the national assembly.[8]

In response, all agents of moderate opinion in Russia pleaded for unqualified support for the national cause. Within the Duma, the *senioren konvent* met daily until 26 July to discuss its patriotic duty and enthuse over the *détente* which had emerged over the constitutional issue. From outside the Duma, the press organs of the moderate parties came out unequivocally in favour of a moratorium on differences with the government. The Progressist *Utro Rossii* (Morning of Russia) declared that 'there are in Russia neither Rights, Lefts, government nor society but only a united Russian nation.' The Octobrist *Golos Moskvy* (Voice of Moscow) asserted that 'the moment has come when all party differences must take second place ... there can only be one party in Russia at this time – the Russian.' For the Kadets, Milyukov preached a suspension of all internal conflict in the face of the common enemy: 'the moment war was declared, all differences faded into the background before a general healthy display of patriotism ... the French call it *union sacrée*, the sacred union.' The Kadet Central Committee published an appeal in the party newspaper *Rech* (Speech) on 20 July urging that 'no matter what our attitude towards the government's domestic policy, our first duty is to preserve the unity and integrity of our country ... let us postpone our domestic disputes, let us not offer our adversary the slightest pretext for relying on the disagreements that divide us.' The same day a manifesto from the Tsar matched the moderates' appeals, trusting that 'in this year of terrible trials, internal controversies be forgotten, the union of the Tsar with his people be strengthened and all Russia stand united to repel the enemy's criminal attack'.[9]

Behind the moderates' unanimous adoption of the principle of *union sacrée* was a blend of genuine patriotism and healthy self-interest. July 1914 found all three moderate parties in disarray and, in different ways, anxious to accept the political respite offered by the war. The Octobrists for example were very ready indeed to welcome the *union sacrée* and the suspension of politics that it entailed. In the years between the death of Stolypin and the outbreak of war, the Octobrists with their basic platform of honourable reconciliation between government and society had undergone a crisis of conscience. The President of the national Union of 17 October, Guchkov, stressed the necessity of abandoning collaboration with the government: what had been permissible in the time of Stolypin was abhorrent in the era of Maklakov and Goremykin, and the Octobrists must return to the principles of the October Manifesto from which they took their name and creed. The majority of Octobrist deputies in the Duma, while voicing their political disquiet, were not prepared to go so far and hoped for a change of heart on the part of the government. At a national conference in November 1913 the Guchkov line won an easy victory but the bulk of Octobrists in the Duma still declined to follow their Union President's conversion to opposition. In the course of December 1913 the Octobrist fraction split into two: the 'Left Octobrists' who followed Guchkov and accepted the mandate of the recent conference, numbering some twenty deputies; and the predominantly landed 'Zemstvo-Octobrists', led by the Duma President Rodzyanko, who mustered some sixty deputies. The schism in the Octobrist national and parliamentary organisations only deepened in the months leading up to the war, so it was with enormous relief that the Octobrists greeted the *union sacrée*. A suspension of all politics offered the battered Octobrist membership an opportunity to recuperate after the exhausting debates of recent months and the chance to rediscover and redefine their fundamental principles. The *union sacrée* could also be seen as the wartime expression of that reconciliation of tsarism and society which the Octobrists had found so elusive in peacetime. Finally, the quasi-Octobrist principles of the rising star in the government, Krivoshein (incidentally an old friend of Guchkov), gave the Octobrists hope that the *union sacrée* was both genuine in conception and tenable in practice.[10]

The Progressists too welcomed the *union sacrée* from motives more complex than selfless patriotism. If the Octobrists in the Duma were the spokesmen for the land interest, it was the Progressist fraction which was the nearest to a mouthpiece for industrial capital. The industrialist class which emerged so rapidly over the last years of the nineteenth century had become indignant that its political influence bore no relation to its enormous economic significance and launched a campaign to make its voice heard in the Duma. After 1909 a group of Moscow industrialists led by the energetic Paul Ryabushinsky decided to convert the small and lacklustre Party of Peaceful Renewal into an industrialist agency, which in 1912 was rechristened the Progressist Party. Industrial backing gave the Progressists a financial security envied by all, but the party was not without its problems. The party was a parliamentary phenomenon, not a national organisation. To quote the leading Progressist P.A. Buryshkin, 'outside the Duma, the Progressist party did not really exist'. Whereas most parties in Russia were intent on maximising their national support in representation in the Duma, the Progressists were concerned to create a national organisation from the Duma centre. This situation was not as incredible as at first appears. Party labels often meant little during elections to the Duma so it was not until the newly-elected deputy took his Duma seat that he was permitted the luxury of the complete spectrum of parties and ideologies from which to choose. The Progressist fraction recruited extensively from previously uncommitted deputies and parliamentary newcomers and thereby contrived to exist at the Duma level without a formal national party. Another problem was that the industrialist backers of the Progressists, having paid the piper, intended to call the tune. Over the year previous to the outbreak of war, the Progressist fraction experienced a deepening rift between the older, more experienced adherents of the Party of Peaceful Renewal led by Ivan Efremov, who resented the takeover by the Ryabushinsky clique; and the new industrialist deputies led by the self-possessed millionaire Konovalov. By mid-1914 the Progressist camp was in a state of continuous internal bickering and its backers were openly disappointed that their patronage had borne so little political fruit. The coming of war changed everything. Russian industry contemplated the demands (and profits) of the war effort and anticipated that the war would hand them the political power for which they had been campaigning so unsuccessfully in the Duma. The Duma Progressists were content that the industrialists' new sphere of operations would relieve the pressure on the fraction and offer more independence than ever before.[11]

The leadership of the Kadet Party found the *union sacrée* particularly timely. Like their moderate colleagues, the Kadets had experienced a growing schism in the pre-war years. A minority in the fraction led by the forthright Nikolai Nekrasov, supported by a growing proportion of the national party, demanded a policy shift to the Left, back to the radical principles of the early years. The fraction majority however still followed Paul Milyukov in attempting to recommend the Kadets to the government by conscientious responsible parliamentary conduct for the furtherance of constitutionalism rather than revolution in Russia. Allied to, but independent of, the 'left Kadet' movement was a growing revolt of the provincial organisation which on the eve of war was seriously embarrassing the party executive. The original rallying-point for the Kadet party and the venue for its foundation congress had been Moscow, but over the years first the emphasis then the physical location of the central Kadet organs had shifted to St Petersburg to be in close attendance on the Duma. By the early years of the Fourth Duma, after long political neglect by the party leadership in the capital, the natural resentment of Moscow at being relegated to the status of leading provincial town found expression. The provincial and left Kadets made a takeover bid for Kadet Moscow in mid-1914, employing the Moscow Kadet Committee to issue a challenge to Milyukov's restrained policies (now widely regarded as obsessively Petersburg-orientated) and daring him to call a full party congress to decide the future direction of the movement:

The raising of these questions bears witness to a ripening crisis within the party, capable sooner or later of creating a schism ... 'Petersburg' is against calling a party congress, which has the power to change broad issues of policy and programme. More accurately, against a congress stands not so much the Petersburg section as a whole but its leader Milyukov, who fears that a congress would sit in judgement on his tactics and snatch the conductor's baton from his hand ... 'Moscow' is more to the left. Here many members are dissatisfied with the tactics of Milyukov and have conducted a campaign against him for some time. The trouble is that the forces in 'Moscow' are almost equally divided and the balance within 'Moscow' means that nothing will be achieved in terms of demands for independent status and dissatisfaction with Milyukov.[12]

Responding to the left Kadet challenge came a riposte from the right Kadets, led by the formidably intellectual duo Vasilii Maklakov and P.B. Struve. In the months before July 1914, Milyukov had made himself unpopular both with the government and his own party by his pacifist beliefs and what were universally interpreted as unpatriotic pronouncements. The right Kadets protested against the primacy of left-wing opinion in the party and the misguided and discreditable foreign policy of the party leader. Just as the whole party was threatened with disintegration, with 'Moscow' on the brink of capture by the provincial rebels and an irreconcilable schism between the left and right wings, war intervened. The unpatriotic reputation acquired by Milyukov now made the Kadet party very vulnerable: on the first day of war *Rech* was summarily closed down by the government. To save his newspaper, reconcile his left and right wings, and preserve the Kadet party nationally, Milyukov had no choice but to become a super-patriot and commit the Kadets unconditionally to the *union sacrée*.[13]

Though the *union sacrée* represented a blend of patriotism and expediency which the government and moderates found immediately acceptable, its adoption was not entirely unanimous. The Duma Left headed by the Trudovik leader Kerensky campaigned to exploit the war to force from the government fundamental reform in the spirit of the October Manifesto. In confrontations with Milyukov which dominated *konvent* meetings immediately prior to the Duma 'historic sitting', Kerensky claimed the support of the Mensheviks, Trudoviks and even some Progressists and left Kadets. To this extent the left Kadets may never have set their signatures to the official party policy of *union sacrée*. However, Milyukov's line gained the enthusiastic support of all to the right of the Kadets and easily defeated the Kerensky proposal. Kerensky was well aware that on this occasion the patriotism of the Duma reflected the nation at large. This is not to say that the Russian masses were as enthusiastic as the architects of the *union sacrée*. In the opinion of Vladimir Gurko, 'the war excited neither patriotism nor indignation among the peasants and factory workers [but] it deeply stirred the patriotic sentiments of the educated classes.' Some have claimed to detect a measure of Okhrana organisation about the enthusiasm of the proletariat and even the French Ambassador Maurice Paléologue had his doubts about the spontaneity of the populace's welcome for the war. Whether the more emotional manifestations sprang from war fever, the hottest summer for a decade or police stage-management, the fact remains that the outbreak of war entirely dissolved the proletarian crisis. A strike of 27,000 Petersburg workers on the day that war was declared represented the last incidence of the already ebbing proletarian upsurge and the collapse of labour agitation for a full year. Conceding that the nation as a whole acquiesced to the principle of *union sacrée*, Kerensky stood down.[14]

The 'historic' Duma sitting of 26 July passed off in the spirit of *union sacrée*. In his presidential speech, Rodzyanko asserted that 'the war has put a sudden end to all our domestic strife [for] the Russian people has not known such a wave of patriotism since 1812.' Goremykin and Sazonov made confident speeches calculated to inspire the Duma and impress the attendant Allied ambassadors. Spokesmen for the national minorities rose to swear allegiance to the Russian cause, followed by representatives of the leading Duma fractions. Milyukov for the Kadets announced 'we are fighting for the liberation of the Motherland from foreign invasion; we are united in this struggle; we set no conditions and demand nothing; on the scales of war we simply place our firm will for victory.' In a gesture to the left Kadets, Milyukov explained that the armistice was only temporary: 'in no sense is the fraction changing its attitude towards questions of internal affairs, only postponing the parliamentary struggle until the general and national danger has passed.' Kerensky resigned himself to the prevailing mood while making his own reservations perfectly plain: 'peasants, workers and all of you who seek the happiness and well-being of our country, steel yourselves for the great trials ahead, gather your strength and, having defended your country, you will free it.' Only the Bolshevik fraction braved the inflamed patriotism of the Duma and even then opted to abstain from voting on the War Credits rather than risk publicly opposing them. The 'historic' sitting served its government purpose of demonstrating solidarity between country and state before national and international audiences. The Duma opposition had decided against making political capital out of the war; the government had secured a virtual blank cheque from the Duma Rights and moderates.[15]

The initial actions of the wartime government seemed in keeping with the *union sacrée*. To symbolise the eradication of German influence from Russian public life, St Petersburg was renamed Petrograd. To instil a high moral tone into the Russian crusade, the Tsar (apparently in the conviction that patriotism was as heady an intoxicant as vodka) imposed Prohibition on the Russian Empire, regardless of the enormous financial sacrifice. To divert or sublimate the political drive of the educated classes, the government was prepared to tolerate the emergence of public organisations: the Union of Zemstvos (which had provided excellent ancillary support during the Japanese War) and the Union of Towns organised themselves to, in the words of Paléologue, 'go to the help of the government in the fulfilment of the complex tasks which the bureaucracy, idle, corrupt and blind to the needs of the people, is incapable of performing itself'. As a result of the government's complaisant attitude, the public organisations rapidly expanded in membership, scope and ambition. The legislation of Alexander III had excluded most of society from participation in local government in the past, with the Municipal Act of 1892 perhaps the most blatant example of discrimination. More recently, the Stolypin circulars of September 1906 and April 1908 debarring members of 'anti-state' political parties from all public and government office had resulted in a nationwide purge of even moderates from the municipalities and zemstvos. Now, with the war, educated Russian society in general and the managerial and technical 'Third Element' in particular saw the opportunity to evade past restrictions on their activities and combine patriotism with public service. With the tacit dissolution of the Duma, it was through the agency of the UZ and UT that society satisfied its ambition to serve the war effort and play its part in the *union sacrée* so essential to victory.[16]

Not all the actions of the government were applauded. Intimidating enough were the exceptional powers assumed by the government over the first days of war. The 'agreement of 25 July' amounted to a declaration that the wartime government would be operating for the most part without the Duma. Although the Duma was not rejected outright, as having no part to play in wartime, its uses were closely circumscribed and its meetings were to be rare and selective. By the same token, legislation through the constitutional Duma and State Council channels was automatically impossible and the government assumed the entire responsibility for legislation by Clause 87 of the Fundamental Laws. The authority of the government was also augmented by powers devolved from the Tsar. Envisaging personal command of the Russian army, Nicholas issued an imperial rescript on 24 July authorising the Council of Ministers to assume extra powers while he was at the *Stavka*, the army headquarters in the field. In the event, the cabinet prevailed upon Nicholas to stand down as Commander-in-Chief but the rescript was not rescinded and the ministers entered autumn 1914 with greater, more independent power than before.[17]

These enhanced powers might have been acceptable as justified by war necessity had not reactionaries in the government employed them to repress society and entrench their own positions. Goremykin for example secured approval in principle for the secrecy of cabinet proceedings at a Council meeting on 9 November; within a week he issued a directive that 'the press can publish no information about the activities of the Council of Ministers except that released through the [official] information bureau.' Though this directive seems less sinister to the modern mind, its contemporary reputation offended many. In the judgement of the president of the Provisional Government Investigatory Commission, it was intended by Goremykin that 'you and your group of ministers should retain power and your activities would be secret and suffer no criticism'.[18]

Predictably, it was Maklakov at the MVD who led the campaign to contain the activities of Russian society. Censorship had been introduced the day that Russia declared war, and was increasingly rigorously enforced in the course of autumn 1914. When Rodzyanko approached him with a request to permit a congress of public organisations (for which he had already secured the approval of the Commander-in-Chief, Grand Duke Nikolai), Maklakov peevishly retorted: 'I cannot give you permission because it would be an undesirable and universal demonstration that disorders exist in supplying the army; besides, I do not wish to grant permission since, under the guise of delivering boots, you will make revolution.' Maklakov's answer highlighted the MVD's fear of Russian society, its preoccupation with the prestige of the government, and its determination (while tacitly accepting the indispensable aid that society offered) to ignore the practical obligations of *union sacrée*.[19]

It was in character that Maklakov's major offensive should be reserved for the Duma. The attitude of the Bolshevik fraction to the war was dictated by Lenin, who from the security of neutral Switzerland demanded unequivocal opposition to the 'imperialist war' by the workers' representatives. In November, the five Bolshevik deputies attended an illegal conference to discuss wartime tactics, only to be arrested on the last day on a charge of treason. With the Okhrana completely informed of developments, Maklakov's pre-arrest report to the Tsar suggests that he was simply rounding up elements suspected of spreading alarm and despondency: 'The members of the Bolshevik fraction are preparing to call a conference … propagandising the idea of the immediate dissolution of the war and the overthrow of the monarchical form of government in Russia.' A.S. Badayev, the leader of the Bolshevik fraction (after the recent flight of the Okhrana agent Malinovsky), substantially agreed: 'The tsarist government had long been searching for a pretext to liquidate the Bolshevik fraction of the State Duma because it was the mouthpiece of the revolutionary movement and the organisational centre of the mass of workers.' But it is also possible that Maklakov was indulging a personal vendetta against the Duma after his defeat earlier in the year on the same issue of parliamentary privilege. It may even be that Maklakov expected the reaction from society to be sufficiently ill-advised as to provide grounds for the dissolution of the Duma in its absence. The MVD-provoked 'Shornikova Plot' had provided the pretext for the dissolution of the Second Duma in 1907 and Maklakov may have hoped that the 'Bolshevik Plot' would serve the same purpose for the Fourth Duma.[20]

Whatever Maklakov's design, the reaction from society was remarkably mild. Even the most partisan Soviet accounts cannot detect a 'workers' response' to the arrests so it may be safely assumed that there was none. The moderates' commitment to *union sacrée* almost entirely smothered their disapproval of the unconstitutional action of the MVD. After his initial attempt at political bargaining, Kerensky too seems to have surrendered and readily postponed the reckoning: 'The living forces of Russian society do not attack or oppose Maklakov. For the time being, our paths run parallel with that of the government. But we expect much more from victory in the war for liberty than the government ... You understand that after the war N.A. Maklakov will be brought to account. In the meantime, we will be silent.' Rodzyanko sent Goremykin a formal letter of protest but made no attempt to raise the issue later as a Duma question or interpellation. Far from protesting, the new super-patriot Milyukov completely disavowed the Bolsheviks, intimating that such traitors deserved all they got: 'The whole population from top to bottom stands for the war; defeatists are not an influential group and may be punished with impunity.' If Maklakov had hoped for an outburst on a scale which could justify the dissolution of the Duma as a seditious assembly, he was disappointed. Though the MVD pressed for the harshest brand of justice for the Bolshevik deputies, and only the intransigence of Grand Duke Nikolai prevented the case from being transferred to a military court carrying the death penalty, the affair finally lent neither credit nor advantage to any of the parties involved.[21]

As the government appeared to be employing its exceptional powers to undermine the position of the Duma, the elation of the 'historic' sitting evaporated, to be replaced by mounting uneasiness among the moderates and the fear – almost too painful to voice, even in private – that their leaders had let slip the supreme moment for negotiation with the establishment. An Okhrana report noted:

The aggregate of relevant factors has completely changed the mood of those Kadet groups which initially hoped that the 'historic' sitting of the State Duma would open a new page in the history of relations between state and society. Complete disillusionment and growing irritation are emerging in speeches, along the lines that some protest or other must be launched against the current tactics and policies of the government.

A succession of Kadet meetings revealed that the familiar rifts in the Kadet party were re-emerging: the left Kadets refused to be gagged by the *union sacrée* and demanded pressure on the government for the immediate recall of the Duma; the centre floated the idea of a discreet deputation to the Tsar; but the right Kadets opposed even a deputation as drawing domestic and foreign attention to society discontent. For the time being, the right Kadets retained control: at Kadet Central Committee meetings on 19 and 25–6 August, it was ruled 'the greatest tactlessness publicly to announce the dissatisfaction of society at this time' and the hope was expressed that informal representations to the government might secure a wartime Duma without the necessity for recourse to an open campaign.[22]

Before August was out, the Okhrana was remarking that although the Duma had been out of session for a month, the Tauride Palace was still the congregating-place for a large proportion of deputies. The pretext for this activity was the Duma Aid Committee, an independent organisation for war work financed jointly by public and Duma subscription, which from the very start performed the function of an information centre for deputies. The 'unofficial Duma' was considering alarming rumours that the last redoubt of the Duma – Budget examination – was under fire within the Council of Ministers. The threat particularly alarmed the Kadets, who 'spiritedly debated the question of the necessity of the recall of the State Duma to discuss taxation matters ... saying that the government wants to dismiss the Duma and "go it alone" over the introduction of new taxes'. A declaration of protest by left Kadets and Progressists reached the pages of the Moscow press and the Moscow Kadets demanded that Rodzyanko and his presidium resign in protest unless the Duma was in session or definitely promised by mid-September. The nerve of the Kadet leadership, which more publicly than any other had put its signature to the *union sacrée*, was under great strain by the autumn of 1914, inducing Maklakov to issue a confidential MVD circular ordering the utmost vigilance regarding political parties and 'in particular, hiding under the flag of the "Constitutional-Democratic Party", the left wing of the opposition with its republican leanings'. The Kadet party became the primary target for Okhrana surveillance.[23]

Much Kadet (and therefore MVD) attention during September and October 1914 rested on the Union of Towns. Inspired by Milyukov, the Kadets battled against their fit of nerves by making strenuous efforts to broaden the basis of their support, mounting a campaign to wrest the leadership of the UT away from the Octobrists (who had largely sponsored its creation only a month before). At its First Congress on 12–14 September, the Kadets toppled the Octobrist N.D. Bryansky in favour of Michael Chelnokov as Director of the UT. Following this coup, a flurry of Kadet meetings took place at which Milyukov repeatedly proclaimed that 'the present time is the most effective for the rebirth of all-powerful public organisations under the flag of (and on the grounds of) philanthropy and aid to war victims.'[24] Maklakov's surveillance over the Kadets was intensified: on 14 October a second circular required provincial governors to present reports on the activities of local Kadets. While subsequent replies were to suggest that the provinces could still be safely disregarded politically, developments in the capital already demanded the Okhrana's constant close scrutiny: 'The Tauride Palace is becoming more and more the centre for the exchange of all kinds of news ... the frustrated are seeking here, at the centre, the solution or explanation of those issues and problems arising in the provinces.' On 19 October Maklakov received the disturbing information that Chelnokov was on a tour of major provincial towns drumming up support both for the UT and the Kadet party. Far from remaining non-political, the UT threatened to become the front for the creation of a nationwide revitalised Kadet movement.[25]

At a cabinet meeting on 18 November, Maklakov demanded that the UT and UZ be strictly confined to medical and sanitary duties; a week later he received authorisation to move against both the expanding sphere of influence of the Unions and Kadet dominance of the UT.[26] An Okhrana enquiry soon confirmed that the UT Director Chelnokov was a Kadet, and of its twenty-two-strong executive committee, sixteen were Kadets and two Kadet sympathisers. Maklakov claimed that this Kadet penetration of the UT was a direct violation of the Stolypin circulars of 1906 and 1908. Maklakov (and his successors at the MVD) was to try repeatedly to reduce the influence of the Unions but was effectively stymied by the shortcomings of the bureaucratic and military establishments, which made the support of the public organisations vital to the war effort. Maklakov also attempted to reduce Kadet control of the UT but Kadet concentration at the executive and administrative levels made it hazardous to remove personnel without a public furore, apart from the military danger of weakening such an indispensable war organisation. On both scores, the Unions (and indirectly the moderates) received a large measure of support from the military authorities and Stavka, who in their own interests protected them from the incursions of the civil government.[27]

While the moderates retained their public allegiance to the *union sacrée* through the autumn of 1914, the original concept of a total suspension of politics was soon abandoned. As the Kadets infiltrated the newly-sanctioned public organisations, the MVD responded by a reassertion of its traditional policy of containment. One of the most enthralling (and little-known) features of late 1914 was the clandestine manoeuvring for advantage on the part of the MVD and Kadet party, a secret war of which few signs ever escaped to disturb the misleadingly bland façade of *union sacrée* assiduously maintained by both sides.

In wartime, the tsarist civil government was ultimately dependent upon Russia's military performance. The exaggerated importance attached to the sensational battle of Tannenberg in August 1914 has overshadowed the principal problem for Russia of adjusting to the concept of a long war. In the introduction to the 'Great Programme' of 1914 appears the revealing statement that 'the present political and economic circumstances of Russia's main neighbours rule out the possibility of a long war'. In practice, this official dogma meant the stockpiling of all the munitions necessary for a brief conflict without thought for the acquisition, still less the production, of more. Thoroughly imbued with the concept of a short Bismarckian war, few combatants were free from a munitions shortage by late 1914 but Russian lack of foresight was crowned by incomprehensible stupidity on the part of the War Minister.[28] As early as August Rodzyanko enquired of General V.A. Sukhomlinov about shortages but received confident assurances of sufficiency. When in September Joffre, the French Commander, asked about Russia's munitions needs, Sukhomlinov answered that no shortage was likely in the foreseeable future. As late as November, an agitated Paléologue was still getting no satisfaction: 'I am getting reports from many quarters that the Russian army is running short of ammunition and rifles; I have been to General Sukhomlinov ... but he keeps answering "Don't worry, I've prepared for everything".' The whole sorry mess was revealed in early December: Paléologue heard from Grand Duke Nikolai himself that operations were being curtailed from lack of ammunition; the British Ambassador Sir George Buchanan received the news independently from the chief of the British military mission at the Stavka shortly afterwards. Confronted by incontrovertible evidence, the War Ministry admitted the existence of a dangerous munitions shortage to the Allied ambassadors on 5 December.[29]

The munitions crisis had three distinct effects on the Russian government. The first was acute embarrassment, rising to terror that the crisis might permanently damage Allied military cooperation. Paléologue and Buchanan complained bitterly, first to Sazonov and then to Goremykin, accusing Sukhomlinov of deliberate and unpardonable deception in his relations with Russia's allies. Stemming from this embarrassment came a perceptible decline in the self-assurance of the civil government. In future, every major military event was to produce a political backlash: victory brought renewed self-confidence to the government to the exclusion of society; defeat sapped the morale of the government, disposing it to turn to society for moral and material support. The third consequence was an awareness that to make good the munitions shortage, the Goremykin administration must establish an immediate and constructive rapport with Russian society. Within six months of the outbreak of war, the Russian government was compelled to appeal to wider society to survive a military crisis largely of its own making. From the moment that the munitions shortage was officially – but not publicly – acknowledged, concessions towards society were inescapable. In legal and financial terms, the government needed at the very least a session of the Duma to authorise the substantial extra sums necessary to remedy the crisis.[30]

The Council of Ministers approached the Duma leaders with a view to contracting a mutually satisfactory political bargain. The degree to which the government recognised the Kadet party as leader of society may be gauged by the fact that initial negotiations were with the Kadets alone. In return for agreement to the new War Budget and a demonstration of unity with the government, Krivoshein (the Council negotiator) offered the Duma three concessions: a government declaration of goodwill towards society, a short Duma session early in the New Year and a promise that the 1915 Budget would be submitted to the Duma without recourse to Clause 87 of the Fundamental Laws. In relation to its needs, the government's terms were laughable. It may be conjectured that Krivoshein did not expect the terms to be acceptable, only to provide a basis for bargaining. In offering the Duma nothing but a brief session when its every utterance was scripted by the government, the Goremykin administration could only gamble desperately that the spirit of *union sacrée* still possessed the Duma majority. In this preposterous ploy the government proved completely successful. Again it may be surmised that the Duma negotiators allowed their gratitude to Krivoshein for his past services to overwhelm their political judgement; but whatever the reasoning, on 20 December Krivoshein secured the agreement of the *senioren konvent* to his terms. Despite its weak bargaining position, the government had achieved its aims without fundamental concession.[31]

Milyukov, who had led the movement for agreement within the *konvent*, now found himself under attack from both wings of his party. In October the Moscow Kadets had become so shrill in their abuse of the MVD that the Petrograd Kadets ordered a halt to 'irresponsible speeches'; the Central Committee 'decided temporarily to hold back from any criticism whatsoever and maintain a policy of restraint towards the government'. This right Kadet line was reaffirmed at a Central Committee meeting on 21 December called to discuss the deal contracted the day before. The *union sacrée* was repledged even to the gross neglect of the recessed Duma: 'if it is foreseeable that the Duma sittings will be employed for a succession of oppositional speeches against the government, it would be better to oppose the recall of the Duma.' However, accepting that it would be unpatriotic to refuse a Duma session offered by the government in its hour of need, the Central Committee agreed to ratify Milyukov's action. Such was the commitment of the Kadet majority to *union sacrée* that the right Kadets had to be wooed by Milyukov into accepting a Duma session, even one granted under the most restrictive conditions.[32]

Not surprisingly, the left Kadets were outraged at the deal and the prevailing mood within the party executive, and were soon agitating for a full congress (a demand postponed only six months by the internal Kadet *union sacrée*) and the employment of the new Duma session for raising such issues as the arrest of the Bolshevik deputies, state censorship and the legality of the extended use of Clause 87. But although the left Kadets won a minor victory in establishing that deputies who signed interpellations against the government would not be disciplined by the fraction, it was clear that the rebels were still in the minority: a combined Central Committee and fraction meeting on 1 January 1915 agreed overwhelmingly to continue the Milyukov policy line and retain absolute allegiance to the *union sacrée*.[33]

There is little evidence to suggest that the Octobrists pursued any independent political line over the first six months of war. Corporate Octobrist policy almost ceased to exist as the fraction members dispersed to voluntary service in the public organisations, most notably the Russian Red Cross and the UZ (to which most Octobrists transferred after the Kadet takeover of the UT). The dwindling circulation of *Golos Moskvy* and its consequent financial difficulties epitomised the general Octobrist decline: in December 1914 the paper's editorial board was broadened to the Left to admit for the first time non-Octobrists (the Kadet N.I. Falbark and the Progressist V.A. Rzhevsky) in a desperate last attempt to save *Golos Moskvy* from liquidation. The Zemstvo-Octobrist fraction surrendered spinelessly to popular anti-German sentiment by expelling its six Baltic German deputies in January 1915, thereby making a fresh contribution to the disintegration and diffusion of the Octobrist camp. The Okhrana judiciously concentrated its attention on the Kadets on the assumption that the leadership (if not necessarily the initiative) of any opposition to the government would come from this quarter.[34]

On 11 January 1915, the Tsar accepted his cabinet's open advice to convene a Duma session on the twenty-seventh (and its confidential counsel to prorogue until November after only three days). With the Duma unwittingly helpless in his grasp, Goremykin informed a delighted Rodzyanko of the convening, though with a warning that 'in view of the war situation, the duration of the imminent session will be of an altogether brief nature'. The government had taken every reasonable precaution before permitting a Duma session by securing the promise of the Duma leaders that there would be no departures from the scripted programme, waiting until the Kadets (the expected troublemakers) had made their harmlessness apparent, and releasing the news of a Duma session only after its three-day duration had already been decided and documented.[35]

With the preparations for the charade complete, the government could afford to be generous. The examination of the Budget in Duma commission commanded the regular and conscientious attendance of all ministers. Krivoshein's protégé, the moderate P.N. Ignatiev was appointed to replace the recently-deceased reactionary L.A. Kasso as Minister of Education, leaving Duma society convinced that concrete advantage had been won from the government. A *Rech* leader enthused: 'the appointment of Count Ignatiev remains at the centre of public interest ... no single appointment has aroused such general satisfaction and hope.' As a final concession, Rodzyanko was permitted to arrange a meeting of the Council of Ministers with the Duma defence commission on 25 January. The atmosphere of the occasion largely accorded with the deal contracted on 20 December. Only Milyukov and Andrei Shingarev introduced a note of discord, attacking the MVD and demanding the dismissal of Maklakov as the 'violator of the *union sacrée*'. Maklakov contemptuously dared the Kadets to attack him publicly: 'Go there [to the Duma], the government does not fear public criticism, we will answer you there.' The meeting of 25 January showed that the government, reassured of the strength of Duma commitment to *union sacrée*, was prepared to meet its critics because of the circumscribed nature of the confrontation. For the modest price of confidential criticism from the moderate leadership, the government gained the credits essential to its military recovery and the placid Duma session necessary for its political self-assurance.[36]

The spirit of *union sacrée* pervaded the Duma session of 27–9 January 1915. As planned, a demonstration of unity between government and Duma was mounted by all leading fractions. The sentiments of A.I. Savenko, spokesman for the Nationalists, serve as a typical example: 'in time of war there are no parties and no nationalities in Russia, only a single, strong, terrible, granite Russian monolith.' However there were signs that the Progressists were starting to follow the left Kadet rebels. Efremov, spokesman for the Progressists, permitted a suggestion of dissent to colour his speech: 'we, the representatives of the people, may not embark upon criticism of the government, even though it sometimes actually hinders the expression of the vibrant patriotism of the people.' For his pains, Efremov was the only moderate leader to have press coverage of his speech censored. With the Bolsheviks physically excluded, it was left to Kerensky to declare against the Duma policy of non-criticism of the government: 'the country has been surprised and shocked by this terrible silence, by this absence of truth over the last six months. It should know that there are people who understand and recognise that this silence cannot continue.' But Kerensky was overwhelmed by the insistence of the majority on continuing the Duma role of the 'historic' sitting. At the closed meeting of 25 January, even the Kadets (the most critical group represented) had been careful to underline that they wanted only to remove 'violators of the *union sacrée*', not dissolve the *union*. In Duma sitting, Milyukov spoke for the great majority of the Duma when he vowed 'just as then, on 26 July [1914], so today, in our appeal for unity, we are performing not a political gesture but our exacting civic obligation.' On the second day of the session, the Duma expressed its civic obligation by passing the Budget without opposition; even the Mensheviks and Trudoviks preferred to abstain rather than oppose credits. On the third day, Rodzyanko was informed that the Duma was prorogued until November. The Duma had again played the role dictated by the government and having outlived its usefulness within three days, was discarded.[37]

At first sight, the Great War fortuitously intervened just in time to forestall a final confrontation between the Duma and the government. In practice, despite the freezing of the Duma's constitutional position, the war permitted the government an authority which it had not approached for almost a decade: the Duma would only be called when convenient to the government; legislation became the monopoly of the government through Clause 87; the principle of parliamentary immunity was tacitly abandoned; and even the precious financial powers of the Duma were under threat. In late 1914 the government achieved what it had failed to do in peacetime. Far from saving the Duma, the Great War provided the excuse to effect a constitutional coup, to reduce the Fourth Duma in practice from a legislative to a consultative assembly. The *union sacrée* was treated by the government (and particularly Maklakov) as a valuable delusion ripe for exploitation. As Milyukov himself conceded later, 'what was meant as a truce was taken as capitulation'. The concept had hardly been a practical one in the first heady days of war but the Duma moderates added unreasonable obstinacy to their earlier gullibility by refusing to learn the lessons of the first months of wartime government and take political advantage of the munitions crisis. If the *union sacrée* had ever really existed outside the Duma, by November 1914 the left Kadet A.M. Kolyubakin was warning that it had disappeared at the popular level: 'an enormous change in the mood of the country has taken place since the "historic" sitting of 26 July ... the mood has collapsed and been replaced everywhere by colossal dissillusionment.' By December 1914 the *union sacrée* existed only in the minds of the Duma Rights and moderates but with a self-delusive tenacity which persuaded the moderates to jettison the political weapons which had been employed in peacetime. The Duma leadership chose to abandon its budgetary powers in favour of a concept which was chimerically sanguine at the best of times and ludicrous in its untenability by the advent of the Duma session of January 1915.[38]

Within days of the Duma closure, leading political figures were alarmed at what appeared to be a government reversion to repression. When the prestigious Moscow newspaper *Russkia Vedomosti* (Russian News) ran an enquiry on the effects of the war on the peasant, Maklakov waited only for the Duma session to pass before ordering 'the necessity of instituting for the future stricter surveillance over *Russkia Vedomosti*' and a general tightening-up of press control. The trial of the Bolshevik deputies, approved by the Tsar in December but prudently postponed until after the Duma session, returned verdicts of guilty and imposed sentences of exile in Siberia on the five defendants. Two months' imprisonment visited on the Kadets Vasilii Maklakov and Struve in March for their conduct during the anti-semitic Beilis trial of 1913 seemed to demonstrate that the moderates too would soon come under fire. An uneasy awareness that the Duma had been cynically used by the government for its own exclusive ends now took possession of public opinion. A desire for a 'real' Duma session stirred, as the official Kadet account (published in September 1915) indicates: 'The general impression was that the session – by no fault of its own of course did not fulfil its function. There was strengthened not only the authority of the Duma but the conviction of the need for a long session. The date "no later than November" seemed too distant.' Kerensky too, possibly fearing that he was next in line to fall victim to the machinations of the MVD, wrote urgently to Rodzyanko on 25 February: 'The authoritative intervention of Russian society is essential. The State Duma must do everything it can to protect the nation from a perfidious stab in the back. I beg you, as official President of the Duma, to insist on the immediate recall of the State Duma.'[39]

The organisers of a concerted campaign for an early Duma were the industrial leaders. Over the first six months of war, industrialists had become increasingly agitated because, to put it candidly, Russian industry was not getting what it had expected from the war. The upset priorities and inevitable dislocation occasioned by the war effort were not being compensated by new business created by the war. In large part, this was deliberate government policy. In responding to the munitions crisis, the government thought instinctively in terms of acquiring more armaments from its traditional suppliers abroad, especially France, Britain and the USA, not of developing already-neglected Russian industry, regarded as both pricey and incompetent. Only when foreign suppliers conspicuously failed to give satisfaction – through giving priority to their own war efforts, arguing about the slide in the international value of the rouble and failing to penetrate the German blockade – was the tsarist government susceptible to a campaign from Russian industry. In early 1915 the Russian industrialists' chance to serve the war effort, thereby combining patriotism and profits, belatedly arrived. The first action of the industrialists was a public relations exercise to improve their national image: the patriotism of Russian industry was played up and the slogan, the 'self-mobilisation of industry', vigorously publicised. A more practical operation was to make the voice of industry more audible to the government and country through the State Duma and State Council. Initially, the State Council seemed the more promising agent. With representation to the elected half of the State Council based on institutional curiae (not geographical constituencies as in the Duma), industry had always found it easier to raise its voice in the upper house of the Russian parliament. Moreover while the recessed Duma maintained no institution out of session except its chancellery (entirely for secretarial functions), in January 1915 the State Council secured permission to run an Economic Commission independently of parliamentary session. The government soon regretted this ultimately fundamental concession. From mid-March, the industrial faction in the State Council headed by N.S. Avdakov employed the Economic Commission to debate controversial issues like the fuel crisis and the spiralling cost of living. While some Commission members deplored accounts of their discussions appearing in the press and urged closed sessions to avoid offending the government, the majority opted for open debates. The first public breach in the *union sacrée* came not from the Duma but the historically much-maligned State Council.[40]

Parallel with the efforts of Avdakov in the State Council came a campaign by Efremov and the Progressists. By late February, a majority of the Duma Progressists had joined the left Kadets in believing a standard – not just a ceremonial or financial – Duma was urgently needed. In late March those Progressist deputies still in the capital voted to initiate a drive for a Duma session and recalled all fraction members to Petrograd. They made little headway among other moderates: the Kadet and Octobrist majorities opposed a special meeting of deputies to discuss a Duma session and also a Duma commission analogous to that of the State Council. The Kadet leadership was particularly dismissive: 'Both Maklakov and Milyukov coldly retorted ... that a long session of the Duma in time of war was inappropriate, and to embark upon a session at such a time (March-April) was undesirable. Milyukov declared himself to be against "switching horses in mid-jump".' But on 1 April the government, hearing that the industrialist faction had tabled for debate the burning issue of the relations between the government and private industry, summarily closed down the Economic Commission. All the industrial lobby's weight was thereafter placed behind the Progressists. On the same evening, the Progressist fraction secretary I.V. Titov angrily demanded (and received) commitment to an immediate Duma session from his colleagues. More important, the Progressists began to make inroads into other moderate party memberships: the left Kadet leaders Nekrasov and S.P. Mansyrev were already converted but a major victory was achieved when the Left Octobrist spokesman I.V. Godnev admitted the only solution 'would be not the creation of a commission like that of the State Council but the convening of the Duma'.[41]

Even so, the *union sacrée* survived the remainder of April 1915. The Russian capture of the fortress of Przemysl ('the key to Galicia and the gate to Hungary'), authoritative rumours about the imminent collapse of Austria-Hungary and Italy's growing commitment to the Allied camp all reinforced the universal belief that the war must end – and victoriously for Russia – very soon. The eve of Russian victory was no time to disrupt the *union sacrée*. On the political level, Milyukov may well have seen the industrialist campaign as dictated by a narrow self-interest which should not be allowed to compromise the unity of Russia at war. Guchkov symbolised the Octobrist exclusive commitment to war at the expense of politics. Guchkov, a former President of the Duma, had experienced bitter defeat in the Moscow elections to the Fourth Duma in 1912, and had spent the months until the outbreak of war in growing frustration outside the Russian parliament. In February 1915, Chelnokov had announced his retirement from the Duma in order to devote himself to the mayorship of Moscow and the Directorship of the Union of Towns. Guchkov was sorely tempted to stand for his old seat in the resulting Moscow by-election but decided to continue his total involvement in the work of the Russian Red Cross. When two such obsessive politicians as Milyukov and Guchkov agreed on a suspension of politics, it was no wonder that the Kadet and Octobrist rank-and-file acquiesced.[42]

In mid May Efremov returned to the capital from witnessing the start of the Russian retreat from Galicia. The transfer of German troops injected higher morale into the Austro-Hungarian army and converted the strategy of the Central Powers from one of defence to attack. Crippled by its munitions shortage and undermined by the lack of coordination between Stavka and the War Ministry, the Russian army was all too soon in headlong retreat. Efremov's news of military disaster shocked the moderates. The government was proved not only tyrannical but incompetent, and the universal self-delusion of a short conflict was replaced overnight by the agonising prospect of a long and, for Russian society, a 'deep' war of attrition. On all counts the *union sacrée* now seemed intolerable and the need for the Duma undeniable.[43]

While Efremov's eye-witness acount made an enormous impact, it was the Ninth Congress of Trade and Industry held in Petrograd from 26 to 28 May that proved the turning-point in the campaign for a Duma session. Two new factors made industrialist agitation even more insistent than before. Although the government was reluctantly admitting the principle of employing Russian industry to serve the war effort, only a favoured few firms, almost entirely in Petrograd, were receiving government contracts. Russian industry outside Petrograd rallied round Moscow's industrialists in their campaign to secure a wider and fairer distribution of war orders. Most alarming of all was the news that the government, anxious to establish greater control over a sector so crucial to the war effort, was seriously considering some form of nationalisation: on 21 April the cabinet offered the Minister of Trade and Industry 'full powers' over war industry. Though Prince V.N. Shakhovskoi refused the offer in some alarm, Russian industrialists awoke to the danger promptly and redoubled their efforts to protect their interests.[44]

The Ninth Congress was planned as a giant publicity-stunt for industry: a general invitation was extended to all Duma deputies and leading government personnel, and larger premises than usual were hired to accommodate the expected throng. The Congress paraded the patriotism of Russian industry in a spirited effort to dissuade the government of the need for nationalisation. The third of the wartime public organisations, the War Industries Committees, was created, establishing local organs of industry designed to improve technical and administrative efficiency and synchronise the resources of Russian industry with the demands of the war effort. This new organisation, again fundamentally a response to the threat of nationalisation, was the institutional manifestation of the slogan the 'self-mobilisation of industry'. The WIC, numbering over seventy local organs within two months, drew together Russian industry into a permanent structure which annual congresses had never been able to provide. After May 1915, industry was organised into a disciplined national pressure group which made its voice more powerful and authoritative than ever before. The Congress also acted as the catalyst for a redefinition of moderate opinion about the *union sacrée*. The speeches which made most impact were from Ryabushinsky and

Avdakov, both stressing the need for closer cooperation between industry and the Duma, both demanding a Duma session. It seems clear that the Congress was regarded as a Duma-substitute: *Birzhevia Vedomosti* (Stock Exchange News) observed that 'there are so many members of the Duma of various fractions together with their leaders in the hall, as well as the instantly-recognisable figure of M.V. Rodzyanko, that the spirit of the national representative assembly blows over this congress.' The Congress provided the venue for the largest gathering of deputies since January and vividly demonstrated that commitment to a Duma session was taking possession of the majority.[45]

The position held by Milyukov and Guchkov was becoming precarious. In April Milyukov had embarked upon a lecture tour of the Volga towns, an area of traditional moderate support, only to discover that his policy of *union sacrée* was not tolerated by audiences unanimously and openly hostile to the government. Disturbed by his findings, Milyukov issued a Central Committee circular on his return requesting urgent information on the provincial attitude to the war, the government and Kadet policy. By late May, the time of the industrial Congress, Milyukov and Guchkov represented a dwindling minority of moderate opinion. The Okhrana reported that the demand for a Duma session found a rare unanimity among deputies of all persuasions: 'the idea did not encounter opposition, even in the ranks of the Right, who in this matter are in complete solidarity with the centre and opposition'. Initiative was slipping away from Milyukov because of his insistence on the by now untenable *union sacrée*. On 29 May, a general assembly of deputies called by the Progressists (as usual masquerading as the Duma Aid Committee) mandated all fraction leaders to recall their members to Petrograd. While Milyukov hesitated, the Progressists were usurping Kadet leadership of the moderates and the bulk of the Kadet party was cleaving dramatically towards the Progressist viewpoint. Though in an interview for *Birzhevia Vedomosti*, Milyukov deemed a Duma recall 'exceptionally important and timely', the Okhrana reported that his agreement to recall Kadet deputies was by reason of pressure applied by Kadets already in Petrograd, not because he had been personally converted: 'Milyukov spoke out against such a recall, declaring it condemned to failure as a poor copy of the Vyborg meeting.'[46]

Milyukov's remark introduces a feature of the Kadet party so potent and enduring that it demands further explanation. In July 1906 the Kadet deputies had responded to the sudden dissolution of the First Duma by decamping to Vyborg in Finland to issue a manifesto of principle against the tsarist government. The Vyborg Appeal demanded a campaign of passive resistance to the Tsar summed up in the battlecry 'Not a soldier to the army! Not a kopek to the treasury!'.

Unfortunately for the Kadets, the national response to the Appeal was minimal. The Appeal which echoed so hollowly in the ears of its aghast and embarrassed authors could not have demonstrated more cruelly that the revolutionary tide of 1905 had receded, leaving the Duma and the Kadet party high and dry. The effect of the Vyborg episode on the physiognomy and psychology of the Kadets was enormous. In December 1907 one hundred Kadet deputies prosecuted by the government for incitement to rebellion were brought to trial, found guilty and sentenced to a lenient three months' imprisonment. The real punishment lay in the fact that the defendants' new criminal records meant they were deprived of all political rights. The force of this judicial verdict amounted to no less than a party tragedy. At a stroke, the flower of the party – I.I. Petrunkevich, M.M. Vinaver, V.D. Nabokov (father of the novelist), F.F. Kokoshkin, S.A. Muromtsev, Prince D.I. Shakhovskoi and Count P.D. Dolgorukov – were excluded from further participation in the Russian parliament. The first and the best generation of Kadet politicians now had no legal or parliamentary outlets for their undisputed talents. Though the 'victims of Vyborg' made the best of it by devoting their energies to the Kadet press – notably *Rech* and *Russkia Vedomosti* – and by making the Kadet Central Committee almost their exclusive preserve for the next ten years, these activities were patently no substitute for the Duma. As what may be termed the revolutionary liberals were purged from the Duma, their places were taken by evolutionary liberals led by Milyukov. Milyukov had every reason to be grateful to Vyborg: because he had been disqualified from standing for election to the First Duma by the machinations of the Okhrana, he could not sign the Appeal and fortuitously (but quite honourably) escaped the punishment meted out to his colleagues. The tsarist government unwittingly fostered the career of Milyukov, for the affair which broke his party rivals (most notably Vinaver and Kokoshkin) indirectly made Milyukov. Though the collective charisma of the Kadet Old Guard was never approached by subsequent generations of Kadet parliamentarians, the price of their martyrdom was relegation to the wings of Russian politics. The legalistic, strictly constitutional, defensive course consistently preached by Milyukov, and apparently vindicated by the Vyborg fiasco, became the leitmotif of Kadet policy in the Third and Fourth Dumas.[47]

The impact of Vyborg on the morale and mentality of the Kadets was equally prodigious. Though the Vyborg drama did not create Kadet misgivings about democratic support, it did confirm and intensify that sense of insecurity into an obsessive characteristic of their political psychology. At its most hysterical, the reaction found expression in an elemental hatred of and contempt for the masses. A classic example is the warning of M.O. Gershenson published in the prestigious and influential *Vekhi* (Landmarks) symposium in 1909: 'far from dreaming of union with the people, we should fear the people more than any government executions and bless this government which alone, through its prisons and bayonets, protects us from the wrath of the people.' At a less apocalyptic level, the mood assumed the form of a profound distrust of the Russian electorate and a determination never again to put the Kadet party and the Duma itself at risk by a precipitate commitment to the country. Throughout its career after 1906, the Kadet party suffered a 'Vyborg complex' which prevented its ever recovering its confidence in Russian democracy or retrieving a healthy relationship with the country which it claimed to represent.[48]

If on this occasion Milyukov's attempt to raise the ghost of Vyborg to undermine the growing militancy of the Kadet majority proved vain, it was not until June 1915 that he was compelled to yield. A party conference on 6–8 June was forced by widespread Kadet revolt against the atrophied Milyukov line. The impression from the conference minutes is of almost universal attack on Milyukov's leadership. The *union sacrée* now seemed so naive that few Kadets could recall how they had ever been persuaded of its value. Milyukov had to suffer a tirade of abuse from provincial delegates (spearheaded by Moscow) while radical resolutions in the Progressist style were passed convincingly, most notably Resolution Five:

> It is considered essential for the practical coordination of the resources of the country and their proper employment in the interests of the homeland,
> (a) To form a cabinet capable of directing the organisation of the home front and of safeguarding the internal peace of the country and the close collaboration of state and society;
> (b) To recall the State Duma immediately.

The bulk of attack came from fourteen leading provincial delegates but five fraction deputies and three Central Committee members joined the witch-hunt. The 'provincials' divided into three groups over future policy: the largest followed the Progressist line that their only safeguard was ministerial responsibility to the Duma; a second urged the immediate development of the ailing provincial organisation to revive a national Kadet movement; and the mildest of Milyukov's critics stipulated a Duma session to implement a programme of solid legislative work. Milyukov (as ever) managed to weather the critical storm. Without the status of a party congress, the conference had no formal authority over the Kadet executive. Of the sixty delegates invited to the conference, only twenty-five were provincial, so the numerical representation was such that a vote of no confidence in Milyukov needed not only the unity of the provincials but the defection of a significant proportion of the fraction. All proceedings of the conference were conducted in closed sitting and the resolutions submitted by the Central Committee were deliberately vague, bearing the nature of recommendations rather then directives. As a result, Milyukov not only escaped with an inconclusive critical drubbing out of the public eye but managed to salvage from the conference his formula demanding 'A Ministry of Public Confidence' over the provincials' slogan, 'A Ministry Responsible to the Duma'.[49]

Yet despite his tactical skill in averting many of the dangers which a congress or conference always presented, there was no denying Milyukov's overall defeat. For Guchkov, the shift was even more traumatic. In the ephemeral philosophy of *union sacrée*, Octobrism had its last chance, a doctrine which united the entire Octobrist camp and briefly revived its favourite policy of collaboration with the government. Though the *union sacrée* was still not liquidated, its dramatic decline closely coincided with the death-agony of *Golos Moskvy*, which published its final edition on 30 June 1915. The winding-up of the official press organ of Octobrism symbolised the final disintegration and disappearance of the national Union of 17 October. By June 1915 the *union sacrée* had ceased operating at all levels of its former influence. At the intra-party level, the rift between the Milyukov Kadets and left Kadets, and between the Left Octobrists and Zemstvo-Octobrists, had re-emerged. At the inter-party level, the initiative of the Progressists revived the jealousy of the Kadet leadership and augured a return to the bitter party politics of peacetime. Finally, at the national level, the *union sacrée* between Duma and government foundered with the moderates' reluctant acknowledgement of both the malevolence and the incompetence of the tsarist administration.

3 The Progressive Bloc

The rout of the Russian army over summer 1915 had a marked political impact on the civil government. In practical terms, the government was compelled to negotiate with society in order to harness the country's energies and talents to the state apparatus; at the level of public relations, the country had to be conciliated with political concessions in lieu of military victory. As the leader of the left wing of the Nationalists, Vasilii Shulgin, remarked, 'for this defeat the government had to pay. But what with? With the only currency which was acceptable in payment – it had to settle its debt by the concession of power, however superficially, however temporarily.' A 'liberal phase' which held sway during the summer of 1915 was forced upon the Russian government by the anonymous pressures of war. It owed little to Russian society and the Duma: the moderates had no power to initiate or sponsor official liberalisation; they could only jump aboard the political bandwagon once it was moving and hope to aid its acceleration by their combined weight.[1]

The government's first ploy in a succession of associated moves to conciliate society was to concede the principle of admitting non-official elements into the structure of the bureaucracy. Though permitting the creation of the non-official UZ and UT outside the bureaucracy, the government had still attempted to meet all problems by drawing on the resources and personnel of the bureaucracy alone, as for example in the formation in early 1915 of the state Fuel and Provisions Committees to tackle the developing crises in coal and food. But in April the Committee of Finances, which hitherto had admitted only a single Duma observer (the Octobrist president of the Duma budget commission, M.M. Alexeyenko), conceded seats and voting rights to five Duma and three State Council representatives. Only too anxious to serve on any organ of crucial financial power, the Duma moderates won the monopoly of representation: Titov and A.S. Posnikov (Progressists), Shingarev (Kadet), S.I. Shidlovsky (Left Octobrist) and A.G. Ratkov-Rozhnov (Centre). Though Duma representation was too small to overawe the Committee of Finances, the principle of Duma participation in government was reasserted for the first time in many months.[2]

As a diehard adherent of the *union sacrée*, Rodzyanko now employed the privileged access to the Tsar of his Duma office to advocate further collaboration between government and Duma. Claiming that the confidential meeting with the cabinet in January 1915 had proved the trustworthiness of the Duma members and the value of cooperation, Rodzyanko advanced a scheme for the Duma and industry to aid the war effort through a commission attached to the Ministry of War. Despite the violent opposition of Sukhomlinov, who won an assurance from the cabinet on 23 May that the proceedings of any such commission would be confidential and its accounts armour-clad (that is to say, neither subject to Duma approval nor included in the annual Budget statement), the Tsar decided to give the scheme a try. Despite the limitations imposed by Sukhomlinov, Rodzyanko was delighted: for the first time Duma and industry delegates were to be permanently attached to one of the most important government ministries and privy to all its deliberations and decisions. Rodzyanko retained his political initiative even when the other Duma moderates condemned his new commission: 'The Nationalists and Octobrists welcomed my efforts but the Kadets, encouraged by their leader Milyukov, entirely unexpectedly ganged up against my undertaking, declaring any contact and joint endeavour with the War Ministry of Sukhomlinov shameful for the Duma ... they, the Kadets, would not participate in the newly-formed Commission under any circumstances.' Rodzyanko exploited the Kadet (and Progressist) boycott to his own advantage: partly from the sour grapes of his moderate rivals, partly by his own machinations, Rodzyanko eventually headed a deputation of four Duma delegates to the Commission – N.V. Savich, I.I. Dmitryukov, A.D. Protopopov and himself – all of whom were Zemstvo-Octobrists.[3]

The attention of the Duma now concentrated on Rodzyanko's Commission to see whether this experiment in wartime collaboration would end in failure and the defiant ossification of a government which refused to mend its exclusive ways, or prove acceptable and engender a succession of similar opportunities for society participation. The first meeting of the Commission on 1 June calmed most bureaucratic fears at the cost of shamelessly neglecting traditional society loyalties. The War Ministry was still toying with the idea of the nationalisation of war industry, and Rodzyanko and his Octobrist colleagues, partly because their predominantly landed fraction had nothing to lose, partly from a craven eagerness to avoid giving offence on the first occasion, offered no resistance to the tentative government move. By this action, Rodzyanko antagonised the industrialist camp and supplied ammunition to those critics who accused him of employing his Duma office for personal and sectional party interests.[4]

Even so, Rodzyanko had contrived a way of promoting the greater authority of the Duma and the Octobrist camp. In the dying weeks of *union sacrée*, the policy of collaboration was reprieved, giving the Zemstvo-Octobrists the first fillip to their self-confidence since the 1913 schism and lending the Duma fraction a revived sense of purpose. Moreover the government was sufficiently reassured of the feasibility of cooperation with select society elements to concede further experiments in collaboration: on 7 June a Commission for Munitions was established, once again admitting four delegates from the Duma. From the two initial Commissions were to spring the five Special Councils created in August 1915 which were to establish permanent institutional collaboration between government and Duma.

The second aspect of official 'liberalisation' was the substitution of more moderate ministers for the most hated reactionaries. The simplest and most dramatic gesture of concession, it was also the most readily reversible. It was less the Duma than Krivoshein, supported by Sazonov, Ignatiev and the State Controller P.S. Kharitonov (the moderate wing of the cabinet), who took the initiative by mounting a vigorous campaign against the most reactionary ministers. With reports of the Russian retreat becoming daily more alarming and Rodzyanko adding his complaints to those of cabinet and country, Sukhomlinov was soon dismissed and replaced by the popular and able General A.A. Polivanov.[5] Maklakov too fell from power. The blocking of his personal ambition, his repeated out-manoeuvrings by Krivoshein and the crushing weight of the MVD discouraged and frustrated Maklakov to the point of actual physical illness. He pursued his vendetta against the Duma to the last: 'The State Duma and its President strive wherever possible to increase their own power and importance in the state and, by the same token, are endeavouring to diminish the power of Your Imperial Majesty ... I have always pressed upon Your Majesty the necessity for pruning the rights of the State Duma and reducing it to the level of a consultative institution.' In June, Maklakov's resignation (tendered since March) was accepted by the Tsar. Unfortunately for moderate hopes, the popularity of his successor Prince N.B. Shcherbatov was matched by his incapacity, a fact in keeping with his only previous administrative experience as Director of the State Stud.[6]

A second wave of dismissals was decided at the Stavka on 13 June, to be made public on Nicholas's return to the capital. The two arch-reactionaries in the Council, V.K. Sabler and I.G. Shcheglovitov, were formally relieved of office on 5 July. Their successors, if less popular than the earlier replacements, were welcomed none the less as symptomatic of the trend away from reaction: A.D. Samarin, the new Procurator of the Synod, was a moderate marshal of the Moscow nobility; Alexander Khvostov, the new Minister of Justice, had a reputation for industriousness and scrupulous honesty. Although Milyukov deeply regretted that Goremykin had not been removed too, Krivoshein's group within the cabinet rested content, as Sazonov described: 'Goremykin had the powerful protection of the Empress Alexandra Feodorovna and under the circumstances it would have been hard to obtain his dismissal. Besides, we thought that without Shcheglovitov ... and his other supporters, Goremykin's part in the Government would be insignificant.' By July 1915, the only survivor of the reactionary wing of the Council as it had existed in early 1914 was its Chairman, whose influence was not expected long to resist the influx of more moderate colleagues.[7]

With Duma and society representatives consolidating a bridgehead on the periphery of government and the arch-reactionaries being purged from the cabinet, only the Duma itself was needed. In June, the collapse of the Duma deputies' commitment to *union sacrée* made political dialogue and negotiation inescapable. As the summoned deputies began to gather in Petrograd, the meetings of the Duma Aid Committee – once again the unofficial Duma – became better attended, unanimously commissioning Rodzyanko to sound out Goremykin about an immediate session. Resigned to the prevailing political climate, Goremykin held out hope for an early session but asked for time to reconstitute the Council of Ministers. Certain ministers would have to be dismissed in order to make government–Duma relations practicable; otherwise, as Goremykin said, 'at the first appearance of Maklakov, every fraction would attack him and willy-nilly I would have to prorogue the Duma'. At an extraordinary meeting of the Duma *konvent* to discuss this reply on 13 June, Efremov and Milyukov clashed violently. Fired by the militancy of a recent Progressist conference in Petrograd, Efremov moved the necessity of 'direct pressure' to force a favourable decision from the temporising Goremykin. Milyukov was still not prepared for so drastic a departure from the *union sacrée*. Recent anti-German riots in Moscow seemed to point the need for restraint and discipline; the dramatic resignation of Struve from the Kadet party the day before in protest at its abandonment of *union sacrée* only confirmed Milyukov's own doubts. Alarmed by the Progressist line, Milyukov rounded on Efremov in rare exasperation: 'I do not understand you Progressists. The government is coming to meet us – they have dismissed Maklakov and Sukhomlinov and given their promise of an early Duma recall ... It's all printed in the newspapers. What more do you want?' Milyukov proposed a cooling-off period of one week to allow the government time to prove its good intentions, a motion carried despite the angry opposition of the Progressists, Trudoviks and Mensheviks.[8]

Milyukov was by now agitated by the success of his moderate rivals. Thanks to the efforts of Rodzyanko, the Duma Octobrists were enjoying a mild revival. Even more dangerously, the Progressists had not only recklessly disrupted the *union sacrée* but thrown down a challenge to traditional Kadet leadership of the opposition. Milyukov's pride was deeply involved: although remarkably little Kadet dirty washing had been publicly exhibited, he was painfully aware that it was public knowledge that the recent party conference had defied his restrained leadership. As Efremov smugly announced, the Progressist record was currently second to none: 'To the credit of the Progressists, it was by their initiative that the collecting together of the Opposition had taken place ... and there was engineered the greatest possible number of Duma deputies at the *senioren konvent* to demonstrate the attitude of the Duma towards a renewed session.' Opportunities for Milyukov to squash his impudent rival were not long in coming. The first chance occurred when the Progressist Central Committee, perhaps over-reacting to Rodzyanko's Commission, published its plan for a supreme executive organ for defence in which the government, Duma and industry would participate jointly and equally to coordinate the war effort.[9] On 23 June the Progressists eagerly explained their 'Committee of State Defence' to the Duma members. The ingenuous nature of the concept, the fundamental questions to which it offered no answers and the Progressists' complete commitment to the plan made it a sitting target for the Kadet leaders. Milyukov and Shingarev cogently argued that the Progressist plan, whilst of course desirable in the extreme, stood no chance whatsoever of implementation. The gains which Russian society had made so far were less victories over the government than concessions made under war duress. The pattern for the future must therefore be to advocate moves which the government would find easy to accept in a spirit of constructive compromise, notably institutional extensions of the existing state structure. The Progressist plan was heavily defeated by the Kadet and Octobrist-dominated meeting, leaving the Progressists thoroughly demoralised. Milyukov's first counter to his challenger was conspicuously successful both in raising drooping Kadet morale and mocking the over-reaching claims of the Progressists to be the new leader of the Duma Left.[10]

Meanwhile on the very same day that Milyukov and Efremov had their first major clash (13 June), the cabinet heard the Tsar sanction not only the second batch of ministerial dismissals but further concessions: 'it is essential to bring forward the date of the convening of the legislative organs in order to listen to the voice of the Russian people ... the renewal of the activities of the Duma and Council will be no later than August.' Goremykin set out to secure the best terms for the government: having announced on 16 June a forthcoming session *sine die*, he attempted to impose conditions on the Duma leaders by refusing to set an opening date until an agenda was agreed. Goremykin's attempt to repeat the stratagem which had proved so successful in January 1915 of only permitting a session if the Duma was guaranteed placid now failed. The political climate of June was very different from that only six months previous and Goremykin could not haggle with the Duma for long without both irritating and compromising the Tsar. At a cabinet meeting on 26 June, the moderate ministers compelled Goremykin to abandon his ineffectual bluff and set the Duma opening date. In the forlorn hope that some element of *union sacrée* might still survive, the opening sitting was scheduled for 19 July – the first anniversary of the war.[11]

The revival of politics affected both the moderate parties in the Duma and the Duma's relations with wider society. The Duma moderates exhibited remarkable tactlessness in their dealings with the fast-growing public organisations. The industrialist sector in particular received very shabby treatment. As already described, Rodzyanko had been so eager to reassure the government of the responsibility of his conduct that he effectively encouraged its move towards nationalisation. The industrialist camp was naturally alienated from the Duma, which appeared to be lightly abandoning the principle of society free enterprise to purchase dubious political advantage for itself. The Duma was staking money not its own to secure winnings which it refused to share. Not content with antagonising industry as a whole, Rodzyanko contrived to estrange Moscow industrialists altogether. Over-anxious to preserve the prerogatives of his precious war commission, Rodzyanko's conception of the infant War Industries Committees was very circumscribed. As a guest at the ceremonial opening of the Central WIC in Moscow, Rodzyanko first delivered a speech in which he dwelt lovingly on the Duma, implicitly denying any other institution political importance, then blandly informed the astonished delegates that the Central WIC would be totally subordinated to the Duma Commission, at most acting as a clearing-house for government contracts. Ryabushinsky, the president of the Moscow WIC, made a scene by flatly refusing to accept this narrow definition of their competence, claiming full executive and administrative independence. With his sights concentrated on the high politics of collaboration with the government, Rodzyanko repeatedly betrayed a chronic insensitivity to social and political forces outside the Duma.[12]

In the course of July 1915, the gulf separating the Duma and industry was confirmed and institutionalised. When in late June the Tsar announced the promotion of the Rodzyanko Commission into a permanent Special Commission on Defence, industrialists were delighted that its composition was extended to include delegates from the UZ, UT and WIC. Joint meetings of the Duma finance and army-navy commissions promptly recommended the creation of three new Special Commissions to cover the vexed questions of fuel, food and transport; but the right-wing representatives, fearing an influx of Bolshevik agitators into privileged offical bodies, insisted that no industrial delegates be invited to serve. Anxious to secure Duma unanimity to present a solid front in negotiation with the government. the two Duma commissions agreed.[13] Once again, industry had been jilted to facilitate Duma ambitions. On 25 July the First WIC Congress met in Moscow, still seething over this rebuff, which was put down to the Duma jealously coveting its monopoly of legal politics. The Congress, which had envisaged institutional contacts with the Duma, now publicly and dramatically dropped the scheme. The Central WIC would instead admit no Duma representatives and appoint no delegates to the Duma. A belated attempt to repair the damage and rebuild political bridges was made by the Progressist fraction (acting for its industrial patrons), who forced a vote in the Duma later on the representation of the WIC in Special Commissions. The Progressist motion scraped through by 141 votes to 138, albeit with a Zemstvo-Octobrist *caveat* stipulating that delegates should be nominated by the Central WIC, not the local committees, in order to exclude agitators. By this time however the damage was done and preserved for all time in the rapidly institutionalising structure of the WIC.[14]

All three public organisations suffered similar estrangement from the Duma. In part this stemmed from the early reluctance of the UZ and UT to make themselves targets for MVD harassment or even closure by becoming involved in politics. Ignorance of political and parliamentary matters also inhibited Union involvement in what was traditionally within the jurisdiction of the Duma alone. But by mid-1915 a major element in the estrangement came from the Duma, with its jealousy of the growing power and labour force of the public organisations, and insistence on its own monopoly of political initiative and access to the government. The public organisations were becoming such a power in the land that they implicitly at least represented a challenge to both government and Duma. An Okhrana report for June 1915 regretted that the technical support which had been the rationale for the official sanction of the UZ and UT was showing unmistakable signs of becoming subordinated to political discussion and manoeuvre. While the public organisations still readily deferred to government and Duma, they were gradually becoming more political. The familiar confrontation of government and Duma was becoming complicated by new society forces to which both traditional protagonists felt hostile.

The forces of society were all the more alarming for their geographical concentration in Moscow. Since the outbreak of war,

Moscow had experienced a rebirth, its strategic situation at the nodal point of the communications system of European Russia making it the natural headquarters for the UZ, UT, WIC and all ancillary home-front organisations. Until mid-1915, partly in sublimation of the political appetites denied by government and Duma, Moscow threw its abundant energies into the war effort alone. After mid-1915, the shortcomings of the government in Petrograd encouraged Moscow society to make a challenge for the leadership of the war effort. By contrast with the energy of Moscow, Petrograd was becoming increasingly introverted, swept by intrigue, rumour and waves of despair which enveloped ministers and deputies alike. The advance of the enemy armies over the summer of 1915 evoked in Moscow a spirit of stubborn resistance which only threw into greater relief the collapse of morale in the capital. 'Lukian', the Moscow correspondent of *Birzhevia Vedomosti*, bitterly recalled how 'on the outbreak of war, the cab-drivers in Moscow made a collection for protective bandages against poisonous gas; in Petrograd, they just doubled their prices.' With the breaking of the Myasoyedov espionage scandal, Paléologue noted the disgust felt by Moscow towards the capital: 'the citizens of Moscow are utterly furious with high social and court circles in Petrograd, whom they accuse of having completely lost touch with national feeling, hoping for defeat and preparing the way for a betrayal.' As Moscow came to regard itself as the heart of the war effort, it developed a political brain and voice. By turns the Duma was regarded either as the society hostage held by the government in its Petrograd stronghold or (less charitably) as an assembly totally out of touch with the realities of wartime Russia. In either case, the moral was the same: Moscow must enter the political arena.[15]

The prelude to the reopening of the Duma was dominated by moderate party politics. From the wings, Guchkov welcomed the new session only as an opportunity 'to remove obstacles to victory and establish conditions essential to constructive work' and relied on the 'political tact' of the Duma deputies to revive and reinforce the original *union sacrée*. The moderates found themselves split over the elevation of Rodzyanko's Commission into the Special Commission on Defence, which again raised the question of the morality of collaboration with the government. The Octobrists of course saw even more reason to participate in the Special Commission than before. The Progressists, as in May, refused to submit a candidate for the Special Commission on the grounds that 'such a framework, while laying upon the members of the legislative chambers great moral responsibility, ... gives the former no real power to influence the decisions of the government.' Both recent Progressist conferences, in Petrograd on 10 June and Moscow on 19 June, had mandated the Duma Progressists to press their militant line. The Kadets in the middle were as usual divided. The left Kadets, long in sympathy with the Progressists, demanded continuation of the May policy of boycott. Milyukov however, desperate to salvage something from the wreck of *union sacrée*, had repented of his earlier stand. Arguing that the substitution of Polivanov for Sukhomlinov removed the greatest obstacle to collaboration, Milyukov won the agreement of the Kadet fraction to the principle of participation by seventeen votes to nine at a suspiciously depleted meeting. A Kadet delegate to the Special Commission, A.A. Dobrovolsky, was duly elected but the volte-face in policy was not without its price: angered by what he regarded as Milyukov's chicanery, the left Kadet leader Nekrasov resigned from the Central Committee in protest. Thereafter Nekrasov and his militant left Kadet clique resentfully pressed their campaign against Milyukov within the Duma fraction, accentuating the trend towards Kadet disintegration.[16]

It was clear from the moment the new session opened on 19 July that any residual hopes for a repetition of the tame Duma of January 1915 were groundless. The independent left newspaper *Den* (Day) spoke for many in asserting that this was the Duma's last chance to redeem itself: 'Though the State Duma has been convened twice since the beginning of the war, it has quite simply neither learned the mood of the country nor understood the nation's activities and ambitions. It has been rhetorical and decorative while the country suffered.' In conversation with Shulgin, even Milyukov conceded the necessity of the Duma voicing the complaints of the populace: 'They expect the Duma to brand the culprits for the national catastrophe. If this safety-valve is not opened in the State Duma, the exasperation will be expressed in other ways.' It is significant that the 'safety-valve concept' of the Duma traditionally associated with the Right had now become characteristic of Milyukov's politics. The much-published Russian traveller Stephen Graham made a similar point in *The Times*: 'the failure of the Russian arms meant the rise of the Duma ... The Duma became the voice of the people, proclaiming anxiety, pain, dread. In great stress, better the people have a voice, otherwise they may go mad. The Duma affords a great relief.'[17]

An outburst of pent-up criticism of the government dominated the first few days of the Duma session. Paléologue sensed 'an atmosphere which is heated, heavy and full of the promise of storms; men's faces seem charged with electricity; the prevailing expression is anger or intense apprehension.' The sitting of 20 July held that individuals responsible for the munitions shortage must be held liable in law as well as morally, pressing the point the next day by passing a resolution demanding legal proceedings against Sukhomlinov for treason. Efremov repeated the Progressist principle that the only guarantee against further government misconduct was an executive constitutionally responsible to the Duma. The antagonism of the Duma towards the government appeared to offer no possibility of compromise nor even the avoidance of immediate prorogation.[18]

Milyukov set out to prevent the Duma committing itself to an unnecessary death though, as Rodzyanko observed, he experienced difficulty weaning even his own party away from furious assault on the government: 'certain Kadets were preparing to raise the question of a Responsible Ministry, and it was no small task to dissuade them. On almost all questions, Milyukov supported the Octobrists against the Progressists.' Despite the bland official Kadet account that 'from the first day of the session, the Fraction of the People's Freedom ... was the ideological leader of the Duma majority', Milyukov had to fight off a serious left Kadet-Progressist challenge. At a special meeting on 18 July of all fractions except the Kadets (who were pointedly not invited), the Progressists tested reaction to their slogan 'A Ministry Responsible to the Duma'. Predictably, its tone was too extreme for the Nationalists, who suggested 'A Ministry enjoying national confidence' as an alternative. Apart from the Zemstvo-Octobrists (who abstained) and the Nationalists (who naturally voted for their own formula), all those present supported the Progressist slogan. With the support of three-quarters of the votes cast, the Progressists anticipated victory on the larger stage: 'this vote gave the Progressist fraction the right to hope that the formula of Responsible Ministry would be accepted by the Duma. The fraction believed this formula alone contained sufficient clarity and exactness, for the formula for the Confidence of Society essentially said nothing at all.' The next day, the rival formulae were advanced in open Duma sitting. To Progressist amazement, the Kadets supported the Nationalist slogan, which in turn prompted the Octobrists to switch from abstention to support for the same slogan. When the votes were counted, the Nationalist formula had a comfortable majority (of 191 to 162) over the Progressist. All the Progressists' careful preparation and reconnaissance had been brought to nothing. Though Milyukov could defend himself by indicating the resolution of the June Kadet conference, his action was motivated by vindictive jealousy of the challenging role of the Progressists. Although, by their latest vote, the Kadets had committed themselves to the moderate Right, ostensibly vacating the leadership of the Left to the Progressists, Milyukov had demonstrated not only that the Progressists were no match for him in political manoeuvre but the Kadet position represented the new fulcrum of Duma politics.[19]

Milyukov's victory lent the Kadets renewed moral authority in the Duma and precipitated a split among the Progressists: a minority group led by N.N. Lvov formally quit the Progressist fraction in the last days of July. Lvov's explanation was significant: 'putting it in parliamentary language, we Progressists must always be to the right of the Kadets ... but for some time now the Progressists have changed their line of conduct and forgotten their primary role. They currently occupy an anomalous position, clearly to the left of the Kadets.' The defection of the Lvov group weakened Progressist hopes of again challenging the Kadets and added solid numerical advantage to Milyukov's moral victory. Soon after the initial spate of denunciation, Kadet authority came to dominate the Duma session.[20]

The government had now to be reassured that the Duma was not merely a spiteful and capricious critic deserving no better than prompt prorogation but a constructive contributor to the war effort. At a Duma closed sitting on 28 July, Milyukov (for the moderate Left) and Savenko (for the moderate Right) warmly supported the endeavours of Polivanov, stressing that the Duma's quarrel lay only with corruption and incompetence, not with the basic direction of the war effort. The Kadets demonstrated their refurbished authority by breaking the traditional Octobrist hold over the Duma army-navy commission to make Shingarev its first non-Octobrist chairman. On 31 July the commission decided to institute closed-session daily meetings, to which the War Minister had an open invitation and the rights of inspection and veto over the commission minutes. While insisting on its own close involvement in the war effort, the commission supplied the initiative for frank confidential relations with the government. Milyukov in particular hoped by this demonstration of rational and responsible behaviour to offset the bad impression left on the government by the ferocious if well-deserved campaign of recrimination which had opened the session.[21]

However by the first week of August it was widely rumoured that those government and court circles hostile to the Duma had already made political capital out of its initial actions. When Goremykin confided to Rodzyanko that in his opinion the Duma would be prorogued in mid-August, a universal belief in imminent closure swept the Tauride Palace, and Duma attendance (particularly on the Right) fell off sharply. In alarm the *konvent* met on 5 August to insist on a full session, a motion endorsed by all fractions except the Right. For the first time, almost the entire Fourth Duma membership followed a policy opposed to leading government circles, and organised a defensive compact soon to be called the 'Progressive Bloc'. The only effective counter-measures against the Bloc in its vulnerable early days could come from the Duma Right, which was uncharacteristically depleted through its precipitate acceptance of the fact of early prorogation.[22]

If the Progressive Bloc was conceived by the Duma moderates, it owed its birth to ministerial support. At this moment of reactionary threat, the moderates in both Duma and cabinet came together to foster the retention of the liberal phase. Learning of the Bloc through its elected president, his old friend S.I. Shidlovsky, and observing the unprecedented unity of the Duma, Krivoshein projected an alliance which would benefit both parties. Vladimir Gurko was in no doubt about Krivoshein's contribution to the Bloc:

> The power behind the formation of this Bloc was Krivoshein, who was anxious to become head of the government. He thought that if he could only effect a union of the moderate Right elements, especially the Octobrists with whom he had long been sympathetically and closely connected, and those elements of the Opposition which at the beginning of the war had declared themselves ready to support the government in the work of defence, he would have support in his campaign to become head of the government. Once he had achieved this goal, he thought that such a bloc would continue to support him and this would mean cooperation not friction between government and legislature.

The political *rapport* between Krivoshein and the Duma moderates which had been in evidence in July and December 1914 reached its climax in August 1915. A 'liberal conspiracy' contracted by Krivoshein and the moderates lent the Bloc its early initiative and impulse towards further development.[23]

As Milyukov later made haste to point out, the Bloc rapidly acquired an independent momentum, outpacing the limited function promoted by Krivoshein and abandoning its early patron en route. The steadily expanding base of the Bloc soon became the critical factor in its development. At a meeting on 10 August the current members, prompted by Milyukov, established the principle of a multi-fraction bloc extending as far towards the Right as possible. The Right fraction itself was patently beyond the bounds of political feasibility but the Nationalists proved within reach. On several previous occasions, differences between the right-inclined Nationalists of Balashev and the left-orientated Nationalists of Shulgin had threatened a permanent schism in the party. The issue of Bloc membership smashed Nationalist unity for all time: the Shulgin group, now dubbed the 'Progressive Nationalists', opted for participation in the Bloc and cast off all links with the Nationalist main body. At the opposite end of the Duma spectrum, the affiliation (though not membership) of the Trudoviks and Mensheviks delineated a Bloc which by mid-August extended from the extreme Left as far as the Nationalist position.[24] The process of broadening the Bloc base involved an approach to the State Council, for it was felt that to unite the moderate elements of both legislative chambers would immeasurably enhance the prestige and bargaining-power of the Bloc. At a first meeting, the leaders of the Bloc were gratified to find representatives of the Academic, Centre and Non-Party factions of the

Council quite as concerned as their Duma counterparts and secured instant agreement to a defensive bloc to agitate against their prorogation. A second meeting nominated four delegates from each chamber to formulate a programme. It took the Bloc working-party just two meetings (on 14 and 15 August) to complete the programme, despite the fundamental disagreement of the Progressive Nationalists and Academic faction with the amnesty and Jewish rights clauses advanced by the Kadets. Even so, an unprecented spirit of fraternal compromise and the application of judicious phrasing narrowly preserved the unanimity of the Duma and Council participants in the parliamentary bloc. The Programme made two basic demands in its preface:

1. The formation of a united government, composed of individuals who enjoy the confidence of the country and have agreed with the legislative institutions on the implementation of a definite programme at the earliest possible time.
2. Decisive changes in the methods of administration employed so far, which have been based on distrust of public initiative.

Eight measures were cited which required immediate attention, the most controversial or far-reaching of which were:

1. By means of Imperial clemency, the termination of proceedings instituted on charges of political or religious transgressions ...
2. The return of those exiled by administrative decree for matters of a political or religious nature ...
3. The complete and decisive cessation of persecution on religious grounds, on any pretext whatsoever ...
4. The immediate drafting and introduction into the legislative institutions of a bill for the autonomy of the Kingdom of Poland ...
5. The inauguration of a programme aimed at the abolition of restrictions on the rights of Jews.

A legislative programme of twelve less urgent measures, including the introduction of a *volost* zemstvo and the confirmation of prohibition, concluded the agreed document. After spending an unconscionable time reconciling itself to the breakdown of *union sacrée*, the Duma majority took less than a fortnight to prepare a political programme uniting the moderates of both parliamentary chambers.[25]

Once again the base of the Bloc was broadened but this time at the initiative of neither its Duma founders, ministerial patron nor Council collaborators. Moscow educated society intervened unasked to organise more general support for the Bloc. In a later account Milyukov shared the honours between the two capitals: 'the political mood which was aroused in the lifetime of the Bloc swung backwards and forwards from Petrograd to Moscow and from Moscow to Petrograd ... it is clear that this mood manifested itself in both

Moscow and Petrograd and that the Progressive Bloc was the product of a joint agreement.' At the time, Milyukov made no attempt to dispute the greater role played by Moscow: 'Time did not wait. In the country the mood of society was heightening and Moscow was the organ which gave this mood definite shape.' On 13 August, the Moscow industrialist and Progressist groups provocatively published in *Utro Rossii* what they called their 'Defence Cabinet': Chairman, Rodzyanko; Minister of Interior, Guchkov; Foreign Minister, Milyukov; Finance Minister, Shingarev; Minister of Trade and Industry, Konovalov; State Controller, Efremov; Minister of Agriculture, Krivoshein; Minister of Education, Ignatiev; and Minister of War, Polivanov. Moscow's ideal cabinet allowed the retention of three moderate ministers currently serving in the Council of Ministers (Krivoshein, Ignatiev and Polivanov) and ingenuously distributed the remaining ministerial posts equally among the moderate parties: two Octobrists (Rodzyanko and Guchkov), two Kadets (Milyukov and Shingarev) and two Progressists (Efremov and Konovalov). Such a blatant example of skinning the bear before it was caught thoroughly embarrassed the Bloc leaders in Petrograd.[26]

Moscow was soon increasing the pressure. On 16 August Konovalov and Ryabushinsky convened a meeting of the leaders of Moscow society 'for the vital organisation of special "coalition" committees, directed by a Moscow Central Coalition Committee, to sponsor widespread agitation to back the programme of the Progressive Bloc'. The Moscow Central Coalition Committee immediately became an arena for conflict between Progressists and Kadets. Konovalov demanded an ultimatum to the Tsar that either the Council of Ministers be re-staffed with society representatives or society would withdraw all aid, material and moral, from the war effort. Vasilii Maklakov headed the Kadet response, desperately indicating the advantages of compromise, the immorality of employing ultimatum tactics in wartime and the feasibility of a joint society and government Ministry of Confidence. Just as the Duma Bloc had quickly outrun the leadership of Krivoshein, Moscow was showing every sign of outrunning the Bloc leadership in Petrograd.[27]

Moscow now floated even more radical schemes. The Okhrana noted with disquiet that 'the Moscow public organisations have come out unanimously in favour of a Society Ministry, the formation of which would be entrusted to Prince Lvov.' Still estranged from the Duma and Petrograd in general (and from Rodzyanko in particular), the public organisations were now thinking of snubbing both government and Duma personnel in favour of their own leaders. The rivalry between the Progressists and Kadets in Moscow grew more intense, the former attempting to expand from their industrial stronghold, the latter fending off bids for their control of the official organs of Moscow civic life. In a closed sitting of the Moscow municipal duma on 18 August, the Progressists attempted to persuade the meeting to switch allegiance from the Kadet slogan 'A Ministry of Confidence' to their own 'Responsible Ministry'. Though defeated, the Progressist bid was not wasted: the Moscow debate was the signal for civic institutions throughout the provinces to introduce political issues on to their agendas and determine their attitudes to political developments in the capitals. Messages of support for the Bloc began to flow from every corner of the Empire. Thanks to the Progressists and to Moscow, at a superficial level at least the Progressive Bloc now had a claim to nationwide support.[28]

In Petrograd the Bloc looked askance at the broadening society campaign and continued to confine its activities to parliamentary channels. The most the parliamentary moderates were prepared to countenance was the informal identification of the Duma with the Bloc. On 17 August the *konvent* agreed that after the passage of essential war projects, more general legislative bills as contained in the Bloc Programme be placed on the Duma agenda. Both this declaration of intent to operate as in peacetime and an attempt by the *konvent* to secure the maximum advantage for the Bloc by cancelling all leave for deputies were intended to demonstrate the harmony of Duma and Bloc. If legally dubious and politically hazardous, this identification seemed justified by the numerical allegiance of the Bloc. With 70 per cent (up to 300 out of 430 deputies) of the Duma membership in the Bloc, it was hardly surprising that by late August the terms 'Duma' and 'Bloc' had become interchangable in the public, parliamentary and ministerial minds.[29]

Confronted by the question of what to do with the Programme, the Bloc chose to duck the immediate responsibility by referring the issue to the individual fractions. The emerging consensus was against publication: the Centre and Progressive Nationalists would not tolerate any hint of ultimatum; it was felt that publication would leave no room for manoeuvre; and the Bloc must make it as easy as possible for the government to concede, a tactical gesture towards official *amour propre* which public negotiation could only impair. The Bloc decided to put the Programme to the cabinet corporately at an unofficial level, with no public limelight to stiffen government resistance or encourage Duma posturings. Unfortunately for this discreet policy of an open treaty secretly arrived at, a slightly garbled version of the Bloc Programme leaked into (significantly enough) the Moscow press. The precise circumstances of the leak remain obscure, but suffice it to say that the 26 August evening editions of the Moscow press boasted a journalistic scoop. The very same evening, the Council of Ministers met to consider the confidential document it had received and, at the suggestion of Krivoshein, commissioned a delegation to approach the Bloc leaders for exploratory talks. The Bloc now found itself in an embarrassing position: 'further restraint was meaningless. On August 27 the Programme was released to the Petrograd papers, even though a group of Bloc adherents (as was subsequently announced by certain State Council members) did not approve of the step.' The cabinet deputation (Kharitonov, Khvostov, Shcherbatov and Shakhovskoi) found itself meeting the Bloc leaders in very different circumstances than those originally envisaged by either side. Despite the full glare of publicity, Kharitonov finally conceded that there appeared to be few serious differences between the Bloc and the ministers but they were sufficiently fundamental to be outside cabinet competence. The unfortunate circumstances of the negotiations notwithstanding, the ministerial delegation reported back to the cabinet on 28 August in a favourable light. The Council expressed its sympathy for the Bloc Programme but, as Kharitonov had warned, declared the agreement of the government to be within the province of the Tsar alone.[30]

It is vital to an understanding of the political crisis to appreciate that the Progressive Bloc was one of two fundamental issues confronting the government at this time. While the month of August 1915 was for the Duma and educated societies of Petrograd and Moscow the era of the Progressive Bloc, the attention of the Council of Ministers was focused on an entirely different stream of events. The summer rout of the Russian forces had persuaded the Tsar that his duty lay with the army and he must assume the role of Commander-in-Chief. On the personal level, Nicholas had been dissuaded from taking military command both in 1904 and 1914, disappointments which had only glamourised the step in his perverse mind. The fatalism to which Nicholas became increasingly subject may have engendered within his complex and elusive personality a desire to sacrifice himself for his country: in Vasilii Maklakov's opinion, 'the Sovereign was not seeking laurels, he was offering himself as a redeeming sacrifice.' The Tsaritsa Alexandra meanwhile was convinced that Grand Duke Nikolai harboured plans to oust Nicholas from the throne. When the Court Minister Count Frederiks attempted to defend the Grand Duke on one occasion, Alexandra angrily retorted:

> Would you prefer that he [Nicholas] should go on giving up his power piecemeal to the Grand Duke Nikolai Nikolaievitch, who exacts it under the pretext that General Headquarters need it and everything must be subordinated to the exigencies of war? He has insisted that the Ministers go and work with him at Baranovichi, he encroaches on the Tsar's authority in every branch of the administration ... The Emperor is dethroned 'de facto' and I can see the time is coming when the Grand Duke will openly take his place.

Returning from an extended tour of inspection of the front in late

June, Nicholas spent the next seven weeks at his palace at Tsarskoe Selo, where the continuous presence and personal dominance of Alexandra must have furnished a vital compotent in his momentous decision.[31]

But Nicholas's assumption of the supreme command was not merely a combination of personal ambition and court intrigue. Since June, Krivoshein had pleaded the necessity of removing Goremykin and establishing a supreme War Council, headed by Polivanov, with Krivoshein himself as vicegerent in charge of civil government. Over the course of July, the arguments in favour of a war dictator were dramatically reinforced by the deteriorating military situation. On 16 July Polivanov delivered his famous cabinet speech 'The Fatherland is in danger', in which he deplored the disorganisation of the Stavka, the defeatism of Petrograd and the chaos of the home front. The most controversial issue was the relationship between the civil government and the Stavka. As the German and Austro-Hungarian armies advanced steadily eastward, enveloping Warsaw on 4 August, Kovno on 17 August, Brest-Litovsk on 26 August and Vilna on 18 September, the war zone under the authority of the Stavka shifted closer to the heart of European Russia. After mid-July, the Russian retreat brought the capital within the war zone and the Council of Ministers felt its powers dwindling to a humiliatingly low level. If Petrograd was in the war zone, was the capital to be administered by the MVD for the civil government or by the Sixth Army for the military authorities? Krivoshein insisted that this dual power was quite impossible and authority must be vested in a single centralised body. Shcherbatov protested that neither MVD nor Stavka could solve this riddle, which must be submitted to the Tsar for judgement. While accepting the serious nature of the dilemma, Goremykin pleaded that court politics favoured extreme caution: with the backstairs campaign against Grand Duke Nikolai at its height, an appeal to the Tsar would be exploited by the anti-Grand Duke caucus. Time and again Goremykin stepped into heated Council debates to warn his colleagues that their open criticism of the Stavka could only lead to the dismissal of the Grand Duke, but inevitably, as Sazonov explained, there came a point when the problem of divided authority was threatening to fragment the entire administrative structure: 'governmental power was divided between innumerable military and civil bodies and there was no one to put an end to the anarchy which continued unchecked, exciting people's minds and shattering the very principle of authority.' Despite general solicitude for the Grand Duke, there was no alternative but to refer the problem directly to the Tsar, the supreme authority alone capable of creating a reformed hierarchy of power to fit the straitened military and political circumstances. It would seem that this submission decided Nicholas to assume military command.[32]

The reaction to Nicholas's decision was everywhere hostile. A protracted Council meeting on 10 August revealed that all the ministers except Goremykin were strongly opposed (and even he later expressed his misgivings about the chance the Tsar was taking). As Sazonov confided to Paléologue, the dynastic risk was immense: 'Henceforth it is the Emperor who will be personally responsible for all the misfortunes with which we are threatened. If the inefficiency of one of our generals involves us in a disaster, it will be not merely a military defeat but a political and social one at the same time.' The danger inherent in the Tsar's personal identification with military performance was not the only problem to tax the apprehensive ministers. With Nicholas safely removed to the Stavka, the inevitable power vacuum in the capital could only be filled by one personality. No minister of even the most diluted liberal tendencies could welcome the entrance of Alexandra on to the political stage. At a cabinet meeting on 20 August, the ministers individually pleaded with Nicholas but made no impression. In desperation, Samarin organised his colleagues to make a corporate resignation issue of the decision. With the signatures of all ministers except Goremykin (who refused to oppose an Imperial decision, however unwise) and Polivanov and Admiral I.K. Grigorovich (whose military oaths precluded such a declaration), a formal letter was sent to the Tsar, concluding with the words:

> We venture once more to tell you that to the best of our judgement, your decision threatens with serious consequences Russia, your dynasty and your person. At the same meeting, you could see for yourself the irreconcilable differences between our Chairman and us in our estimate of the situation in the country and of the policy to be pursued by the Government. Such a state of affairs is inadmissible at all times and at the present moment it is fatal. Under such conditions, we do not believe we can be of real service to Your Majesty and our country.

The letter was despatched on 22 August, the same day that Nicholas left for the Stavka to assume military command, the same day that the Duma leaders put their formal signatures to the Bloc Programme.[33]

The reaction of the Duma to the Tsar's decision was equally disapproving, as Gurko described:

> The news created a tremendous sensation, especially among members of the opposition. The Duma members present were all monarchists, opposed to and afraid of revolutionary movements during the war, and among them the Tsar's decision aroused many fears. They regarded the Stavka, headed by the Grand Duke Nikolai Nikolaievitch, as a sort of corrective to the extreme Right policies of the Tsar, but they felt that under Nicholas II the Stavka would lose its corrective influence.

Rodzyanko hysterically begged the Council of Ministers to petition Nicholas not to assume military command, an attitude certainly endorsed by the Duma majority. When the news was publicly released on 14 August, the response was again unfavourable: 'The news has produced a deplorable impression; it is objected that the Emperor has no strategic experience; he will be directly responsible for defeats; and lastly, he has the "evil eye".' At just this moment, the Duma army-navy commission presented its report on the war effort to the Tsar. After predictable complaints about the chaos caused by divided power, the commission recommended the immediate resolution of the problem of authority by the appointment of a war dictator. The intention of the commission was in fact to support Krivoshein's plans for the elevation of Polivanov but the report, couched in diplomatic language intended to avoid offending Imperial sensibilities, was apparently taken by the Tsar as Duma corroboration of his decision. As on so many other occasions, mutual misunderstanding served only to widen the gulf between Duma and Tsar.[34]

Although the submission of their Programme to the government coincided with this crisis of relations between the cabinet and the Tsar, the Bloc leaders had high hopes that the heightened atmosphere would benefit their campaign. It did not seem possible for the Bloc to be refused when so many factors were in its favour: the Duma was united as never before and enjoyed the support of a large sector of the State Council; the Bloc demands were modest, partly to accommodate the unprecedented variety of participants, partly to make it as dignified as possible for the government to concede; Petrograd and Moscow society was organised to lend effective moral backing to the Bloc; the provinces had woken up to the significance of the campaign being staged in the capitals; with the exception of Goremykin alone, the entire Council of Ministers accepted the Bloc Programme; and by attending the ceremonial inauguration of four new Special Councils on 22 August, the Tsar had apparently set his official seal of approval on state-society cooperation. For adherents and critics alike, it was difficult to imagine why or how the Progressive Bloc could fail.[35]

On 29 August Goremykin set out for the Stavka with a brief from the Council of Ministers to secure the sanction of the Tsar to compromise with the Bloc. Neither cabinet nor Bloc would have greeted his mission with such optimism had they known Goremykin's real intentions. Goremykin had made an attempt in mid-August to reduce the Bloc's allegiance to the familiar confines of the 'professional Opposition' by inviting the Octobrists and Nationalists to form an official grouping which would enjoy government patronage and privilege, and create a stabilising bond between government and Duma. When this cynical ploy was rejected, Goremykin's political philosophy permitted no other recourse but prorogation of the Duma. Accordingly, when Goremykin was received in audience by

Nicholas on 30 August, he pleaded not for negotiation with the Bloc but instant Duma closure. Nicholas's response was on this occasion uncharacteristically decisive: Goremykin returned to the capital the next day with a signed imperial authorisation for prorogation.[36]

Very soon rumours and counter-rumours were circulating in Petrograd. The Progressists swore that, in the event of prorogation, they would withdraw their delegates from the newly-created Special Councils as a first step towards complete abandonment of the war effort, and would disobey the command to disperse, instead appealing to the country for support. The Kadets were only a little less strident: in the unlikely event of prorogation, the Bloc would appeal through the Duma presidium to the Tsar, maintaining a total boycott of the war until its demands were met. All too soon the Bloc leaders found themselves having to justify their threats: when the apprehensive deputies assembled in open Duma sitting on 3 September, they were met with a *fait accompli* to which they mounted no challenge or show of resistance. In the watchful presence of government officials, a crestfallen Rodzyanko meekly announced the prorogation of the Duma.[37]

Shocked into submission by the cool arbitrariness of this unexpected coup, the fighting spirit of the Duma leaders abruptly disappeared. At a *konvent* meeting, the militants were prevailed upon to abandon or at least postpone immediate action in the interests of Bloc unity. The official Kadet account attempted to play down the extent of the blow: 'it was unanimously decided to receive the break in activities with complete composure in order to set an example to the country ... by this decision was demonstrated the unity of the Bloc'. A hastily-convened Octobrist Central Committee stipulated no withdrawals from legislative or administrative institutions and urged the Bloc 'to maintain its role of an organisation bringing pacification to the country'. The Kadets, only too aware that their recent threats were embarrassingly ineffectual, were easily persuaded; even Nekrasov conceded the necessity of 'operating only by parliamentary means'. The Progressists were considerably harder to convince but acceded to the Bloc majority after a tussle with their consciences. A depressed Bloc meeting on the evening of 3 September decided that although the prorogation was 'an uncharacteristic and transitory episode', the Bloc was an extension of the Duma and could not function independently of it. The Bloc which commanded the loyalties of over two-thirds of the Duma dissolved not because of government persecution but from an internal crisis of confidence. The self-assurance of the Bloc evaporated quite literally overnight. The decision of the Tsar not only prorogued the Duma but, at one remove and with the defeatist complicity of its members, had the effect of proroguing the Progressive Bloc. The Bloc went into voluntary liquidation until the morale of its members recovered from the brutal shock of the rejection of its campaign.[38]

While the Bloc surrendered unconditionally, its sympathisers within the Council of Ministers fought hard. On his return from the Stavka, Goremykin informed an astounded cabinet that the Tsar had decided against further negotiations with the Duma, which would be prorogued until November; as to their collective letter of resignation, all ministers were to remain at their posts. With time to consider the enormity of the decision, the cabinet mounted a full-scale protest on 4 September. Goremykin was accused of deliberately flouting the wishes of the cabinet by delivering a report to the Tsar which gave a false impression of the mood of the Duma and the recommendations of the Council of Ministers. Goremykin argued in reply that as the sole official channel of communication between Tsar and Duma, the Chairman was perfectly within his rights to follow his own advice. The meeting ended in uproar, leaving Goremykin determined to resolve his present intolerable position by appealing to the Tsar. Nicholas promptly summoned all ministers to a 'showdown' meeting at the Stavka for 16 September.[39]

The ministers were put in no doubt that they were in disgrace: pointedly uninvited to dine with the Tsar, they were compelled to seek sustenance at the buffet on Mogilev railway station. At first Nicholas may have hoped for an accommodation with the moderate ministers: to quote Goremykin, 'all of them got a good scolding from His Majesty the Emperor for the August letter and their behaviour during the August crisis.' But Nicholas quickly perceived that there was no possibility of the two fiercely antagonistic groups continuing in the same cabinet. There does not seem to have been any doubt in his mind as to who should remain: 'I hope henceforth that you will unhesitatingly follow my orders as well as the instructions of Ivan Logginovich, whom I intend to retain at the head of the Council of Ministers for a long time.' In a letter to Alexandra, Nicholas observed that 'yesterday's sitting has clearly shown me that the Ministers do not wish to work with old Gor. in spite of the stern words which I addressed to them; therefore, on my return, some changes must take place.' The purge of the cabinet awaited only Nicholas's return to the capital. The ministerial letter of 21 August had identified the disruptive elements and, as Sazonov described, 'it decided the fate of the ministers who signed it: six of them, including myself, were gradually got rid of during the following year and only two, supposed to be less dangerous, remained in office till the downfall of the monarchy.' Within ten days of the Stavka meeting, Shcherbatov and Samarin had been summarily removed, clearing the way for the refurbished authority of Goremykin and the reactionary zeal of the new occupant of the MVD. Totally downcast by the collapse of his 'moderate conspiracy', Krivoshein knew that his days were numbered: a month later, on 26 October, his dismissal symbolically brought to an end the liberal phase of 1915 and the last hopes of a meaningful *union sacrée*.[40]

The third protagonist in the crisis was the collection of public organisations centred on Moscow. At every level, the prorogation, which elicited only disappointment and resignation in the capital, generated a more dynamic response in Moscow. While Petrograd could muster only some 2500 strikers, over 18,000 came out in sympathy with the Duma in Moscow. It may well be, as one Soviet authority claims, that the official statistics are grossly misleading and that the total striking force in the capitals touched 70,000; but whatever the exact figures, this unexpected manifestation of proletarian outrage alarmed the Duma. Far from being cheered by the workers' support, the Bloc leaders dreaded the approach of a fresh revolutionary upsurge. Konovalov for the Progressists considered 'it is essential immediately to take every measure to prevent the nation from sinking to that state of morale when it is so overwhelmed by despair that there appears to be only one course open – the path of force and every kind of excess.' Kerensky suspected the government was attempting to provoke the Left into committing itself to premature revolution: 'to prevent the government seizing the opportunity to explain away its military failures and growing repression, the Trudovik fraction must maintain its tactics of restraint and appeal to the workers not to strike ... the activities of the government must be viewed as provocation.' At a meeting on 5 September, the Kadet deputies and Moscow Kadets regretted what they regarded as a potentially explosive situation in Moscow. Guchkov too felt constrained to make the Octobrist position clear: 'we demanded the government enter into an agreement with society not for revolution but to strengthen the government for the purpose of defending the homeland from revolution and anarchy.'[41]

At higher levels of Moscow society, the sense of outrage was equally widespread but inhibited by the Bloc's appeals for restraint and the very real spectre of violent disorders in the city. At a giant open meeting in Moscow on 5 September, unmistakable antagonism towards the government was muted by fear of the terrible consequences of forthright criticism. All eyes turned to the UZ and UT congresses scheduled for 7–9 September, which were the obvious rallying-point for political protest and opposition. Even before prorogation, *Den* reported that 'Duma deputies are decided in the event of dissolution to "go to Moscow" for the zemstvo congress opening there shortly and convert it into a political demonstration'. The Tsaritsa too was alive to the possibility of the congresses becoming a substitute for the recessed Duma: 'now the members of the Duma want to meet in Moscow to talk over everything when their work here is closed – one ought energetically to forbid it, it will only bring great troubles. If they do that – one ought to say that the Duma will then not be reopened till much later – threaten them.' However, from outside and within the congresses the Bloc leaders pleaded for calm. To the Moscow Kadets on 8 September, Milyukov played down the interruption in the Duma's activities and condemned the militancy of the Progressists as criminally irresponsible. At the volatile UT congress, Guchkov and Shingarev called for restraint and self-control. The efforts of the moderates proved successful: though the debates of the congresses were stormy, the final resolutions were relatively mild. The moderate Kadet element prevailed over the militant Progressist minority within the UT to lend support to the restrained criticisms put up by the joint Kadet and Left Octobrist establishment within the UZ.[42]

Public interest was reduced to following the inglorious career of a joint deputation from the UZ and UT to the Tsar. Anticipating that the UT might elect radical representatives, the UZ deliberately selected delegates of moderate views, the right Kadet Prince Lvov (the UZ Director) and the Octobrists P.V. Kamensky and A.I. Maslov. As it turned out, the moderate cause was not lost within the UT: the Kadet Chelnokov was elected together with the Progressists Ryabushinsky and N.I. Astrov. Overall, the deputation membership of two Octobrists, two Kadets and two Progressists once again gave the Kadets a pivotal leadership. Though the UT delegates argued that neither congress should disperse until the deputation was received, as a guarantee against treachery or faint-heartedness, the delegation itself (by a predictable four-to-two vote) proposed adjournment. When the UZ congress agreed, the UT reluctantly acquiesced. The fears of the UT were soon realised: on 20 September Nicholas announced that he could receive no delegation of a political nature. The impact of this snub upon the UZ and UT was hardly less shattering than that of prorogation on the Bloc members some three weeks previously. Again the result was not to provoke the moderates into more direct action but to convince them of the uselessness of further agitation. The UT made a public statement amounting to a despairing apology for the political impotence of the public organisations. On 29 September, the six members of the delegation sadly reviewed their situation, voted against fresh congresses in the near future and gloomily dispersed. In the face of the intransigence of the Tsar, the public organisations, like the Duma Bloc and the Bloc sympathisers in the Council of Ministers, brought to an end the political campaign which they had already restricted to narrow confines of their own choosing.[43]

When seeking explanations for the defeat of the Progressive Bloc, the circumstances of the Tsar must figure prominently. With so many advantages favouring the Bloc, only the Tsar himself was sufficiently powerful to upset the odds. Nicholas's assumption of military command and endorsement of the Special Councils were expressions of his own idiosyncratic reinterpretation of the *union sacrée* in the straitened circumstances of late 1915. Travelling from Petrograd to the Stavka on 22–3 August, Nicholas felt the burdens of political leadership slipping from his shoulders with immense relief. In a sphere far removed from the demoralising defeatism of the capital and the claustrophobic domesticity of life with Alexandra, Nicholas experienced a feeling of elation which he himself compared to the emotion following Holy Communion. Refreshed by his welcome remoteness from the 'poisoned air of Petrograd', Nicholas quickly absorbed from his energetic Chief-of-Staff, General M.V. Alexeyev, a soldier's contempt for the antics of office-bound civilians. The spirit of cautious optimism which pervaded the front contrasted starkly with the extravagant despair of those safe in the capital, as Nicholas remarked to his son's tutor, Pierre Gilliard: 'You have no idea how depressing it is to be away from the front. It seems as if everything here saps energy and enfeebles resolution. The most pessimistic rumours and most ridiculous stories are accepted and get about everywhere ... At the front there is only one thought – the determination to conquer.'[44] Into this fresh atmosphere of hope and action, all the more intoxicating because of its brief duration, burst Goremykin with tales of rebellion inside and outside the government. With hindsight, it is plain that the greatest mischance of the political crisis was that the two issues of the Bloc campaign and Nicholas's assumption of military command coincided. To Nicholas, now remote from political events at Mogilev, it can hardly have seemed coincidental that the Duma Bloc should consort with the moderates in the Council of Ministers precisely at the time when he received an illegal attempt to force his hand from those same ministers. The ministerial letter of 21 August and the Bloc Programme of 22 August were interpreted as expressions of the same coalition aimed at forcing fundamental changes in the midst of war and preventing him continuing as Commander-in-Chief. This impression of conspiracy was accentuated by the single biased inspiration to which he was subjected, that of Alexandra; and the single tendentious account to which he had access, that of Goremykin. Browbeaten by the correspondence of the Tsaritsa and irritated by the account of Goremykin, Nicholas allowed his exasperation to manifest itself in a precipitate decision which many considered contradicted the recent direction of his thought.[45]

However, the circumstances of the Tsar provide no insight into the collapse of the Bloc after the prorogation of the Duma. Politically and psychologically, the moderates were no match for the tsarist establishment. At base there could be only two approaches to the government: clandestine pressure or an open campaign. The first method was infinitely better suited to the moderates, guaranteed the widest measure of society support and offended few patriotic scruples as to the morality of extracting concessions under war duress. To quote a perceptive Okrana reporter, the Kadets in particular wanted 'to effect a peaceful revolution, clandestinely, with the sanction of the government itself'.[46] Unhappily, the almost conspiratorial early rationale of the Bloc was soon compromised. Widening membership multiplied the chances of a public confrontation with the government, Moscow initiated its own unsolicited campaign of radical support, the Programme leaked into the national press and the whole Bloc enterprise escaped from the confidential confines of the Tauride Palace into the streets. By the time the Bloc approached the cabinet, the runaway development of the society campaign had sabotaged any lingering hopes of clandestine pressure and stiffened the resistance of the Tsar and reactionary establishment.

The only alternative now was to abandon constitutional petition and pass on to overt rebellion. In the heat of the moment, wild threats were indeed made by some moderates. Fedor Rodichev, for example, insisted that 'after the dissolution of parliament, the Bloc must transfer its agitation to the country and embark upon the organisation of the populace.' But Rodichev was far from typical. A radical who would undoubtedly have signed the Vyborg Appeal had he not been attending a conference of the Inter-Parliamentary Union in London at the time, Rodichev was an uneasy, almost guilty survivor of the lost generation of Vyborg casualties. Out of place and almost self-consciously anachronistic in the Milyukov-dominated fraction of the Fourth Duma, Rodichev's chosen role as the conscience of the Kadets could be interpreted as courting that political martyrdom from which he had involuntarily escaped in 1906. Nothing came of his bluster. The moderates were alarmed enough at the end of August by the broadening of the Bloc campaign and becoming agitated by their responsibility for opening a Pandora's box in wartime Russia. Even when the surprise prorogation of the Duma dashed their inflated hopes, the Bloc leaders were incapable of attempting any raising of the populace. The only precedent – the Vyborg Appeal – had proved an unmitigated disaster and few with any experience or close memory of that traumatic event could ever muster the self-confidence to follow Rodichev and suggest a repetition of the experiment. In short, the Bloc leaders found the sphere of operations permitted by their constitutionalist scruples condemned them to political impotence. Clandestine pressure was the only weapon the Bloc allowed itself in wartime and once this approach was spent, there was no permissible alternative. The moderates' allegiance to *union sacrée* was compromised but never abandoned. The arbitrary closure of the Duma in early September meant only the official rejection of the moderates' application to renegotiate the *union sacrée* from a better bargaining position. In its last stages, the Bloc campaign was consciously or unwittingly an exercise in bluff; when that bluff was called by the Tsar, the realisation of their political failure hit the moderates harder than ever before.[47]

To wider groups of society, many politically activated for the first time, the lessons of the crisis were rather different. Support for the Duma was now more a society convention than an ideological commitment. The 3 September issue of *Den* reported that 'it may seem a paradox but without doubt the dissolution of the State Duma is making more of an impact on the country than the existence of the Duma. It may well be that the country has not seen the Duma as the incarnation of its dreams and aspirations but the closure of the Duma means their total liquidation.' Moreover the conduct of the Progressive Bloc had been controversial in the extreme. It had always been assumed that in the event of a confrontation between government and country, the Duma would act as the general staff of the national campaign. With their first tentative foray into the political arena in mid-1915, the public organisations had looked to the Progressive Bloc for guidance and direction. Far from welcoming the arrival of powerful reinforcements, the Duma Bloc jealously discerned a potential challenge to its political monopoly and not only neglected to give the public organisations a strong lead but positively discouraged their assumption of a political role. After the prorogation, in fear of a more general political crisis, the embarrassed and apologetic moderates made every effort to contain the unsolicited broader movement which had incidentally evolved. Well into September, the faltering impetus of educated society was less the product of the defensive and repressive actions of the MVD than the result of the insistent restraining influence of the Duma Bloc. Contemporary interpretations of the conduct of the Bloc varied. The Left was angry: the craven response of the Bloc to prorogation amounted to a sell-out to the Tsar. An obscure imprisoned revolutionary at the time, Joseph Stalin later contemptuously wrote off the moderates' campaign as 'a revolt on their knees'.[48] The Right was content: the behaviour of the Bloc under stress demonstrated that the moderates represented no real danger to the tsarist establishment. The consensus opinion was that the greater the crisis, the more likely were the moderates to support the status quo. In the heightening political and social atmosphere which developed relentlessly after mid-1915, this reputation could do the Russian moderates no good at all.

4 Crisis of Confidence

After the prorogation of September 1915, the reactionary *revanche* gathered momentum. Even before prorogation, the Duma Nationalists and Rights responded to the challenge of what they called the 'Yellow Bloc' by planning their own 'Black Bloc'. Outside the Duma, the United Nobility agitated vigorously against any suggestion of official concession and a series of monarchist congresses (the only large public gatherings now permitted by the MVD) flaunted the victory of the Right in the faces of the crushed moderates and kept the general public well aware of the primacy of reaction. Goremykin had already ensured that the position of the Duma was weaker than ever before. Since the Duma's greatest authority stemmed from its perusal of the Budget, Goremykin reasoned that to remove (or even only threaten to remove) this prerogative would render the Duma harmless. In June 1915 Goremykin persuaded the Council of Ministers to consider the principle of taxation by decree. If the government could raise taxes without recourse to the Duma, the national assembly would survive merely as a luxury which could be dispensed with whenever circumstances dictated. On 27 June, encouraged by guarded cabinet agreement to his *ballon d'essai*, Goremykin conceded the Duma summer session; but a mere five days before the Duma convened, it was brazenly announced that under the terms of Clause 87 of the Fundamental Laws, taxation might be raised by decree for the next two-and-a-half years. At a stroke, the financial rights of the Duma were threatened with suspension until January 1918. Only the Tsar's indulgent attitude towards the Duma kept Goremykin from summarily dismissing the legislative assemblies. The moment that the Tsar's opinion coincided with that of Goremykin, the Duma could be safely prorogued. That moment came at the Stavka on 30 August. After prorogation, Goremykin contemptuously offered the Duma the most menial form of financial collaboration: to pass the 1916 Budget in the certain knowledge that refusal would mean the withdrawal of even this servile function. With morale lower than at any time in the history of the Duma, the Bloc leaders were prepared to accept this travesty of its financial prerogatives rather than attempt to argue the point.[1]

But it was the new Minister of Interior, Alexei Khvostov

(confusingly, the nephew of the Justice Minister Alexander Khvostov), who proved the pacesetter of the reconstituted Council of Ministers. As befitted a minister recruited from the Right fraction of the Duma, Khvostov's chief concern was the future role of the legislative institutions. From the very day of his appointment, Khvostov demanded maximum Okhrana surveillance over political parties and a detailed weekly report on deputies' activities. Only in mid-November did Khvostov judge the political crisis to be over, reverting to the standard practice of relying on the judgement of the Director of Police to place the most important decisions and information before the Minister. Given that political calm was restored, Khvostov followed the example of his predecessor Maklakov in seizing the opportunity to undermine the recessed Duma. The rescript which prorogued the Duma had promised a new session 'not later than November 1915' but on 23 November another rescript baldly stated that, 'owing to special circumstances', the November session would not now take place. The next day Goremykin announced that a new session would be convened only when the Duma budget commission, the only permissible institution of the Duma in recess other than the chancellery, had completed its examination of the 1916 Budget. It seemed that the future Duma, should it exist at all, would be limited to the purely financial functions of July 1914 and January 1915.[2] Khvostov looked further ahead still. If the Fourth Duma ran its full course, its last session was scheduled to close in June 1917 but with the uncertainties of war and the recent agitation of the moderates, Khvostov felt justified in making preliminary preparations for the Fifth Duma. Of eight million roubles set aside for expenses in future Duma elections, Khvostov spent some 1,300,000 roubles over late 1915 and early 1916. A proportion went to the subsidisation of the Right press and support of the Right organisations. Most went into preparing a detailed psephological examination of the Duma elections of 1912. This analysis, known as the 'Khvostov Memorandum', became the blueprint for a state-created Fifth Duma designed to exclude all parties to the left of the Zemstvo-Octobrists.[3]

It could have been worse. Khvostov's Memorandum still amounted to an assertion of qualified support for the Duma as an institution. A pragmatic Right politician like Khvostov saw many reasons for retaining the Duma; the only problem lay in concocting a Duma with a membership sympathetic to the government. Even Goremykin, who was more committed to the eventual abolition of the Duma, had no immediate plans for its reduction or liquidation in late 1915. For the Duma moderates however, their morale at an unprecedented low, the future of the Duma could have been bleaker only with the prospect of imminent dissolution. The government had secured legislative and financial independence of the Duma, the plans for its successor were already under way, and all that remained for the Fourth Duma was to eke out its remaining term in the pitiable and ignominious role of part-time government auditor.

The moderates could not overcome the disappointment of the defeat of the Bloc. The first (and arguably the only) moderate fraction to stage any kind of recovery was the Kadet, but even so the process by which the Kadets threw off the despair which enveloped them was slow and sporadic. On 22 September the Kadet fraction resigned itself to a government hardened against the Progressive Bloc and was troubled by the political torpor which by now possessed Russian society. In the words of a *Rech* leading article, was this 'calm or indifference'? – a tribute to their own influence or an expression of profound insouciance? There were no plans for a further approach to the government, only the forlorn hope that events would turn their way some time in the future. A plenary session of the Kadet Central Committee on 5 October confirmed this Micawber-like course: Kadets everywhere were enjoined to watch, record and document all instances of government abuse and maladministration for a future day of reckoning. This resolution was subsequently issued as a circular to the provincial party, with a sanguine footnote suggesting that good behaviour on the part of the populace might still win over the government. The sterility of this exercise, betraying just how far Kadet confidence had fallen since August, overshadowed the ten-year anniversary of the October Manifesto and the foundation of the party. The eminent historian who headed the Kadet movement employed the months of political defeat to convert his party into an historical research team. With a hopeless political situation confronting him, Milyukov abandoned practical activities in favour of an academic exercise, in the belief that any occupation was better than none in preventing a further collapse of morale.[4]

The autumn of 1915 did see attempts by Kadet groups to break away from Milyukov's fatalistic prescription. The left wing refused to be bound by the defeatist complacency of the Central Committee. The left Kadets interpreted the Bloc defeat as demonstrating the stark necessity of abandoning any dealings with the government and proving the need for close alliance with the Left parties and the labour movement. On 1 October they organised a giant open meeting in Petrograd to create local residents' committees to make the voice of the proletariat more powerful and articulate. By parading as the sponsors of the residents' committees, the left Kadets hoped to build bridges between the Kadet party and the re-emerging workers' movement. Unhappily, a second meeting a week later resulted in a chaotic fracas between the various workers' groups, each claiming the monopoly of legitimate representation of the proletariat and united only in scornfully rejecting Kadet patronage. A similar effort to reach the Moscow workers on 15 November was indignantly boycotted. The Okhrana reports paint a sorry picture of Kadet failure: of the new residents' committees, a few were taken over by the workers themselves, more were captured by the Left parties but the great majority simply withered away from lack of support. In disgust, the left Kadets abandoned the workers' movement to the Bolsheviks and Mensheviks. A simultaneous approach to the parties of the Left had a similar reception. The Trudoviks of Kerensky had been tuned to the workers' movement since early September and entered into close alliance with the Mensheviks soon afterwards. Although they were the left Kadets' closest neighbours, the Trudoviks were committed to a move away from the Kadets and three separate meetings in October only emphasised that no hope of collaboration existed. Neither the direct approach to the workers nor the indirect approach by way of the Left parties proved remotely encouraging to the dispirited left Kadets. While the Milyukov line seemed unnecessarily defeatist, the left Kadets quickly learned that their radical schemes could provide nothing more constructive.[5]

The activists on the Kadet right wing were hardly more successful. In seeking (like their left colleagues) to broaden the base of the Kadet party, the right Kadets moved in the surprising direction of the traditional bastion of conservatism, the United Nobility. Over September, a group of the nobility, disconcerted by official treatment of the Progressive Bloc, broke away from the main body to form what came to be known as the 'Young Nobility'. On 10 October the Moscow Kadets debated the significance of the breakaway group and opted for contact: 'It is essential to exploit by every means the incipient movement within the camp of the nobility. Every Kadet with connections in that quarter must use all his influence for its development, and by the patronage of the growing movement ... to draw this movement under the Kadet flag.' To split the United Nobility with its congress only a month away, enhance the authority of the Progressive Bloc by claiming the active adherence of a sector of the nobility, and increase the practical resources of the Kadet party were prizes which the Kadets could not let slip. Feelers were extended, though in an atmosphere of mounting doubt. Finally, on 1 November the Moscow Kadets decided to call a halt on the grounds that the move could well split the Bloc should details of the confidential negotiations get out, and that approaches towards the Right were suicidal in this period of a reviving labour movement. The Okhrana, which had been watching this development with some anxiety, reported on 8 November that the Kadets appeared to have abandoned all moves in the direction of the 'Young Nobility'. A week later the police dossier on this fascinating but short-lived Kadet enterprise was closed.[6] Both left and right-wing Kadet attempts to extend beyond the conventional orbit of the moderate camp and recruit traditionally more extremist support had come to nothing.

The Kadet opposition to the Milyukov establishment secured just one victory. On 3 September the Kadet sub-committee on the next party conference recommended a full congress be held to determine the national response to the current crisis. Over the course of September the provincial pressure for a party congress proved overwhelming, constraining the Central Committee to agree formally on 5 October to hold a congress in the first week of the new Duma session, at that time scheduled for November.[7] Provincial conferences were convened throughout October to elect delegates to the promised congress and evaluate the Kadet position. The opinions expressed were very mixed, representing the whole Kadet spectrum from the crypto-Trudovik to the crypto-Octobrist positions. The Saratov conference of 10–11 October supported the Milyukov line, preferring steady persuasion of the government to any attempt at wider agitation. The Samara conference of 20–1 October condemned Milyukov, demanding the Kadet fraction jettison the Progressive Bloc in favour of alliance with the Left and the labour movement. (The Samara Kadets were not to know that left Kadet attempts to do just that in the capitals were currently collapsing.) The Kiev conference, also held on 20–1 October, adopted a central position, rejecting the militancy of the left Kadets in favour of concentration on the Progressive Bloc to increase pressure on the government. The convening of provincial Kadet conferences should not incidentally be interpreted as an indication of the party's robust health: the Samara conference attracted only twenty-six members and the Saratov conference twenty-two — and five of these were not locals but Duma deputies! To Milyukov's relief, it appeared there was no unequivocal mandate from provincial Kadetism. In these circumstances it seemed legitimate for the fraction and the Central Committee to follow their own advice until the congress met.[8]

As Kadet and Bloc leader, Milyukov decided to test the political temperature of society. On 25 October he summoned the leaders of the Bloc and public organisations to a consultation, which only exposed divisive and contradictory attitudes. Guchkov (for the WIC) demanded firm action against the government, Chelnokov (for the moderate leadership of the UT) advocated a 'wait-and-see' policy, Astrov (for the more radical rank-and-file of the UT) stipulated opposition to the government, and Lvov (for the UZ) attempted to play the trimmer while making plain his sympathy for Chelnokov's restraint. The internal divisions between the various public organisations were matched only by their common profound mistrust of the Progressive Bloc. Three days later Milyukov, dismayed at the latest evidence of the trend towards reaction in the dismissal of

Krivoshein, called the first meeting of the Bloc since 3 September. Seeing little chance of a long Duma session in the immediate future and worried lest the moderates atrophy through lack of exercise, Milyukov voiced the opinion that the Bloc must learn to function independently of Duma sessions. The State Council delegates countered that extra-Duma activity must be left to the public organisations and the most the Bloc could legally do was to prepare for the next session. It was graphically plain that its Council delegates were condemning the Bloc to virtual impotence. A second Bloc meeting only repeated the stalemate, for the imminence of the promised Duma session encouraged the Council delegates in their stand. On 5 November the Bloc drew up a formal Resolution comprising six 'military' recommendations and six 'political' demands, the latter carefully muted to avoid offending the sensibilities of the Council delegates. To no avail. On 12 November, the Bloc dramatically split three ways: the Council delegates accepted only the military section of the Resolution; the right-wing Duma Blocists were prepared to countenance the political demands but only if the Resolution were presented to the Tsar confidentially; and the left-wing Duma Blocists led by Efremov insisted on the publication of the entire Resolution. All three groups threatened to quit the Bloc unless their views were respected. Appalled at the fragile nature of the Bloc alliance, Milyukov deliberately temporised over another meeting to allow time for passions to cool.[9]

On 23 November the bombshell landed: the promised Duma session was indefinitely postponed. A Bloc meeting three days later presented Milyukov with an appalling dilemma: if the Bloc stepped up its activities in protest, it would lose its Council representation; if it accepted the postponement without complaint, it stood to lose the Progressists. On 28 November the Duma Progressists showed they were not bluffing by publicly withdrawing their delegates from the Special Councils. In despair, Milyukov and the Bloc president Shidlovsky agreed that the Bloc mount some form of agitation, if only to keep the Progressists within the Bloc. The challenge, if not affront, to the Council delegates was implicit and on 9 December the Centre faction of the State Council formally quitted the Bloc. All the painful concessions and compromises to accommodate the Council members had proved vain against the tide of events, and yet, far from purging the Bloc of its least reliable elements and clearing the way for an energetic campaign, this defection only impressed more deeply upon the Bloc's remaining adherents the fragility of the coalition and the necessity of most careful consideration before the smallest action. The secession of the Council Centre faction shocked the Bloc back into non-activity and it was a full two months before the members mustered the courage to call a fresh meeting. Even the schemes of the experienced Milyukov were fruitless: the public organisations were too quarrelsome and independent-minded to be of use to the Bloc, while in defeat the Bloc itself showed every sign of proving the sum of its members' weaknesses rather than the aggregate of component strengths.[10]

If the Kadets only with difficulty began a recovery from the prorogation crisis, their fellow moderates fared even worse. The rejection of the Bloc seems to have administered a profound shock to Guchkov. A flurry of Octobrist Central Committee meetings over autumn 1915 show Guchkov undergoing a personal shift from allegiance to *union sacrée* back to his pre-war political militancy. Guchkov's reconversion was augmented by a growing sense of personal frustration. By 1915 he had antagonised almost every political organisation by his capricious conduct, leaving him with minimal support in the world of Russian politics. In September 1915 this widespread dislike was dramatically demonstrated when Guchkov was badly defeated in the UT Congress elections to the delegation to the Tsar. For this candidacy, regarded as a formality in the Bloc, to be defeated rammed home the new isolation of Guchkov. Though he quickly rallied, securing election from the industrial curia to the State Council only days later, Guchkov's fear that his political star was on the wane had been pointedly confirmed. A note of desperation enters Guchkov's public statements from this time, as for example his cryptic remark in an interview with *Den*: 'Political life is changing and at the present time of crisis it is altogether likely that tomorrow will bring surprises which will reverse yesterday's conditions.' Though this opinion could be interpreted as mere political Micawberism, it is probably a first indication of the Octobrist leader's commitment to a palace revolution.[11]

The Octobrists within the Duma suffered the blows of the government with the fatalistic resignation of a party whose spirit is broken. The attitude of the Zemstvo-Octobrists was best expressed in the famous 'mad chauffeur' parable published by Vasilii Maklakov in late September. As the most right-wing of Kadets, Maklakov was very close to the Octobrist position and provided a striking metaphorical apologia for the weakness of Octobrist policy. The author (the Progressive Bloc), travelling by car over dangerous mountain roads, is appalled to discover that his chauffeur (the government) drives so badly that he threatens all his passengers (the Russian people) with almost certain death. Maklakov describes the dilemma of the leading passenger:

What must you do? Force the chauffeur to vacate his seat? That would be fine in a cart, in ordinary times, at slow speed and on the flat. At such a time it would save the situation but can it be done on a winding road in the mountains? He still has the wheel and drives the car – if you are not strong and skilful, one false move or hasty arm movement will crash the car. You know this, and he knows it too and smiles at your fears and impotence: 'Don't try to grab.' He is right. You dare not try to grab the wheel. Perhaps fear or exasperation might lead you to forget the danger to yourself and make a grab for the wheel and risk a crash – but wait! It's not just yourself who is involved. Your mother is with you and your action would kill her too.

The only rational course to take in such a situation is not to distract the chauffeur and hope for the best, judiciously ignoring the complaints of those whose judgement is inferior to one's own:

So you restrain yourself. You postpone the reckoning with the chauffeur until the danger decreases and you are on the flat again. You let the chauffeur keep the wheel. More than this, you try not to get in his way, even helping him with advice, directions and cooperation. You are quite right – this is necessary. But what will you endure at the thought that even your restraint will not carry you through, that even with your help the chauffeur cannot drive! What will you suffer if your mother, seeing the danger, begs you for help and, not understanding your behaviour, accuses you of inaction and fear?

Maklakov succinctly sketched the mentality of the Octobrists (and in large measure the entire moderate camp) in Aesopian language, stressing the apprehensive terror of a political group whose policies were reduced to hoping for the best and whose energies were debased to the level of humouring a government which it knew to be incapable. Not surprisingly, the decline of Octobrism inside and outside the Duma was reflected in its continuing organisational death agony: after the closure of *Golos Moskvy*, the Central Committee was hard put even to organise the traditional celebrative jubilee to greet the tenth anniversary of the October Manifesto.[12]

The Progressists were hardly in better shape. In the stunned wake of prorogation, the Progressist leadership adopted the same defeatist line as the Kadet: while Milyukov converted his party into an historical research team, *Utro Rossii* proposed employing the redundant Duma deputies as the staff of 'an itinerant popular university'.[13] But it was not long before Efremov returned to his earlier militancy and moved the Progressist fraction into direct opposition to the government. Although the Moscow industrialist-dominated Progressist Central Committee stipulated on 2 October that 'the Fraction must under no circumstances depart from the path of parliamentary struggle and must remain within the Progressive Bloc', the directive barely survived the month. Early in November, Efremov threatened the

Bloc with the withdrawal of the Progressists; on the twenty-eighth, he withdrew the five Progressist delegates from the Special Councils. A fraction statement released two days later claimed that the Special Councils were under government not Duma control, Duma representation was too small to have any chance of outvoting the government, Duma delegates were channelled into sub-committees where they were out of their depth in technical minutiae and, in that they had no legislative or executive authority, the delegates were allowing the government to 'use' the Duma to share responsibility for misdeeds over which they had no control.[14]

While Efremov and the bulk of the Progressist fraction pursued their policy of boycott, their backers were profoundly unhappy. In view of the stiff competition for ministry contracts, the high profit margin on orders and the continuing background threat of the nationalisation of war industry, the industrialists were most anxious to secure the maximum possible influence over the government. Far from promoting this policy, the provocative line of the Duma Progressists almost invited government reprisals against Russian industry. The Okhrana noticed that the Progressist withdrawals from the Special Councils had so agitated industrialist circles that they were seriously considering transferring their support to the Kadets: 'the indecision of the industrialists, oscillating over whether to associate with the political platform of the Kadets or Progressists, is exciting the Kadets to the greatest possible degree, for they eagerly wish to attract the industrialists to their party.' Tactical considerations also weighed with the industrialists: with the Progressists consistently defeated by the Kadets over 1915, was it more advantageous to support the perennial challenger or the regular winner? Now that the Duma Progressists had forfeited the confidence of industry by their intemperate conduct, would it be expedient to transfer support to the more professional and tractable Kadets, whose moves to effect compromise with the government seemed so much more appropriate than the Progressists' ill-judged antagonism? The doubts of the industrialists were echoed by Progressist opinion in the provinces. The shock of the decision of 28 November shattered the already desperately weak Progressist provincial movement: the majority of local Progressists deserted *en masse* to the Kadets and even the loyal remainder showered the Central Committee with complaints about the leadership of Efremov and urged an immediate return to the Special Councils. A similar protest movement raised its head among the Duma Progressists and in December a group of deputies led by Prince E.N. Trubetskoi quit the fraction to associate with the Kadets. Efremov's militant line had precipitated a crisis which threatened the party with disintegration at every level.[15]

The passage of time only served to exacerbate the Progressist crisis.

In early December, the scandalously excessive profits of the oil monopolists prompted the Special Council on Fuel (currently without Progressist representation) to recommend the compulsory fixing of oil prices. Fearful that the oil issue might become a test case for nationalisation, the Council of Congresses of Trade and Industry hurriedly agreed to a system of price-fixing on the understanding that no plans for oil nationalisation were entertained. However public indignation against the oil monopolists reached such a pitch that nationalisation was widely advocated as the only answer to the abuse. On 22 December, a set-piece contest took place in the Duma budget commission: for nationalisation stood the Left Octobrist I.S. Klyuzhev; for price-fixing stood Titov, the embarrassed Progressist champion of industrial free enterprise. In the vote that concluded the debate, Klyuzhev won a striking victory and an assurance that oil nationalisation would be put to the Duma the moment it reassembled. The Duma as well as the government was entertaining the principle of nationalisation of industry. As the position of industry deteriorated, the despairing industrialists saw even more reason for abandoning the Progressists in favour of the Kadets.[16]

By New Year 1916 the government expected little trouble from the moderates. The arbitrary postponement of the Duma in November had proved that its membership was in no condition to launch a counter-offensive. The Progressive Bloc had sunk in the early days of September, to resurface in a grotesquely waterlogged condition for a brief period in November, only to disappear again. Among the Duma membership, the Right was content with a recessed assembly, the Left was powerless until the labour movement assumed greater proportions, the Octobrist fraction was silently decomposing and the Progressists showed every sign of tearing themselves to political shreds. Only the Kadets posed a potential threat. Khvostov instituted close surveillance over the Kadets throughout the autumn: on 30 October an Okhrana circular demanded information on the various Kadet projects to expand their support; a supplementary circular on 7 November requested detailed reports on the Kadet provincial conferences. An end-of-year summary by Police Director S.P. Beletsky ruled out all parliamentary parties as dangerous except the Kadets.[17] The Kadets were indeed the only party which could be said to have weathered the September crisis. By December, they seemed likely to secure the monopoly of organised moderate opposition, for the internal dissensions of the Progressists made possible their elimination as a Duma force and the transfer of their personnel and resources to the Kadet party. Though they had suffered enough, the Kadets salvaged more from the defeat of the Bloc than their moderate colleagues: the crisis had relatively enhanced the Kadet position within the moderate camp even while the fortunes of the moderates and

Duma as a whole suffered a profound slump.

In early 1916 the position of the Duma improved a little, though, given the desperate weakness of the moderates, it is hardly surprising that its partial recovery owed nothing to the efforts of the Duma parties and was essentially a by-product of ministerial politics. Goremykin's reactionary conception of the Duma function was causing unease at the highest level by the winter of 1915–16. While Goremykin assumed that prorogation and a cabinet purge gave him *carte blanche* in the pursuit of reactionary policies, the Tsar does not seem to have wished to sever contacts with the Duma irrevocably. When, for example, Goremykin and Khvostov jointly proposed the extension of pre-publication censorship from areas of 'reinforced protection' to the whole Russian Empire, the cabinet agreed but Nicholas, as on so many other occasions the despair of his ministers and critics alike, turned the proposition down flat. Soon after the November postponement of the Duma, Alexandra ventured some advice to her husband: 'Our Friend [Rasputin] has been with the old man [Goremykin] who listened to him very attentively but was most obstinate. He intends asking you not to call the Duma at all (he loathes it) – and Gregory told him it was not right of him to ask such a thing of you – they must be shown a little confidence.' It is likely that during autumn 1915 Nicholas became increasingly unsure of the correctness of his prorogation decision of 30 August and instinctively played the trimmer against the reactionary ambitions of Goremykin.[18]

On 19 December 1915 Rodzyanko accused Goremykin of inexcusable neglect of the supply situation in Russia, concluding: 'if you, Ivan Logginovich, feel that you lack the strength to bear this heavy burden and use all available means to help the country to emerge on to the high road of victory, have the courage to own this and make way for younger and more energetic men.' Exasperated by this scathing personal attack, Goremykin was confirmed in his determination to ignore the Duma completely. As the cabinet crisis crystallised, two candidates emerged as possible successors to Goremykin. Perceiving the area of Nicholas's dissatisfaction with Goremykin, Khvostov set out to prove himself the only individual with the expertise to resolve the troubled relationship between government and Duma. At a secret assignation in January 1916, Khvostov promised Rodzyanko and Milyukov a standard Duma session in exchange for a guarantee of Bloc good behaviour. Rodzyanko eagerly gave the required assurance and even Milyukov was prepared to express guarded agreement (whilst hedging his assent with sufficient provisos to make repudiation practicable should the deal turn sour). Khvostov could now advertise that his adroit management had secured in advance the tranquil Duma desired by the Tsar. Unfortunately for Khvostov, the powerful machinery of backstairs influence also advanced a candidate. In late December an anonymous document entitled (ironically enough) 'What is to be Done' was brought to the attention of Alexandra, who was so favourably impressed that she passed it on to Nicholas. The paper called for a break with the brittle reaction of Goremykin which, by refusing a Duma session, only inflamed the country against the government and cast the Duma in a thoroughly undeserved heroic role. The alternative was a new 'soft line': the Duma was to serve not as the spokesman of troublemakers but as the safety-valve for society tensions; by feeding the Duma a frugal but savoury diet of small reforms, a tolerable simulacrum of concord could be achieved between the government and country. Neatly packaged and irresistibly simple, the scheme was sold to the Imperial couple at precisely the right psychological moment. Once its acceptance was assured, the document's author was identified as Boris Sturmer. As rumours of the succession crisis grew, the moderates were cheered that the hard line of Goremykin was under pressure and both rival replacements had committed themselves to a milder line towards society and an early reconvened Duma.[19]

On completing its examination of the 1916 Budget, the Duma budget commission challenged Goremykin to redeem his November pledge and call the Duma. On 13 January 1916, there occurred a fundamental split in the Council of Ministers. Together with three colleagues, Goremykin opposed anything more than a 'financial Duma' and proposed that five days were ample for the Duma to complete these functions. Intuitively aware that the time was ripe for Goremykin's downfall, Khvostov and the other ministers denied the feasibility of recreating the Duma of January 1915 and pressed for a standard session. Goremykin responded as in late August 1915 by appealing to the Tsar to support him and overrule the Council majority: on 17 January Goremykin demanded of Nicholas a Duma prorogation blank, with spaces for dates and conditions which would be inserted by himself. It was clear that Goremykin was too set on the ruin of the Duma to be suffered any longer and he had departed from the 'butler' role which had carried him through the earlier crisis. The very next day, Nicholas summoned Sturmer and asked for his reaction to Goremykin's contention that 'the Duma must be limited in its activities exclusively to the examination of the Budget'. Mindful of the flexible image projected by his promoters, Sturmer replied 'I think that if the Duma exceeds the permitted limits of its work, it can always be quickly prorogued but I see no reason for lack of faith in the Duma ... I consider that the Duma can and should function.' Nicholas had already decided against the elevation of Khvostov, which would have signalled a combination of premiership and MVD reminiscent of the superministership of Stolypin. Satisfied with Sturmer's attitude of hopeful pragmatism, two days later Nicholas officially substituted him for Goremykin as Chairman of the Council of Ministers. In point of fact Sturmer, the puppet of a clique which included Rasputin and N.V. Gurlyand (who 'ghosted' his manifesto), had little sympathy for the Duma but he knew that the circumstances of his appointment bound him to the Duma ticket: in keeping with the undertaking made to the Tsar in interview, Sturmer was compelled to attempt a working relationship with the Duma and set a date for a new session.[20]

The response of educated society to the prospect was relatively lethargic. What spirit of urgency existed was injected by the public organisations. The ailing Russian cooperative movement (another potential avenue for moderate expansion and recruitment) had already largely succumbed to MVD repression, a dreadful warning to the more established UZ, UT and WIC. Moreover an imperial edict of 26 January stipulating that future orders for foreign merchandise must be placed through the government held far-reaching implications for the public organisations: if they could not order independently of the government, the edict amounted to the first stage of forcible incorporation of the public organisations into the state structure. Alarmed (like industrialists) by the trend towards nationalisation, the public organisations were very concerned to consolidate and expand their links with the Duma in the interests of self-defence.[21] But the Duma moderates who prepared for their first public platform for five months seemed anything but inspiring. When on 28 January the Progressive Bloc met for the first time in two months, its participants contented themselves with chatter about the change in premiership. When more serious business was contemplated, the familiar rows soon re-emerged: the Progressists again found themselves in a minority supporting the Responsible Ministry slogan and again Efremov, supremely unaffected by the crisis afflicting his party, threatened to quit the Bloc. By 8 February the quarrels of November over a Bloc Resolution had been revived: now the right-wing fractions in the Bloc would accept only war legislation while the left-wing fractions insisted on extensive political reform. The day of the reconvening of the Duma dawned to reveal a Bloc quite as divided as at any point since the previous September.[22]

Nicholas confirmed rumours of his sympathy towards a new session by unexpectedly attending the Duma opening ceremonies on 9 February. Although the Duma deputies welcomed the visit as a last-minute gesture of goodwill, Nicholas had in fact been considering the move for some months. In her idiosyncratic shorthand, Alexandra was reminding her husband of the idea as early as November: 'One must call the Duma together even for quite short, especially if you, unknown to others, turn up there it will be splendid, as you had thought before of doing.' By 4 February Nicholas had reached his decision: 'I want to return in order to be present at the opening of the State Duma and State Council. Please do not speak of this as yet.' Of the success of the Tsar's visit there was no doubt. Nicholas's appearance was greeted with an enthusiasm and facile optimism summed up in Rodzyanko's outburst 'The Tsar is in the Duma, Praise be to God, now everything will change for the better.' Perceiving that Nicholas was quite as moved as the Duma, Rodzyanko seized the opportunity to attempt a constitutional *coup de théâtre*: 'Your Majesty, use this glorious moment to announce here and now that you are granting a responsible ministry. You cannot imagine the greatness of this act which would without question pacify the nation and favourably resolve the war.' However, Nicholas was not so overwhelmed by emotion as to forget himself completely, and he shrugged off Rodzyanko's 'Progressist petition' with a non-committal 'I shall think about it.' The euphoria generated by the visit overlaid the poor impression made by Sturmer's first ineffectual appearance in the Duma and the disappointing government declaration that followed. The veteran reporter Stanley Washburn echoed the opinions of the optimists in an article for *The Times*: 'For the first time in history the Emperor attended the opening of the Duma ... a step of great resolution and tremendous significance, irrespective of party, which has instantly shed radiance on internal affairs and will effectively purge the poisoned currents of domestic policy.' It was in this atmosphere that the sitting of 9 February reached the final item on its agenda, the Resolution of the Progressive Bloc. The document which had been desultorily bickered over since November by now represented no more than the lowest common denominator of the Bloc's varied adherents. It offered no constructive programme but rested content with a forlorn appeal 'urging the government to give ear to the voice of the people'. The Bloc had been thoroughly upstaged by the Tsar: even if the Bloc had been able to mount an impressive Resolution, it is doubtful whether it could have overcome the artificially-elated atmosphere of the first sitting. The relief which attended the opening of the long-awaited Duma session blended with the optimism generated by the Tsar's visit and the fortuitously-timed Russian capture of Erzerum on the Caucasian front to promote a benign parliamentary atmosphere in which the militant line of the Progressists evoked neither support nor sympathy.[23]

It was in this climate that the Kadets, by far the healthiest party in the Bloc by early 1916, were confronted by perhaps their most dangerous crisis to date. Party congresses were hazardous exercises for the moderates, and the Kadet Central Committee had gone to great pains to avoid convening one for over eight years. Milyukov in particular had a number of reasons for not wanting a congress. First was the unpalatable but undeniable fact that the Kadet party was only a shadow of its former self. The fall-off since late 1905 (when Kadet membership had touched one hundred thousand) had been judged alarming by the Fifth Congress in October 1907 (when the figure had dropped to twenty-five thousand).[24] The collapse of membership in the provinces was spotlighted in a Moscow Kadet report of 1910: 'for the last three years our party organisation has suffered still more – administrative and judicial persecution, the absence of contacts between deputies and electors, the unaccustomedness of society to continuous political activity and many other reasons have led to the still greater disarray of our local organisation.' It is difficult to reconcile the Petersburg Kadets' own estimate of 12,540 party members in the capital (as reproduced in an Okhrana report for February 1912) with the total membership of 25,000 lamented by the Fifth Congress without conjecturing that the so-called national movement had shrunk to the confines of the capital cities. Of course it is possible to view the figures with healthy scepticism, bearing in mind that the Petersburg Kadets were eager to perform well in the imminent elections to the Fourth Duma and were boosting their morale by elaborate whistling in the dark. Even so, the lesson still seems to be that the Kadet party was strong in the capitals (later in 1912 the Kadets won all four Duma seats in Moscow and conceded only two out of six in Petersburg) but becoming chronically weak almost everywhere else in Russia.[25]

The membership crisis in its turn undermined Kadet finances, for the party had little regular income apart from membership subscriptions and dues. Time and again leading Kadets had to bail out the party by acts of personal generosity. In autumn 1912 for example, the party was only able to complete its Duma electoral campaign through the financial intercession of the Central Committee president Petrunkevich. Even so, the party effectively bankrupted itself: when the Central Committee met after the elections on 8 November 1912, it was to announce that it could only subsidise the electoral expenses of local Kadet branches to the tune of ten per cent; as a direct result of incurring the remaining ninety per cent of expenses, many local branches were compelled to close down. The 1912 elections both pauperised the Kadet party and provided a dramatic stimulus to the already disastrous collapse of its provincial support.[26]

Time brought only a further deterioration in the provincial party. At a Central Committee meeting on 14 May 1913 it was revealed to the shocked delegates that only nine provincial branches survived of the twenty-seven represented at the 1907 congress. Though the branches remaining were unnamed, independent Kadet and Okhrana evidence would suggest that they were (in approximate order of strength): Kiev, Samara, Saratov, Kostroma, Riga, Don, Kaluga, Yaroslavl and

Irkutsk. With unconscious humour A.V. Tyrkova voiced the fears of all in forlornly describing the Kadet party as 'a head without a body' and the Kadet leaders as 'the last of the Mohicans'.[27] Traditional recruiting-grounds for the Kadets were becoming apathetic or transferring their allegiances elsewhere. The teaching profession was a case in point. An Okhrana report covering the First Congress of Teachers in December 1913 advanced the following tentative figures for the political affiliations of the delegates: 40 per cent were non-political, that is to say uncommitted to any party; of the remaining 60 per cent, some 55 per cent were SR, 20 per cent SD, 10 per cent Right or Nationalist, 12 per cent Kadet or Progressist and 2 per cent Octobrist. If this spread of affiliation was typical of a traditional area of Kadet support, the national outlook was very gloomy indeed. Other evidence pointed the same lesson. The number of provincial newspapers with which the Kadet press bureau had formal contacts fell from 26 in 1911 to 16 in 1913; by early 1914 the bureau chief A.S. Izgoyev was reporting that 'it can be confirmed that there is no Kadet press in Russia at present'. A rather half-hearted campaign to exploit the recent Octobrist crash by a recruitment drive in the provinces in January 1914 only exposed Kadet local weakness: the Okhrana estimated that only seven hundred individuals participated in the entire Empire.[28]

After the outbreak of war, the increasingly unpopular philosophy of *union sacrée* confirmed the plummeting membership and deteriorating finances of the party. By the winter of 1915–16 reports from the local Okhrana registered an all-time low in the Kadet provincial organisation. A report from the province of Estland (later Estonia) seems to have been typical: 'there are no organised groups of the Party of Popular Freedom in the city of Reval, and where there are individuals adhering to the afore-mentioned party, they retain no close links with the central party executive.'[29] In such a situation a full Kadet congress was, to say the least, an unnecessary hazard. While past efforts to disguise the extent of the provincial collapse by claiming that all meetings were hastily-convened unrepresentative conferences had been passably successful, a formal congress could betray the Kadet disaster for all to see. A Kadet congress might well reveal the fraction's Duma politics as sheer bluff and destroy the reputation and credibility of the party as a whole.

It is hardly surprising in these circumstances to learn that the Sixth Congress was forced upon Milyukov and the Central Committee. The Bloc defeat in September 1915 exasperated Kadet 'Moscow' and fed the conviction that only more radical proposals and militant tactics could meet the critical political situation. An Okhrana report for October 1915 noted the mood of 'Moscow':

Despite all efforts to conceal growing rifts within the party, this meeting has demonstrated that ... a quite significant group is speaking openly of a profound split. For some time there has existed within this group sharp dissatisfaction with Milyukov for ruling the party too 'autocratically' ... Most recently, the most bitter personal attacks on Milyukov have proliferated in the ranks of the Moscow Kadets.

The early localisation of the opposition within the Kadet party became more and more pronounced until by late 1915 'Moscow' had assumed the role of spokesman for the entire provincial organisation against the tyranny of Milyukov and 'Petrograd'.[30] However a wider anti-Milyukov movement existed which needed no local Muscovite allegiance to lend it expression. Dissatisfaction with the concept of collaboration with a reactionary government which cynically exploited national patriotism grew until by mid-1915 the Kadet provincial organisation had moved so far left that it approximated more closely to the line of the Progressists (or even Trudoviks) than to official Kadet policy. The Kadet conference to test provincial opinion held in early June had clearly demonstrated the danger to those still not blinded by the discredited *union sacrée*. Thereafter Okhrana reports provide ample evidence of the growing gap between the provincial Kadets on the one side, and the Kadet fraction and Central Committee on the other. In late July the Kadets in the Kaluga and Don provinces opted for the Progressist slogan 'A Ministry Responsible to the Duma'. By late October rebellions against the Milyukov line were well advanced in Samara and Kiev. In late December the Kostroma Kadets joined the rebels in agitating against the possibility that future Duma sessions might be strictly budgetary. Finally, in January 1916 the Samara Kadets refused direction from the Central Committee and pointedly formed an alliance with the local Mensheviks.[31]

The scale of the provincial rebellion forced a congress of the party. Even the Central Committee's authority over the Kadet press was yielding under provincial pressure: the official line preached by *Rech* in Petrograd was being compromised by rebel campaigns in Moscow's *Russkia Vedomosti* and Kiev's *Kievskaya Mysl*. By the eve of the Congress, the Okhrana confirmed that there existed a full-scale revolt: 'in the last few days, numerous protesting members of provincial Kadet groups have moved a declaration against the Kadet fraction amounting to a threat to defect to the Progressists in the event of basic principles of the Kadet programme.' Although a congress could reveal the pitifully reduced state of the national organisation and although a congress had the 'constitutional' right to override the Central Committee and mandate the Kadet fraction, the central Kadet organs had no choice but to concede. Despite the dangers, including the possibility that the Kadet party might share the fate of the Octobrist Union after its own crisis congress in 1913, the Sixth Kadet Congress was essential to prevent the disintegration of the party and the defection of its remaining provincial organisation to the Left.[32]

When the Sixth Congress convened on 18 February 1916, one fear at least was quickly laid to rest. The attendance at the Congress, while considerably lower than at any previous (or subsequent) Kadet congress, was not so low as to provide incontrovertible evidence of national collapse. One hundred and twenty-seven delegates claiming to represent twenty-eight Kadet groups attended the congress, though it is more than likely that a number of provincial representatives spoke only for themselves. But however dubious the credentials of individual delegates and whatever the contribution of the Central Committee to drumming up an artificially high attendance, on one score the Congress proved less an embarrassment than expected. But the Central Committee was at a disadvantage whatever the Congress attendance: if the numbers were down, the decline of the party would be recognised as an accomplished fact; if the numbers were respectable, the reputation of the party was saved but the opposition to the Kadet establishment appeared in strength for the first time for years. The latter eventuality was realised. The fortuitously high provincial attendance at the Congress answered one of Milyukov's problems by posing another.[33]

The most dramatic manifestation of Kadet rebellion occurred in the general debate which followed Milyukov's 'Report on the Kadet Fraction and its Tactics', which had to be extended to accommodate the speeches of twenty provincial delegates, with only three exceptions fiercely antagonistic to the Milyukov line. As expected, the provincial rebellion was spearheaded by Moscow. The Moscow spokesman M.L. Mandelshtam attacked Milyukov personally for 'leading the party to a dead end, into a swamp' by his fatuous insistence on *union sacrée* and refusal to come to terms with the leftward swing of public opinion. The true interests of the party lay in three uncompromising principles:

1. The chief task of the party must be the transfer of power to a ministry supported by a majority in the Duma and capable of implementing the Bloc Programme and organising the forces of the nation for victory ...

2. In the pursuit of these aims, the party must not hesitate at open conflict with the government and even the dissolution of the Duma.

3. The party must steadfastly advance the interests of the democratic masses and rights for nationalities, and wherever possible support contacts with all democratic parties.

Mandelshtam was equally concerned about the monolithic nature of the Kadet party, the responsibility for which again lay with its leader: 'Milyukov's cardinal error consists in the fact that he is absolutely ignorant of, and unwilling to get acquainted with and take into account, the mood of broader circles of the party. He sees only the Duma Kadet fraction, persons totally immersed in the Petrograd atmosphere, and he judges all Russia by them.' The remedy for the lamentable collapse in communication between the provinces and the central organs was simple: 'we express the wish that party congresses, as laid down in the party rules, he convened annually; this would bring new life to the provincial branches of the party, and the composition of the Central Committee would be renewed with fresh forces.' Provincial delegates queued up to embellish the theme. A prominent spokesman was D.N. Grigorovich-Barsky, representing what the Okhrana called 'the centre of the Kadet provincial periphery', Kiev:

> The present congress is making a dispiriting impression. For what have we waited for a congress for eight years? What will we take home with us? The subtleties of Duma politics in no sense satisfy our colleagues in the provinces. We wanted to sort out and establish mutual understanding ... but we are told 'You are not needed, we here in Petrograd watch for all and never make mistakes' ... The provincial delegates to the congress have found no indication that the Central Committee wants to employ party forces at the local level or concerns itself with closer links with them.

Only the predictable abstentions of the delegates for Petrograd and Kursk spoiled the unanimity of the Kadet provinces' chorus of complaint.

As leader of the left Kadets (and – as Duma deputy for Tomsk – a provincial himself), Nekrasov now anticipated an alliance with the provincial rebels which would lend him greater authority than ever before. In two speeches to the Congress, Nekrasov expressed his sympathy for the militant leanings and internal party grievances of the provincial delegates, winning warm applause for his slogan 'Remember the Progressive Bloc but never forget the people'. By offering himself as the spokesman for the provinces within the 'magic circle' of the Kadet establishment, Nekrasov anticipated a massive rebuke to Milyukov which would overthrow his policy of restraint and transfer the initiative to the left wing of the party. At this juncture it did not seem beyond the bounds of possibility that the Sixth Congress would break Milyukov as leader of the Kadet party.

Almost incredibly, Milyukov survived. Having been compelled to concede the congress, the Central Committee had taken care to ensure that all its practical aspects favoured the leadership. On the eve of the provincial conferences in October 1915, the Okhrana noted that 'the Central Committee of the Kadet party is sending out delegates through the provinces to inform themselves at the local level of the general state of affairs and the mood of the masses.' It soon emerged that these delegates – like Maklakov at Saratov and Shingarev at Kiev – were personable and responsible 'trouble-shooters' despatched to explain the party line to the provincial hotheads. The intention of the Kadet establishment to fashion as sympathetic a congress as possible was clear, although imperfectly realised.[34] The timing of the congress was deliberate: convening only days after the start of the first Duma session in almost six months, the congress was influenced by the spirit of cautious optimism which currently held Petrograd. Moreover, although the provincial rebellion was dangerous enough, Milyukov was well aware that the parties to the left were at present in no position to exploit a Kadet crisis: the Trudoviks had decided that links with the Kadets were politically damaging while the Progressist party was on the verge of complete disintegration. What may be termed the psychological advantage lay with Milyukov: February 1916 was the first moment since the Bloc defeat that his political philosophy seemed tolerable and the alternatives suspect. The Congress venue was set for Petrograd on the pretext that the current Duma session necessitated the presence of the Kadet deputies in the capital; the Central Committee thereby ensured that it would meet its critics on home ground. The duration of the Congress was to be three days, so not only was the Sixth Congress the shortest to date but the time elapsed since its predecessor ensured that 'historical reports' would take up an unprecedently large proportion of the agenda. The time remaining for general debate (and therefore criticism) was proportionately brief, and even then was to be invaded by necessary procedures like the election of the new Central Committee. Finally, the Central Committee imposed almost news-tight restrictions on the Congress. The Congress was not announced to the public either before or during its sitting. Security was stringent: the press was specifically excluded and before each session the credentials of all delegates were meticulously scrutinised before admission. It was only on 22 February, the day after the Congress dispersed, that the inquisitive and by now frustrated press was granted an official statement, a bland and jejune summary which satisfied no one. All in all, no practical detail of the Congress remained unexploited by Milyukov and the Central Committee to safeguard their entrenched party position.[35]

Milyukov forestalled a certain volume of criticism by publishing the Bloc Declaration on 9 February, in an attempt to demonstrate the vitality of Kadet leadership of the moderate camp. He underlined the point the next day when he impressed upon an audience of Moscow Kadets the need for a more militant Bloc policy, a course which he admitted to be hazardous but necessary. The timing of these rather surprising opinions, the circumstances of their delivery and Milyukov's subsequent conduct lead one to the cynical conclusion that they were made entirely for effect. The fact that Milyukov's most radical wartime opinions were expressed in Moscow, the centre of internal Kadet opposition, one week before the party congress can hardly have been coincidental. By proclaiming a shift in policy towards the position expected from the imminent congress, Milyukov hoped to steal the thunder of his critics.[36]

An analysis of the Congress attendance figures also reveals that Milyukov's position was not as vulnerable as at first appears. Of the total 127 delegates, seventeen were from the Central Committee, thirty-six from the current Duma, thirteen from past Dumas, three from the State Council and fifty-eight from the provinces. Numerically, the provincial element was in the minority by fifty-eight delegates to sixty-nine. Just as significantly, the so-called provincial representation was weighted in favour of the more tractable capital cities: fourteen Petrograd and eleven Moscow delegates gave the capitals a total of twenty-five of the fifty-eight 'provincial' places. The authentic provincial element amounted to only thirty-three delegates of the total 127, a measure of the decline of the provincial organisation and of the Central Committee's efforts to exclude the most quarrelsome elements. The weakness of the provincial party saved Milyukov: when the all-important division occurred after the policy debate of 19 and 20 February, the official line had a slim but adequate majority of some twenty votes over the rebels.

Though confident that a major upset was now unlikely, the Central Committee rallied to the defence of the official line. On opening the general debate on Milyukov's report, the session chairman Prince P.D. Dolgorukov emphasised that Milyukov had spoken not just for himself but for the Committee as a whole. Prince D.I. Shakhovskoi refused to share left Kadet trepidation about the masses and insisted that 'in the State Duma and our party, the workers see their allies'. Shingarev poured scorn on left Kadet demands to quit the Progressive Bloc: 'You say "get out". But where can we get out to? Into our own government? On to the streets?' Rodichev too chose to toe the official line: 'I do not understand these demands not to forget the democratic masses; we ourselves *are* the democratic masses.' Finally Milyukov took the opportunity to reply to his critics, though in the patronising manner of the leader who knows his opponents are beaten and is unconcerned if his arguments still fail to give satisfaction.

The last ploy of the left Kadets was to force through an expansion of the Central Committee, apparently in the hope that the larger its size, the greater its provincial and therefore left-wing representation. Conceding to provincial pressure, the Committee itself recommended an increase in membership from the present forty to forty-five seats, but Nekrasov and the left Kadets won a further increase to fifty places. In practice, Nekrasov's scheme backfired badly. The provincial delegates could not organise swiftly enough to secure unanimity behind their candidates, the central organs and capitals were better prepared, the establishment successfully victimised the most prominent troublemakers (like Mandelshtam), and the sheer distance and time involved precluded the regular attendance of all but a handful from the provinces. When the election results to the new expanded Central Committee were released, it emerged that left Kadet representation had improved marginally (with Nekrasov and M.S. Adzhemov making the Committee comfortably) and five of the six Moscow candidates had been successful (ironically, the single failure was their leader Mandelshtam). The Milyukov camp lost little: a full half of the new Committee were Milyukov's colleagues from the outgoing Committee and he had the support of six Petrograd delegates and nine fraction deputies. Milyukov could count on the backing of some thirty-five of the new Committee, more than adequate as a working majority. The martyr on both sides was the provincial representation, now numbering just three – F.F. Shteingel (Riga), Prince G.M. Shumanov (Caucasus) and Grigorovich-Barsky (Kiev) – the lowest proportion in the history of the party.

The balance of the new Central Committee served to emphasise the bleak prospects for further opposition against Milyukov within the Congress. In the final debate over congress resolutions, the left Kadets did win a significant victory by getting their motion to command party approaches to the Left passed easily (46 to 27) but Milyukov countered by securing overwhelming support for Kadet allegiance to the Progressive Bloc (73 to 14) and a comfortable majority for the official slogan 'A Ministry of Public Confidence' (52 to 32). The shrill protests of the authentic provincials achieved little: the Congress's response to Grigorovich-Barsky's plea to revive the provincial party was to refer the issue to the new Central Committee; so effective was the Committee's procedural expertise that Mandelshtam's demand for annual congresses was not even tabled for debate, let alone put to the vote. By the last day of the Congress, the thirty-three provincial delegates were at best tolerated as voting fodder in the conflicts between Petrograd and Moscow, and between the official and left Kadet forces. Safe now until the next congress, the last two speakers at the Sixth Congress permitted themselves a measure of self-congratulation which must surely have had the rebel groups burning with frustration. M.M. Vinaver, the Congress chairman, provocatively dwelt at length upon the democratic structure of the party: 'We are a democratic party and as such need no alliance with left parties to be democratic. Let them come to us. Democracy is not just a political ploy with us but one of the principles of our faith, the single premise which unites us ... the foundation upon which we confidently build our organisation and policies.' After a standing ovation, Milyukov chose to flaunt his victory before his enemies with the cool observation 'differences of opinion have never alarmed this party ... the Central Committee has emerged from the Congress debates revitalised by the healthy exchange of opinions.' On this pharisaical note the Sixth Congress closed, its only direct legacy a clutch of vague and contradictory resolutions and the membership of the new executive.

The Central Committee met immediately after the closure of the Congress on the afternoon of 21 February to prepare a press release and elect its officers (both exercises from which the Congress itself was debarred). During the Congress Petrunkevich, president of the Central Committee since 1907 and an elder statesman whose unapproachable prestige and declining physical powers suited Milyukov's purpose admirably, had announced his long-expected resignation on grounds of ill-health. In anticipation of the first election to the presidency in almost ten years, Kokoshkin obsequiously proposed that 'it would be helpful for the greater unity of the fraction and Central Committee if the president of both party organs were the same man.' And so it proved. At the Committee meeting on 21 February, Rodichev received one vote, Shakhovskoi seven votes and Milyukov twenty-two votes. President of the fraction since 1907, Milyukov now added the presidency of the Central Committee. Though only lending formal and retrospective recognition to a state of affairs which had existed for some time, the election represented an advance in Milyukov's rule over the Kadet party. The accompanying elections to vice-presidencies confirmed Milyukov's stranglehold over the party organisation. Loyal colleagues were rewarded, critics were humbled: four vice-presidencies were adroitly divided between Petrograd (Shakhovskoi and Vinaver) and tame Moscow (Dolgorukov and N.M. Kishkin); Nekrasov's candidacy met with humiliating defeat. Despite considerable dissatisfaction, the Central Committee had emerged from the Congress with increased administrative power and Milyukov had officially extended his formidable authority from the fraction to the Central Committee to institute a more monolithic centralised executive than had ever before existed in the history of the Kadet movement.[37]

Although Milyukov had turned an anticipated disaster into a resounding personal triumph, there were factors which made the victory a hollow one. At the same Committee meeting of 21 February, the Kadet leaders gazed despairingly at the twin problems of membership and finance. A Congress resolution had urged the Committee 'to prepare a plan to develop the party in the country and immediately to embark upon its implementation but the Committee saw no realistic prospect of accomplishing this. Shingarev warned that 'if this task is to be pursued seriously, it demands substantial financial resources, which the Central Committee simply does not possess.' A.A. Kornilov, re-elected secretary of the Committee, agreed that even when the party numbered one hundred thousand, its finances had been unsound; with the much reduced membership of 1916, even after the Committee had sold its office premises and pared its expenditure to the minimum, receipts barely covered the unavoidable expenses of the central party organs. Tyrkova tetchily remarked that 'it is a pity that when the Sixth Congress laid this difficult commission upon us, it said nothing about the means by which it could be effected.' There seemed no escape from the vicious circle: the provincial organisation could not be developed for lack of finance, but the only sizeable source of regular income was an enlarged national party. Prompted by Milyukov, the Committee came to the interim decision 'to postpone consideration of the finances of the Central Committee until the discussion of an overall plan for reorganisation, as commissioned by the congress; in the meantime to ask the provincial members of the Committee to raise at the local level the question of the improvement of the financial resources of the central organs of the party'. At a subsequent Committee meeting on 30 March, after protracted but fruitless debate, the issues of membership and finance were referred to a party commission, there (almost inevitably) to lie buried until the February Revolution prompted an hurried exhumation.[38] The national future of the Kadet party in 1916 was bleak. While Milyukov was extending his power over the executive organs of the Kadet movement, wider developments in the country at large were corroding its provincial organisation. Milyukov's tactical expertise had won a superficial victory at the Sixth Congress but he could offer no solution to the fundamental problems which were undermining his authority in the broader context. Milyukov was assuming greater and greater power over less and less.

The Sixth Congress was considered a success for Milyukov only because it had been expected to break him. Far from benefiting Milyukov, the Congress not only failed to solve Kadet problems but exacerbated them. The left Kadets made inroads into the power structure of the party as well as the Moscow Kadets (though neither secured the coup they planned). The composition of the new Central Committee, though safer than Milyukov had feared, tacitly testified that the party could no longer claim to be a national movement. The expense of holding a congress only further depleted the meagre Kadet coffers: though it was customary for the Central Committee to bear the cost of a congress, a registration fee of fifty roubles per delegation was levied in advance as a vital subsidy. The provincial delegates were alienated en masse by the vivid impression of being superfluous in a metropolitan-dominated and orientated movement. The rifts within the party were widened significantly: the rebuffs suffered by the rebel groups only increased their sense of frustration; the slight gains made only whetted their appetites for more. Far from being a triumph for Milyukov, the Sixth Congress was no more than a holding operation to stave off the complete disintegration which threatened the Kadet party.[39]

By contrast with the drama of the Kadet Congress, the atmosphere of the Duma in early 1916 was languid and purposeless. There was no attempt on the part of the moderates to resume the Bloc campaign of) August 1915 except by the most incorrigible Progressists. In part the explanation lay with the absence of many political leaders. Guchkov suffered a near-fatal heart attack, necessitating a long period of convalescence on the Black Sea which kept him out of politics for the first six months of 1916. Ryabushinsky was unable to take up his newly-won seat in the State Council through pneumonia. Kerensky too was *hors de combat* until the early summer recovering from a major kidney operation. Even Milyukov, though possessing the essential autocratic attribute of unfailing robust health, chose to spend over two months away from the Duma in western Europe.[40].

The personal indispositions of individual leaders cannot alone explain away the low morale of early 1916. Both Duma and government had made their positions clear in autumn 1915 and now had little to say to one another. As Milyukov remarked in one of those metaphors so favoured by the moderates, the government and Duma were now 'in the position of fellow-travellers, seated in the same train compartment but avoiding acquaintance with each other'. Sturmer held aloof from the Duma, refused to answer interpellations and ignored appeals from Rodzyanko for better relations. The Progressive Bloc continued to devote itself to the misgivings of its membership at the expense of action. Most significantly of all, the poor and still deteriorating health of all three moderate parties predisposed them against any action which might precipitate irremediable collapse. When Rodzyanko, in accordance with his undertaking to Khvostov the month before, warned the Bloc on 25 February against launching assaults on the government, the moderates put up only statutory complaint. Dovetailing neatly with Sturmer's soft line towards the Duma, the Bloc policy was to settle down to a plodding programme of petty legislation. By this tactic of finding things to occupy their minds, the moderates hoped to pass the time until they recovered their spirits and nerve. In the meantime the Duma continued on its constitutional way, inexorably conscientious, as though the events of 1915 had never been. A contented Okhrana report of 29 February confirmed that the Duma was still cowed after its traumatic defeat in September and remarked that while the Bloc maintained its oppositional stance towards the government, its campaign was effectively undermined by its internal divisions and constitutional and patriotic scruples. The government was encouraged to believe that for the duration of the war at least the moderates presented no great threat and the Duma could be tolerated with an acceptable margin of safety.[41]

External events conspired to exert stress on the Bloc despite its adoption of the lowest of profiles. The flood of war refugees from the western provinces invading the towns and cities of European Russia constrained the Kadets (in concert with the UT) to advocate prompt municipal reform to permit Moscow and Petrograd in particular to cope; but the Octobrists discerned an ulterior Kadet motive, suspecting that at base the reform was designed to rescue the town-based Kadets from the political ruin which confronted them. The government sequestration of the mighty Putilov works in early 1916 occasioned a similar split between the wings of the Bloc over the militarisation of industry. When the issue was debated in closed Duma sitting on 7 March, the right wing led by the Zemstvo–Octobrists (who had no industrial interests to respect) favoured militarisation while the left wing, led by the Kadets and Progressists (who were well aware that they were competing for the backing of the powerful industrialist lobby), opposed militarisation. Tragically, this episode was to occasion the dismissal of the War Minister Polivanov, one of the few remaining friends of the Duma in the cabinet and an irreparable loss to the war effort.[42] The third issue of the session both confirmed the fragility of the Bloc alliance and indicated a renewed reactionary impetus in official policy. In January the Police Department had issued a circular hinting that a few pogroms for the populace to let off steam would not come amiss, a suggestion taken up with gusto in the western borderlands of the Empire. After the introduction of an inter-pellation against official anti-semitism submitted by the Left, an open Duma sitting on 8 March revealed yet again a split between the Kadets (who being financially indebted to Jewish sources had practical as well as ideological cause to wave the banner of racial equality vigorously) and the Zemstvo–Octobrists and right wing. The argument of the author of the circular, Police Assistant Director A.N. Kafafov, that his motive had been to inform rather than direct deceived none but with the Bloc right wing cynically accepting his expla-nation, the Kadets felt forced to acquiesce in the interests of maintaining the Bloc. The March anti-semitism debates again underlined the precarious nature of the Bloc, the elision of principle required to main-tain such a broad alliance, and provoked a crisis in Jewish circles which was to threaten the integrity of the whole moderate camp.[43]

The government had every cause for satisfaction with the record of the Duma session of early 1916. The only area of concern was that the lacklustre conduct of the Bloc was undermining the public organisations' allegiance to the moderate course, which might lead to their radical politicisation. Khvostov was alarmed on hearing from the Okhrana that the Bloc had established a permanent bureau for liaison with extra-Duma bodies but was relieved to learn that the Bloc was quite as apprehensive about the public organisations as the MVD, only setting up the bureau to establish a braking machinery over the campaigns of broader society. While the left Kadets in particular were agitating for the public organisations to adopt a more political line, the UZ and UT congresses of March 1916 demonstrated that their governing echelons, though under growing criticism and pressure from a more spirited rank-and-file, had no wish to provoke the wrath of the MVD with the doubtful patronage of the Duma Bloc as their only protection.[44] The government knew that although wider society developments were becoming more threatening, the Bloc-dominated Duma represented no danger: the sharp lesson administered in September 1915 had brought the moderates to heel for the rest of the war; the adoration accorded the Bloc in August 1915 had been dissipated by the Bloc's own neglect of the major issues of 1916 and refusal to resume the offensive against the government. Although the Duma completed its examination of the Budget in late March and was no longer strictly necessary to the government, its patent harmlessness encouraged all but the most reactionary elements to take a tolerant view of its future. As Sturmer acknowledged, the Duma was playing the role demanded by the government: 'I was deeply content that the first session of the Duma passed in the most desirable fashion and ended without any misunderstandings and entirely agreeably.'[45] The passivity of the early 1916 session virtually guaranteed an immediate successor.

Milyukov missed the entire subsequent session. The Kadets had always been the Russian party in closest contact with western Europe and on 5 October a Central Committee meeting had reiterated the necessity of even more intimate links. Milyukov approached the Allies through the British Ambassador Buchanan and in February 1916 an Anglo-Russian banquet sealed an agreement that a Russian parliamentary delegation would be welcomed in Great Britain in April. But while a delegation for mutual information and encouragement seemed a good idea in late 1915, by the time that April approached its wisdom was seriously in doubt. A row sprang up over the delegation in the Kadet Central Committee. At a meeting on 30 March the Committee argued energetically against Milyukov's participation: no other party was sending its leader in the delegation, the two-way trip via Scandinavia was too dangerous, and Milyukov would miss the next Duma session at a time when the Bloc was at a critical stage in its career. But so set was Milyukov on leading the delegation that on 31 March he agreed to withdraw only if the overwhelming majority of the Committee opposed him. Shingarev, also committed to the delegation, stated that if forbidden by the Committee he would withdraw his candidacy but would also resign the chairmanship of the Duma army-navy commission in protest. The obduracy and scarcely-veiled threats of Milyukov and Shingarev overcame the opposition of the Central Committee and they got their way. On 16 April 1916 the parliamentary delegation left Russia on its scheduled two-month trip to western Europe; by the time it returned to Petrograd, the repercussions of Milyukov's absence had been felt throughout the Duma.[46]

With every objection raised by the Central Committee well-founded, it is important to isolate Milyukov's fundamental motive for participating in the delegation. As the only party leader present (for both Rodzyanko and Efremov declined membership), Milyukov dominated the attention of Western leaders to an extent that flattered his formidable ego. In his public statements Milyukov attached most importance to identifying the Kadets with political progress in the eyes of the Allies: 'for me personally, this was an opportunity to reinforce the Russian progressive tendencies through public European recognition and thereby open a new door for our influence just at the moment when another door was being slammed in our faces.' And yet the fact that Milyukov and the Kadets were readily accepted by the West as the champions of the Russian constitutional movement, while lending them a pleasing cosmopolitan aura, seemed to offer little beyond moral encouragement for the improvement of their predicament within Russia. It may be that Milyukov, the 'Russian European', simply overestimated the domestic impact of international moral support. But it is also possible, especially in the light of his penchant for opportunism, that Milyukov had an ulterior political coup in prospect. At its most modest, it may have taken the form of instituting a channel of publicity about the Progressive Bloc outside Russia: since 1913 at least the Kadets had been considering publishing a French-language Kadet newspaper in Paris; by early 1916 Bloc circles were debating the establishment of a Duma Information Bureau in London or Paris. Milyukov may have been more ambitious. On 29 February the Okhrana described a right Kadet scheme for persuading the Allied governments to lend money to the now impecunious Russian government, with Duma auditing as a condition of the loan. During the Sixth Congress, Milyukov had stated categorically that 'a reactionary government, not responsible to the Duma and not enjoying the confidence of the country, will get no money from either France or England after the war … and it is thus, through the State Duma, that Russian liberalism will reach its goals.' The Kadet leader was probably right in believing that only by exploiting the Duma's financial prerogatives could permanent concessions be extracted from the tsarist establishment. Since the ukaze of July 1915, Duma perusal of the Budget had been little more than the contemptuous gesture of a government which appreciated the value of projecting a moderate image to its Western allies. In such a situation, means to exert financial pressure on the government through the good offices of a sympathetic third party had to be investigated.[47]

But while the direction of Kadet thought is clear, evidence about the precise steps taken is scanty. Since the Kadet Central Committee opposed Milyukov's participation in the mission, it may be surmised that he had received no official commission from the party but was pursuing a personal line of action. Whether Milyukov ever broached the subject in official western European circles or not (and I have found no records of such a conversation), a project of this kind could have little hope of implementation. While sympathetic to the predicament of the Duma, the British, French and Italian governments were prepared to take action only to reinforce Russian obligations towards the Allies and ward off any threat of a separate peace. To this end, all three calmed Milyukov's fears about Allied reluctance to accept Russian acquisition of the Dardanelles at the end of the war. But to have promised Milyukov one iota of the ambitious Kadet scheme would have justifiably irritated the Russian government and might well have accelerated its suspected pro-German drift. On the other hand, if the tsarist government were to contemplate a separate peace, a Duma committed to the Allies would prove a valuable agency to oppose the move. Accordingly, the Allied reception of the Russian parliamentary delegation was friendly and respectful but deliberately apolitical: as Milyukov was feted and flattered through Britain, France and Italy, he must have recognised that the most ambitious of Kadet grand designs to save Russian constitutionalism stood no chance.[48]

If Milyukov's performance on the international scene exposed his limitations, his absence from Russia highlighted his domestic indispensability. Within the Kadet party, elements hostile to Milyukov's 'dictatorship' seized the opportunity to attempt coups which, they hoped, he would have no alternative but to accept on his return. The first rebellion came from Moscow. Burning with frustration at his failure at the Sixth Congress, Mandelshtam had ordered a Moscow post-mortem on the congress for 28 February, when he once again violently attacked Milyukov, accusing him of leading the party into crypto-Octobrism, arrogantly ignoring wider circles of Russian society and, in his obsession with the Duma, refusing to acknowledge that the solution to the crisis could only lie with the leadership of the peasant and proletarian masses.[49] Despite the wide support for his views among Moscow Kadets, Mandelshtam was unable to translate this moral backing into political reality while Milyukov was personally in command. Once Milyukov departed the scene, however temporarily, Mandelshtam was prepared to take action. The Moscow Kadet minority who supported the official line, headed by Kornilov, were soon swamped by the rising tide of rebellion. On 26 April, a bare ten days after the delegation left Petrograd, the Moscow Kadets attacked, demanding the immediate adoption of the Responsible Ministry slogan and full rights for Moscow within the Kadet movement. When the Central Committee curtly retorted that it could not meet the dictates of an 'unrepresentative cabal', the Moscow Committee arranged a plenary meeting for 10–11 May which demanded equality with the Petrograd Committee, the subsidised development of the provincial organisation and regular channels of communication between the central organs and the provinces. Resolutions in the spirit of Moscow took pride of place on the agenda of a Central Committee meeting in Petrograd on 19 May: regular information about both the Petrograd and Moscow committees was to be circulated in future; the party must join battle with the government by all parliamentary means to win fundamental reform; contacts with the public organisations were to be developed; and a party commission must be appointed to prepare for the elections to the Fifth Duma.[50]

Coordinated with the Moscow rebellion came a separate movement within the fraction. Nekrasov and the left Kadets too had found the Sixth Congress a frustrating experience but likewise preferred to bide their time rather than challenge Milyukov to his face. On the very first day of the new Duma session, made bold by the knowledge that their party boss was at that moment in Paris, the left Kadets rebelled against the official line and petulantly voted with the Progressists and Left in defiance of the Bloc. Thus two associated rebellions against Milyukov's authority were mounted, threatening the Kadet party with the disintegration which Milyukov's skill had averted at the recent Sixth Congress.[51]

To these more predictable challenges was added a third. The Jewish lobby had always exerted a disproportionately large influence over the Kadets but until 1916 had preferred to remain in the political background. It was a great shock when, in deference to the prejudices of the Progressive Nationalists, Milyukov struck the Kadet principle of 'the immediate removal of all religious and national restrictions' from the Bloc Programme in favour of a formula of 'gradual advance along the road to Jewish equality'. *Evreiskaya Zhizn* (Jewish Life) bitterly condemned this act of betrayal: 'Before us now is the question – is it time we broke with the Kadet party and withdrew our deputies from the fraction completely? With regard to the Jewish question, the

Kadets have moved further to the right than even the Octobrists and government.' In despair at continuing civil and military persecution, the wretched plight of Jewish refugees whose pale of settlement in western Russia was now occupied by the enemy, and the inefficacy of Kadet patronage, the Jewish community in the capitals split into two camps. One rejected the Kadets as champions of the Jews, particularly in view of Milyukov's apparent condoning of police anti-semitism in the March debates, and turned to the Left. The leader of the Jewish deputies in the Duma, N.M. Friedman, dramatically quit both Bloc and Kadet fraction in protest in June. The better-connected camp sought to employ its influence over the Kadet party to force through the reforms discarded by the Bloc. In March the Jewish group within the Central Committee, led by Vinaver and I.V. Gessen, attempted to secure Kadet sanction to the attaching of a Jewish rights' clause to the *volost* zemstvo bill. Milyukov, realising that the Nationalists and Octobrists would never tolerate such an unwelcome graft, argued that Jewish rights must be temporarily postponed. It became plain to Jewish Kadets that the initial impediment to Jewish rights was Milyukov himself, always ready to sacrifice them to the principle of the unity of the Progressive Bloc.[52] The critical Central Committee meeting of 19 May saw an *ad hoc* alliance of the Moscow Kadet, left Kadet and Jewish Kadet factions against the Milyukov establishment. Long jealous of Milyukov, Vinaver made a spectacular bid for power. Though it had been agreed in March that Shakhovskoi would deputise for Milyukov during his absence, the rebel alliance secured the election of Vinaver as interim chairman of the Central Committee. Counting on the gratitude of Moscow and the left Kadets for his sympathetic chairmanship, Vinaver promptly proposed that a Jewish clause be inserted into the bill on peasant rights currently taking shape in Duma commission. Without Milyukov to argue the wider political context, Vinaver's proposal passed the Central Committee by seventeen votes to thirteen. Within the confines of the Kadet party, the Jewish group's coup was conspicuously successful: for the first time in the Fourth Duma, the Kadets were committed to immediate legislation for full Jewish rights.[53]

This final internal Kadet coup set off an astonishing political chain reaction. The peasant deputies in the Duma had resented the proposed Peasant Rights' Bill from its inception, discerning a deceitful attempt by the Bloc to win undeserved wider support. The new Kadet proposal to tack a Jewish rights' clause on to the already discredited bill roused the peasant deputies to fury. Convinced that nothing in the true interests of the peasant could come from the existing parliamentary spectrum, a movement sprang up in May for the creation of an independent peasant fraction. The instigators of the move were the three peasant deputies in the Kadet fraction led by P.A.

Levanidov, thereby posing yet another threat to the unity of the Kadets. All fractions regarded this development with the gravest concern. The peasant revolt affected the right-wing parties more seriously than the moderates and Left: with two-thirds of the peasant deputies (31 of a total 47) currently members of the Right and Nationalist fractions, the Duma Right had no cause to welcome this particular Kadet crisis. But the Jewish rights' clause angered not only the peasants but the right wing of the Bloc as a whole. The Centre, Zemstvo-Octobrists and Progressive Nationalists categorically refused to countenance any Jewish concession, threatening (as Milyukov had anticipated) to withdraw from the Bloc rather than concede. The Jewish Kadet coup rocked the entire Duma boat. Hardly a single fraction benefited from the absence of Milyukov: the Kadets were rent as never before by factional conflict, the whole spectrum of Duma parties was menaced by the loss of large proportions of its membership, and the precariously-maintained Progressive Bloc was confronted by the final polarisation of the left and right wings of the moderate camp.[54]

The government and Duma tacitly combined to draw the parliamentary session to an early close. On 1 June Sturmer informed Nicholas that the documentation for the summer prorogation was complete and needed only the Tsar's decision on a date. A week later Sturmer argued the case for immediate prorogation. Over the first three weeks of the session, the Duma had held only four open sittings attended by an estimated 150–200 deputies. The low morale indicated by these figures rendered the Duma undesirable to government and political parties alike. By contrast, the State Council was being stirred up by Bloc sympathisers like the ex-premier Kokovtsov; the remedy lay in prompt closure and a purge of unreliable elements at the Council elections scheduled for the autumn. Persuaded by Sturmer's argument, Nicholas ordered the prorogation of the Duma and Council on 20 June until November.[55]

Far from complaining about premature prorogation, the Duma moderates were complaisant. Some years later, Rodzyanko's memories of the weary defeatism of the Duma in mid-1916 were only too vivid: 'The deputies were not conscientious in attending sittings and often there was no quorum. The Rights made violent speeches in the hope of cutting short the Duma and in general the atmosphere was so strained that it was hard to achieve anything. The perpetual conflict seemed fruitless, the government refused to listen, disorder increased and the country went to the dogs.' Many moderates saw practical sense in accepting early closure: Godnev for example spoke in the *konvent* against continuing the session after June on the grounds that war work and the absenteeism of the Right would render a constitutional quorum impossible. Rodzyanko openly advocated prorogation as the only way of saving the reputation of the Duma and the unity of the Progressive Bloc, though his perverse dedication to this end provoked some complaint. In a letter to Nicholas, Alexandra gleefully anticipated Rodzyanko's downfall: 'there is a good chance that he won't be re-elected because his party is furious he did the thing clumsily and asked you to close the Duma because they were tired.' The fact that criticism of Rodzyanko concentrated on his tactlessness only underlines the point that the moderates could find no alternative to their president's policy of deliberately courting prorogation for the Duma.[56]

On the very eve of prorogation, Milyukov burst back onto the Russian political scene. Arriving back in Petrograd late on 17 June, still largely unaware of the deterioration of the Bloc and Kadet party in his absence, Milyukov gave enthusiastic assurances that the European constitutional movement was firmly behind the Progressive Bloc but brought little comfort to the moderate deputies as they packed their bags for home. On 19 June, at the penultimate sitting of the Duma session, Milyukov argued that, with Allied victory in sight, it was time for the Bloc to act and for the Russian parliament to sell itself to Europe to extract maximum constitutional concession from the tsarist government at the forthcoming peace conference. No one appears to have been so tactless as to point out either that the Bloc and the Duma now seemed incompatible or that to demand action on the day before the Duma closed for over four months was politically grotesque. The Russian parliamentary situation had changed so rapidly from bad to worse during Milyukov's absence that even his charismatic authority could make no impression on the moderates' collapse of morale.[57]

Over the early summer recess the activity of the moderate camp was minimal. The moderate leaders were little in evidence: Guchkov, still in delicate health, devoted his reduced energies to the WIC; Rodzyanko toured his estates in the provinces; Konovalov plotted in his Moscow mansion; and Efremov and Milyukov spent long periods in Western Europe. No record survives of any formal meeting of the Bloc between 20 June and 3 October 1916. The policy formulated in September 1915 that the Bloc would operate only during Duma sessions was still closely adhered to a year later, though the original scrupulous legalism was now reinforced by concern for the unity of the Bloc alliance. As for the moderate parties individually, an almost total political languor reigned. A lengthy report by Police Director E.K. Klimovich submitted to Sturmer on 24 June dwelt contentedly on the divisions within the moderate camp and argued persuasively that the unity of the Kadet party had never been so unsure. In peacetime, the long Duma recess had traditionally served as an arbitrary yet acceptable 'guillotine' on national politics and in mid-1916 there appeared to be an atavistic return to the apolitical summers of 'the day before yesterday'. An Okhrana report of 15 August suggested that while the moderates were branding the government for the tribulations of Russia, even the most active group – the Moscow Kadets – was at heart unwilling to precipitate further fragmentation by joining battle over major issues and was content to accept the enforced period of recuperation offered by the Duma recess. In mid 1916 the Bloc and, most especially, the Kadet party were so split that their members preferred to avoid national politics in fear of irreversible disintegration.[58]

Far from recovering from the defeat of September 1915, the Progressive Bloc spent the next year undergoing a profound crisis of confidence which was expressed in collapsing morale, internal schism and deliberate shunning of the most pressing issues of the day. Minor improvements in the position of the moderates, like the granting of a Duma session, were incidental by-products of ministerial or imperial politics and owed nothing to the efforts of the parliamentary parties. The long-awaited Duma session proved more a curse than a blessing: Bloc problems which had been confidential to its membership proliferated with exposure to the general public. The last straw was the temporary absence of Milyukov, the sole authority acceptable to the majority of moderates and the only politician with the expertise to stem the deterioration in the health of the Bloc. However well-intentioned Milyukov's visit to Western Europe, his absence exacerbated the problems of the Kadet party and Bloc to the point of final disintegration. The moderates had come to a sorry pass. Soon after the granting of the standard Duma session for which they had been hoping since the outbreak of war, they discovered in despair that Duma politics put an intolerable strain upon their newest creation: having agreed in late 1915 that the Progressive Bloc should not operate *out* of Duma session, they discovered in mid-1916 that it could not survive *in* Duma session. It was left to the unfortunate Rodzyanko to pursue the thankless task of securing early prorogation to prevent the ruin of the parliamentary Bloc. Without resource for the future, the moderates greeted the summer recess with immense relief, postponing all thoughts of national politics until the day when the reconvening of the Duma brought them face to face with their many problems. Just six months away from the Revolution, the Russian moderates featured a lower morale and greater disunity than ever before.

5 The 'Storm-signal of Revolution'

Time would not stand still to favour the Progressive Bloc, and before the summer of 1916 was out the moderates found themselves more than ever at the mercy of the government and the country. While the Bloc parties embraced the prolonged period of political convalescence offered by the early summer recess, the Tsar planned a fundamental reorganisation of his government. Krivoshein's scheme for civil dictatorship had been advanced as long ago as July 1915 but Nicholas's assumption of military command and later inclination to allow greater play to the Duma had effectively shelved the idea. By late spring 1916 the deteriorating situation in the country, the product of poor organisation rather than ultimately debilitating shortages of raw materials and manpower, had revived active discussion of a civil dictatorship. A colleague of Milyukov stressed the dilemma of authority: 'There was no one to put things in order. The authorities were everywhere, supposedly giving orders, and there were a lot of them. But there was no directing will, no plan, no system.' In the increasing chaos of authority, a greater centralisation of civil government seemed essential to the maintenance of the war effort.[1]

The courage to attempt radical reorganisation was linked with military success. The recent collaboration of government and industry in the Special Council on Defence was starting to bear fruit: the Russian army faced the campaign season of 1916 in better condition than the previous year and the munitions shortage was becoming a thing of the past. On the Caucasian front, only two months after the taking of Erzerum (the first feat of Russian arms since 1914 itself) came the capture of Trebizond. On the European front, in late May was launched the Brusilov offensive, which inside a month claimed over 200,000 prisoners alone in a steady advance to the Carpathians and destroyed the independent morale of the Habsburg army for ever. With the apparent turn in the tide of Russia's military fortunes, the government experienced a resurgence of self-confidence and Nicholas attempted answers to problems which hitherto he had been content to ignore.[2]

The circumstances of the Tsar were, as ever, a vital component. Nicholas had gallantly assumed the command of the Russian army partly in the hope of resolving the critical relations between the military and civil authorities but in practice no one individual could sustain both commands. After some months of conscientious (if militarily superfluous) attendance at the Stavka, Nicholas was forced to make a choice between his political role as Tsar and his chosen office of Commander-in-Chief. The prospect of the 1916 campaign season and the vision of a triumphant progress into Europe reminiscent of Alexander I decided Nicholas to opt for military command. After April 1916 he abandoned the practice of making regular visits to the Stavka from Tsarskoe Selo in favour of making his permanent domicile at the Stavka, from which he made rare and reluctant trips back to the capital. On committing himself primarily to his military role, Nicholas attempted to fill the resulting vacuum in civil authority by the creation of a dictator. In June, the conditions for establishing a civil dictatorship were uniquely favourable. Recognising that the four-month summer recess offered the opportunity to attempt a bold political experiment without a Duma audience, Nicholas argued in a letter to Alexandra that 'it is imperative to act energetically and to take firm measures to settle these questions once and for all; as soon as the Duma is adjourned, I shall call all the Ministers here for the discussion of these problems and shall decide upon everything here.' If, when the Duma reconvened, the experiment had proved successful, the Bloc would be compelled to accept the new system because of its efficient prosecution of the war; if the experiment failed, the failure would owe nothing to the Duma and relations could be reinstituted without serious government embarrassment or loss of face.[3]

Commissioned by the Tsar, General Alexeyev produced a detailed report outlining the weaknesses of the home front which recommended that

> Just as in the military theatre all power is concentrated in the supreme commander, so throughout the internal provinces of the Empire ... power must be concentrated in the hands of a single all-powerful figure, who might well be called the Supreme Minister for State Defence. Such a person, enjoying the highest possible confidence of Your Majesty, would have the following responsibilities: to unite, lead and direct by his sole will the activities of all ministers, state and society institutions situated outside the limits of the theatre of war ... For his activities and prerogatives he would answer to Your Majesty alone.

The Council of Ministers was summoned to the Stavka to discuss Alexeyev's memorandum on 28 June, a week after the prorogation of the Duma. The bulk of the ministers were in their own interests opposed to the scheme but were understandably reluctant to condemn a project so evidently fostered by the Tsar. To avoid the basic direction of criticism and save embarrassment, the ministers reduced the issue to one of personality, questioning the availability of a suitable candidate for the new post. Nicholas however had already settled the candidacy in his own mind. Since March, when Alexei Khvostov was dismissed for plotting against Rasputin, Sturmer had temporarily filled the offices of both Council Chairman and MVD, a combination which in Nicholas's eyes prepared him admirably for the role of civil dictator. Dismayed attempts to dissuade Nicholas from outside and within the government met with no success. Rodzyanko, commissioned by moderate leaders to plead the rival cause of collaboration with society, made no headway with Nicholas who (not for the last time) remarked that 'Rodzyanko has talked a lot of nonsense'. The moderate Minister of Agriculture, A.N. Naumov, resigned in a vain attempt to sink the dictatorship project. Even Sturmer protested at his candidacy, arguing that the combination of Council Chairman and MVD was onerous enough without the addition of the role of dictator. Yet despite the protests of the candidate, the antipathy of the recessed Duma and the muted opposition of the cabinet, the will of the Tsar proved (as in September 1915) powerful enough to override all other factors combined.[4]

The dictatorship was hurried through without regard for domestic or foreign sensibilities. On 1 July Sturmer assumed the role of civil dictator. His admittedly heavy load of responsibilities was lightened by a ministerial reshuffle: Sturmer himself dropped the MVD in favour of the 'lighter' Foreign Ministry, from which Sazonov (away on leave blissfully unaware of recent developments) was casually dismissed. The impact of Sazonov's removal upon Duma circles and Russia's Allies was prodigious, being universally interpreted as confirmation of rumours of a separate peace. Paléologue and Buchanan pleaded with the Tsar for Sazonov's retention but to no avail. Even so, the most sinister interpretations of the cabinet changes were mistaken. The dismissal of Sazonov was only incidentally an international event: although Nicholas must have appreciated the damaging effect of the change upon Russia's relations with her Allies, he was temporarily obsessed by the necessity of subordinating all considerations to his design for a civil dictatorship.[5]

Unfortunately for Nicholas, good timing was the only merit of the attempted dictatorship. It had been apparent from Sturmer's earliest days that he had neither the stature nor skill to command respect from the Duma, still less obedience from his ministerial colleagues. Beyond the unsuitability of the candidate, the very first move in creating the dictatorship was demonstrably foolish: no matter how onerous the MVD might be, it was quite impossible to effect a dictatorship of the home front without control of the MVD. The decision of 1 July, designed to make Sturmer's tenancy of the dictatorship feasible, doomed the operation in practice from its inception. The transposition of the unambitious Alexander Khvostov to the MVD only offered the 'dictator' an opportunity to operate without the traditional rivalry of the Minister of Interior; but what he needed was the practical authority which only the MVD could provide. Without that authority, even the delegated powers of the Tsar proved insufficient to implement dictatorship.[6]

Sturmer's attempts to expand his field of operations met with the stolid resistance of vested interests within the government, who had little choice but to raise their hats to the concept of dictatorship but were not prepared to concede without a struggle when their own positions were threatened. Badgered for decisions on subjects about which he understood little and overwhelmed by the sheer volume of work for which he was held responsible, Sturmer played more and more for effect. Making no headway at the expense of established ministries, he attempted to prove his authority by simply adding to the government structure. In August, for example, he tentatively suggested the creation of a Ministry of Health, a proposal rejected out of hand by the Council of Ministers and only implemented when Sturmer went over ministerial heads direct to the Tsar. But although Sturmer won his point, the Ministry of Health contest only highlighted the three-fold nature of his weakness. Sturmer was only contriving new and relatively inoffensive bureaucratic accessories because he was unable to make headway within the traditional government structure; the new institutions he created only served to exacerbate the critical problem of divided authority; and on contentious issues Sturmer was able to defeat vested interests within the government by appeal to the Tsar alone, which defeated the whole point of the exercise. By late August the fundamental failure of the dictatorship was universally acknowledged and even Sturmer settled for the less demanding role of 'government co-ordinator'. The practical outcome of the dictatorship experiment was the reverse of its intention, not the enhancement and centralisation of authority but a further contribution towards what Milyukov called 'paralysis of authority'.[7]

Such was the political lethargy of the moderates over summer 1916 that the Sturmer dictatorship passed almost without comment until it opted to settle the fate of the Fourth Duma. In March, Alexei Khvostov had hesitated in his preparations for the Fifth Duma to ask himself whether this course was either practical or desirable. Would it not be more convenient for all concerned to extend the life of the Fourth Duma? The practical difficulties of conducting a general election in wartime were daunting enough, what with large areas of the Empire occupied by the enemy and much of the remainder under military jurisdiction, but the political imponderables were just as worrying. By early 1916 Russia had lost all or part of fifteen provinces to the enemy (Vilna, Volynia, Grodno, Kovno, Courland, Minsk and the Polish provinces); and another seven could be considered at risk (Bessarabia, Vitebsk, Kiev, Lifland, Mogilev, Podolia and Chernigov). In parliamentary terms, these provinces returned 122 deputies, or well over one quarter of the Duma membership. Most significant was the fact that by the operation of the electoral laws of 3 June 1907 these provinces had been overwhelmingly right-wing in 1912, returning 10 per cent of the Octobrists in the Duma (9 out of 99), 25 per cent of the Rights (16 out of 64), 28 per cent of the Centrists (9 out of 33) and a massive 60 per cent of the Nationalists (52 out of 88). It was only too plain that the territory lost to the enemy constituted the bastion of the political Right, and a general election in the remainder (even assuming the outdated political affiliations of 1912) would produce a Left landslide. Worse still, Okhrana information left the MVD in no doubt that the recognised leftward shift in public opinion after 1912 had accelerated over 1915, raising the likelihood that the electorate would have altered so dramatically that, even granted the peacetime extent of the Russian Empire, the artifice of the MVD electoral process would be unable to fabricate an assembly more 'suitable' that the Fourth Duma. Declining either to risk a radical Fifth Duma or to take the ultimate step of abolishing the Duma altogether, a large body of bureaucratic opinion within the government preferred to retain the Fourth Duma in a spirit of *pis aller*, backing its tactical decision with the precedent of the extended parliaments of Russia's European Allies.[8]

The members of the Fourth Duma split fundamentally over the issue. The only elections since 1912 which might serve as an indicator of current political trends was the voting to the Finnish Diet in June 1916, by which the Social Democrats secured for the first time an overall majority. As a result the Duma Left (including the Progressists and left Kadets) were inclined to welcome a Fifth Duma, confident that the MVD would be unable to concoct an assembly more conservative than the present Duma. The Duma Right (including the official Kadets and Octobrists), appalled at the prospect of a general election which could wipe them out as a parliamentary as well as a national force, tacitly appealed to the government for protection and fervently supported an extension of the Fourth Duma. The decision over the Duma appears to have been one of the very few issues settled by the civil 'dictator'. In part Sturmer's argument was legalistic: since the maximum duration of the Duma was laid down as five years in Clause 101 of the Fundamental Laws, a rule which could not be overriden even by the often-used and much-abused Clause 87, an extension of the Fourth Duma past mid-1917 necessitated altering the Fundamental Laws. Such a giant step, especially in the prosecution of so dubious a policy, turned Sturmer against extension. Moreover, at the same time the decision was to be made, the success of the Brusilov offensive, with its recapture of large tracts of the western borderlands, engendered an atmosphere of optimism in which the reinstitution of the Right electoral bastion was not beyond the bounds of possibility. Ironically enough in a career littered with instances of failures of initiative, the Sturmer dictatorship bequeathed a single important legacy: commitment to the dissolution of the Fourth Duma in 1917.[9]

The agitation of the Russian moderates was all the more keen because of the lack of a Duma forum and, once again, the absence of Milyukov. As on a number of earlier occasions, Milyukov's actions over summer 1916 have attracted adverse criticism. If the internal state of both Kadet party and Progressive Bloc was so precarious, what possessed him to spend all August and early September on lecture tours in England and France? Not only would a further absence prevent him mending his trampled political fences, it could logically be expected to exacerbate the condition caused by his previous expedition. Milyukov could be accused of gross irresponsibility in repeatedly deserting party and Bloc when they so demonstrably needed his presence and leadership. It is possible that Milyukov the historian had not completely succumbed to Milyukov the politician: despite the parliamentary professionalism which marked him out from his Duma colleagues, Milyukov was not a complete political animal, never abandoned the pursuits of the academic profession and retained some features of the dilettante. It may also be that Milyukov's ideology and scholarship led him to place excessive stress on contacts with the West to the regular neglect of domestic Russian developments. If Milyukov was on this occasion over-modest, he probably reasoned that the Duma could play no part during the summer recess so his own presence or absence would have only marginal impact. In later accounts Milyukov is both defensive and infuriatingly vague: 'I must admit now that in spite of all the tenseness of the situation, I left my post for a second trip abroad without great misgivings. This, apparently, was due to my belief that in the developing drama the Duma would not be a decisive factor.' Milyukov's highly selective absent-mindedness also 'apparently' extended to the internal disunity of the Kadet party and Bloc: for the duration of the recess, it could do no harm to put the whole taxing unity problem of the moderates 'on ice'.[10]

September 1916 saw a quickening of Russian political life for reasons less factional than the moderates' *frissons* at the prospect of a general election. It was in September that the Russian capitals first experienced that heightening atmosphere caused by the growing economic and social repercussions of the war which was to culminate in February 1917. Milyukov blamed the new tension on the fact that top-level politics escaped into the streets: 'everything previously known only to the more or less tight circle of the devoted became during this time the property of the public at large, including the rank-and-file citizen. The barometer of the domestic mood rose accordingly.' As yet it was still basic discontent with their social conditions rather than political commitment which excited the masses. The Okhrana noted that

> By the beginning of the month of September this year, an unusual rise in opposition and animosity was clearly noticeable among the widest and most diverse strata of the residents of the capitals. Again and again complaints against the administration and harsh merciless condemnations of government policy were heard ... but the mood of the broad masses is 'oppositional' and not 'revolutionary', standing outside the strict confines of party platforms.

The Duma moderates' political self-interest became compounded by concern for the impact of the war on the cities, and the resulting militancy of the proletarian masses. Threatened by both government and country, the moderates returned to political life. A campaign by worried Kadet, Progressist and Octobrist deputies persuaded Rodzyanko to call an unofficial meeting of Duma members for 10-11 September, which expressed grave concern over the labour movement, condemned the government's handling of the supply crisis and demanded an immediate Duma session. Taking advantage of the absence of Milyukov, the militant wing of the moderate camp began to organise a political offensive after the manner of August 1915.[11]

The faltering dictatorship of Sturmer was now challenged by the Tsaritsa. After April 1916 initiative within the government largely devolved upon Alexandra, for Nicholas was too remote at the Stavka at Mogilev to exercise close political control and too absorbed in the successes of the Brusilov offensive to check the increasingly arbitrary actions of his consort. Alexandra's appetite for power grew immeasurably, to the extent of totally conquering her former social awkwardness: 'I am no longer the slightest bit shy or afraid of the ministers and speak like a waterfall in Russian ... they see I am energetic and tell all to you and that I am your wall in the rear.' By September Alexandra was heading the attack on Sturmer's collapsing dictatorship with the object of persuading Nicholas to abandon civil politics to her alone, and was advancing her own protégé Alexander Protopopov. Nicholas had taken a liking to Protopopov at their first acquaintance and was disposed to believe that he would improve relations with Russian society by favouring the Vice-President of the Duma. Alexandra emphasised this point in her campaign to get Protopopov installed as Minister of Interior: 'Gregory begs you earnestly to name Protopopov. You know him and had such a good impression of him, happens to be of the Duma (is not Left) and so will know how to be with them.' Though worried by Sturmer's performance, Nicholas did not welcome the intrusion of a potential rival: 'While it seems to me that this Protopopov is a good man ... Our Friend's opinions of people are sometimes very strange, as you know yourself – therefore one must be careful especially with appointments to high offices.' But Nicholas had to admit that the protest against Sturmer was not merely a product of his wife's fertile imagination, for a majority of the cabinet led by the Minister of Communications, Alexander Trepov, was currently pressing for his dismissal. On 10 September, Nicholas acceded to Protopopov's appointment, although demonstrating his reluctance to declare the dictatorship a failure prematurely by insisting that Protopopov serve a probationary term as acting Minister of Interior. The challenge of the Tsaritsa had been substantially successful: with the public announcement of Protopopov's elevation on 18 September, the failure of the Tsar's civil dictatorship experiment was tacitly admitted.[12]

The moderates were not sure how to greet Protopopov's translation, and speculation polarised into mutually exclusive interpretations. In the optimist camp, the Russian industrialists and Allied ambassadors hailed the move as promise of a new era in relations between government, Duma and country. Many moderates hoped privately that Protopopov, as an Octobrist well aware of their predicament, would become their political saviour by ordering an extension of the Fourth Duma. The most sanguine of all discerned a new moral responsibility of the government to the Duma stemming from the fact that, as an Octobrist deputy, Protopopov owed obedience to Rodzyanko both as party leader and Duma President. But the pessimists' belief that the appointment was nothing more than a sop to the Duma and Protopopov personally either a dupe or a careerist was soon dramatically reinforced. The news that Protopopov had met German agents in Stockholm in June fed the view that his promotion was part of the long-rumoured but now definitive government move towards a separate peace. Moreover, only days after taking office, Protopov extended the ban on public gatherings instituted by his predecessors: henceforth all meetings whether open or closed were to have police representation, which was empowered to terminate the proceedings without explanation or appeal. Although directed not against high society and Duma circles but against the labour movement of the capitals, this repressive measure incited all sectors of the populace against Protopopov and added to the mounting tension.[13]

Even so, the moderates showed no signs of rushing to the barricades. The Octobrists and Progressists debated their precarious parliamentary position. The Petrograd Kadets waited for Milyukov to return from abroad on 15 September to reassert the traditional policy of restraint. The Moscow and left Kadets too, though rather more active, were unnerved by fears for the future. At an unofficial Moscow Kadet meeting on 18 September, discussion concentrated on the agenda item 'Party strength on the eve of the Fifth Duma elections.' On 23 September, at the first formal meeting of the Moscow Kadet Committee since June, the principal regret was that patriotism disarmed any wartime opposition movement against the government. Kishkin could not imagine revolution until at very least the end of the war. A. A. Kizevetter believed the Tsar was relying on that Russian lethargy which had always been the decisive factor maintaining the existing government in power: 'I am very much afraid that this silent infinite patience is not an expression of conscientious patriotism but only that dull submissiveness and downtroddenness that has characterised our whole Russian history.' Paléologue's contacts with the moderates led him to expect no trouble from this quarter: 'The liberal parties in the Duma have made up their minds not to take up any of the Government's challenges and to defer their claims. The danger will not come from them.'[14]

October 1916 saw the opposition movement accelerating and broadening to a degree alarming to all moderates. Inflation had spiralled so uncontrollably that wage levels lagged far behind prices which were overall four times those of July 1914. The widening gap between wages and prices could only mean social hardship and desperation. The transport and supply crises were so advanced that the living conditions of the town populace were deteriorating dramatically. Washburn noted that 'nowadays the food problem comes first in public interest, with almost every other topic, the war included, nowhere in comparison.' This economic collapse provided the decisive factor in promoting a revolutionary situation in the capitals. An Okhrana report for October was fully alive to the emergency:

> In the opinion of the spokesmen of the labour group of the central WIC, the industrial proletariat of the capital is on the verge of despair and it believes that the smallest outbreak due to any pretext will lead to uncontrollable riots with thousands and tens of thousands of victims. Indeed the stage for such outbreaks is already more than set. Groups of responsible workers find it difficult to prevent the masses from bursting into demonstrations growing out of the lack of necessities and the rise in the cost of living.

It was in October that the first all-city political strike occurred in Petrograd in protest at living conditions. In later conversation with Bernard Pares, Konovalov too judged that 'it was in October that living conditions really became alarming and it was from this time that the revolutionary mood must be dated.'[15]

Another factor in the crisis was that the military success which had buoyed up government confidence and deferred society grievances over the past few months was over. The Brusilov offensive had been halted and replaced by a campaign to reinforce Rumania, which had joined the Allies in August. With hindsight, it is plain that Rumania was militarily so weak that she would have been preferable as a neutral – or possibly even as an enemy – than as an ally. The German armies of Mackensen and Falkenhayn, supported by their Austrian and Bulgarian allies, proved more than a match for the Rumanians: by December the advance of the German army necessitated the transfer of almost one-third of the Russian forces to defend the Rumanian front. The enormous length of the Russian front by late 1916 stretched Russia's military resources to the point that she became incapable of anything more than a defensive 'holding the ring'. At the same time the military emergency increased the need for efficient organisation of the home front and rendered the problems of the civil government all the more acute. As in the previous year, with the adverse change in military fortunes came a familiar ebbing of government self-confidence and initiative.[16]

As was to be expected after its contribution to the Bloc campaign in 1915, Moscow now played a major role. As early as 27 September *Russkia Vedomosti* announced that Moscow was on the verge of a bread and flour shortage amounting to a famine, a state of affairs which Petrograd (though hard pressed) had still to reach. Popular pressure on the political groups of Moscow lent their traditional radicalism a fresh militancy. Against the advice of Milyukov, the Moscow Kadets came out boldly in favour of attacking the government. For the Progressists, Konovalov arranged meetings of Moscow society to discuss the political situation, flagrantly exploiting his position as organiser to hit out at the Kadets. To quote the Okhrana, 'Konovalov hurled at the leaders of the Kadets charges of being inactive, doctrinaire, over-academic and – most important – estranged from democracy.' He glibly equated the Kadets with the Octobrists as willing or unconscious stooges of the government: 'After the Octobrist-ministers, as if we have not suffered enough, will come the Kadet-ministers. Maybe in a few months we shall have a ministry of Milyukov and Shingarev. Everything depends on us – the imminent session of the State Duma must be the decisive onslaught on authority, the final assault on the bureaucracy.'[17] Continuing the steady 'politicisation' which had been their most striking feature over the past year, the Moscow-based public organisations followed the same militant line. At a WIC congress held in defiance of the MVD ban, 'Guchkov announced that an agreement to take up arms in battle against the state power was essential to save Russia ... and the congress, under the chairmanship of Guchkov, passed a resolution of struggle against authority.' The militant rank-and-file of the UT compelled a reluctant Chelnokov to follow suit and even the cautious and apolitical Lvov pledged the full support of the UZ to a Duma stand against the government. Finally, on the streets of Moscow, demonstrating workers precipitated the first isolated incident in which troops sided with the insurgents against the police. With this ominous episode, the social unanimity of Moscow's commitment to political militancy was complete.[18]

Moderate and conservative circles in Petrograd were by now acutely anxious. A shocked Milyukov confessed that a Moscow meeting which he attended on 1 October had proved a rude awakening: 'There has been a metamorphosis in the mood of Moscow. The most naturally inert and ignorant circles have begun to speak in the language of implacable revolutionaries. I would think that the mood of Moscow still outstrips that of Russia as a whole; meanwhile it seems that it has still to reach Petrograd and the provinces ... Moscow wishes to express her own feelings and she cannot and will not be silent.' To Milyukov's alarm, he realised that the London and Paris of 1916 were more familiar and comprehensible than the Moscow of 1916. The effect of this discovery was to reinforce Milyukov's belief in the necessity of controlling and channelling the groundswell of militancy. He expressed this conviction at Bloc meetings in early October but found the participants as far from unanimity as ever. At a meeting on 3 October, the first since June, a meandering debate closed with a jeremiad from Shingarev, 'I don't know whether it is too late for us – we are on the brink of catastrophe.' A second meeting proved equally unconstructive while a third (on 13 October) vividly demonstrated the incompatibility of the members' opinions. Count Kapnist argued the case for 'breaking the neck of the government', Efremov once again declared 'a responsible ministry is the only remedy' but Maklakov insisted that 'this Duma is not a politically mature institution, the majority is volatile and rejects the principle of a responsible ministry ... more than a ministry of confidence is quite beyond us.' The problem of inducing the varied members of the Bloc to adhere to a single coherent policy seemed as insuperable as ever.[19]

The moderates' failure to speak out was depriving them of all popular support. A joint meeting of SRs and SDs on 9 October 'registered an indisputable fall in the influence of the progressive-liberal political current led by the Kadets and remarked the complete bankruptcy of the Duma and Progressive Bloc'. Another Okhrana report noted that 'outside traditional political allegiances, the broad mass of the people are little interested in the State Duma.' Moreover public opinion about the Duma was shifting from indifference towards open hostility: 'at the lower levels of society, they accuse the Duma ... of deliberately refusing to come to the aid of the masses in general; the most bitter accusations in this respect are levelled not only at the Octobrists but the Kadets too.' Despite the glaring absence of any policy consensus and notwithstanding fears for the unity of their parties and the survival of the Bloc, there was no alternative for the moderates but to re-enter the political arena.[20]

The government was as apprehensive as the moderates. In late September the Okhrana predicted that any future Duma session could only be oppositional and anticipated a critique of official policy in Rodzyanko's opening speech. Uneasily aware that his stated preference for a Fifth Duma had alienated all moderate and right-wing support in the Duma, Sturmer was convinced that the entire membership would attack the government in order to play to the electoral gallery: 'the whole Duma is preparing to speak, impelled by considerations of the new elections in 1917 and by the desire to distinguish themselves before their electorates in the interests of re-election.' The Duma threat had the effect of polarising the cabinet into 'soft' and 'hard' camps, those who favoured the political 'carrot' and those who relied on the traditional 'stick'.[21]

The 'carrot' was offered by the rising power in government, Protopopov. Having helped to discredit Sturmer, the Tsaritsa planned to expand the authority of Protopopov at the MVD to effect her own dictatorship of the home front. The dictatorship projected by Nicholas had been an artificial superimposition on the traditional structure of government; Alexandra chose to back the most promising development *within* the government, the rise of the MVD to challenge the premiership for supreme executive power. By October 1916 Sturmer had been effectively demoted to the function of Council Chairman and authority within the government was flowing to Protopopov. The Tsar's candidate for civil dictatorship had been replaced by the Tsaritsa's.

Various enticements were dangled before the moderates by Protopopov to strengthen their instinct for restraint. Rumours from 'usually reliable bureaucratic sources' asserted that the prevailing opinion within the government still favoured extending the Fourth Duma. Journalistic intelligence suggested that Protopopov preferred not be be seen to take the initiative: if the Duma desired extension, it should submit a parliamentary bill, which would safely pass the State Council and become law; if the Duma did not want extension, the government would continue its preparations for the Fifth Duma. It is difficult to conceive of a more effective counter to moderate militancy (to frame a paradox) than this subtle approach by Protopopov. The advantages to both sides were clear: the government bought off the moderate opposition and isolated the Left; and the moderates gained at least a respite from the political ruin which currently confronted them. Only the unprecedented pressure from outside the Duma prevented the parliamentary moderates from accepting the deal in their own interests.[22] Protopopov now broke cover to attempt direct negotiation with his ex-colleagues at a meeting on 19 October. Aware that their militant supporters suspected a sell-out, the Bloc negotiators adopted a more intractable line than they would otherwise have done. Although there was a serious attempt at political bargaining, the circumstances of the meeting (which forced the Bloc to play to a wider militant gallery), Protopopov's sullied reputation (especially over his assignation with German agents in the summer) and the radical demands of Efremov (representing the broader opposition movement) proved impossible to surmount. In exasperation, Protopopov played his last conciliatory card: an offer to legalise the Kadet party. This attempt to buy off Milyukov by guaranteeing the legal security the Kadets had always craved was too blatant for the Bloc leaders, let alone their watchful audience. With his last throw indignantly rejected, Protopopov departed: 'Gentlemen, I have made the experiment of cooperation but unfortunately it has proved unsuccessful. This is my last attempt. What more can I do?' The 'soft' approach to the Bloc had been rejected (despite Protopopov's well-judged ploys) and the government now had no option but to fall back on its 'hard' line.[23]

As in the past, the government was less concerned about the violence of Duma criticism than the wide currency it enjoyed. Sturmer toyed with the idea of enforcing closed sessions 'to exclude the possibility of the publication of the stenographic records and their appearance in the press'. The desirability of imposing a political quarantine on the Duma was underlined by the Okhrana: 'the opposition mood has reached exceptional proportions which were not attained in the broad mass of the population even in the period 1905–6 ... Russia is on the brink of revolution and Petrograd is more than close to an armed uprising.' By the last days of October, Sturmer's nerve was giving way. In a report to Nicholas, he voiced his conviction that the Duma was committed to 'the path of systematic battle with the government ... and the publication from the height of the Duma rostrum of criminal propaganda throughout the country demanding a revolution in the existing structure of government'. Panic-stricken and desperate to avert such a calamity, Sturmer resorted to open threats: 'I draw the attention of the members of the Duma to the fact that the immediate consequence of the dissolution of the Duma would be the speedy despatch to the front line for military service of all members of the legislative chambers in the liable age group.'[24]

The moderates were confronted by the most critical manifestation to date of a familiar dilemma: the war bound them to some allegiance to *union sacrée* but the mood of the country was so heightened that their traditional policy of restraint would destroy what little wider support they still enjoyed; conversely, to express the antagonism of the country on the principle *je suis leur chef, donc je les suis* would incur the wrath of the government and their own political annihilation. In the words of Maklakov, 'the indignation of the country had risen to such heights that the Duma did not wish to be left behind', but precisely what form should Duma action take? Efremov, Konovalov, a majority of Progressists and the left Kadets proposed adding their weight to the opposition movement to avoid being overtaken as political leaders, despite the risk of revolution or military collapse. Milyukov, most Kadets, a minority of Progressists, and the whole Octobrist camp led by Rodzyanko, fearing revolution more than the Tsar, proposed employing the Bloc to channel the opposition movement into securing particular concessions from the government. A succession of Bloc meetings over the last ten days of October became the principal arena for the clash between the two viewpoints. On 20 October debate centred on that crucial but incalculable point, the degree of support which the Duma might expect in a crisis. B. I. Krinsky for the left Kadets argued that to attack the government 'would earn colossal popularity' but Shingarev feared that popularity was an ephemeral factor in politics: 'The Vyborg Appeal was a mistake. The people did not rise and the Appeal was incomprehensible even to the intelligentsia ... In general I am a great sceptic of revolution. Instead, let us launch a campaign of parliamentary action.' At a meeting two days later, the two-way split became three-way: the Progressists and left Kadets were committed to attacking the entire tsarist system; the official Kadets and Octobrists proposed concentrating fire on the Sturmer administration; but the Progressive Nationalists were unconvinced that any campaign should be mounted. On 24 October Milyukov achieved a considerable personal success by persuading Efremov and Shulgin that his centre line was preferable to the ascendancy of the opposite wing, and securing grudging acquiescence to his policy of selective opposition. In this fragile consensus, Milyukov won a crucial tactical victory. Thanks only to Milyukov's moral authority, the first Bloc crisis since the previous Duma session had been narrowly surmounted.[25]

Milyukov had now to convince his own party. The Kadet autumn conference which met in Petrograd on 22–4 October was the first platform for the rebel groups since the internal coups of May and jeopardised any hopes for restraint. Anticipating bitter censure, Milyukov adopted his usual practice of excluding the public and press, then desperately defended his position on tactical grounds:

> In its struggle with this upheaval, the government will find itself in a vacuum – it will have no one to lean on ... At the last moment, frightened, it will reach out for us and it will then be our task not to destroy the government, which would only aid anarchy, but to instil

a completely different content, that is, to build a genuine constitutional order. That is why, in our struggle with the government, despite everything, we must retain a sense of proportion ... To support anarchy in the name of the struggle with the government would be to risk all the political conquests we have made since 1905.

As Dolgorukov remarked, the difference in emphasis was becoming daily more marked: 'Milyukov sees the centre of attention as the parliamentary struggle with the government; the "provincials" insist on shifting the centre of attention to the organisation of the masses and a *rapprochement* with political groups to the left.' Far from convinced by Milyukov, the left Kadets and provincial delegates hit out harder than ever before: 'Finally, as always, Milyukov succeeded in defeating his opponents and made them follow him but this was accomplished only after a prolonged and heated struggle. The conference showed that the party's left wing is growing constantly stronger.' Although the Kadet party showed every sign of becoming ungovernable in the near future, Milyukov had for the time being run the gauntlet of Kadet criticism and emerged physically unscathed. By sheer personality and political expertise, Milyukov had engineered tactical victories for a policy of restraint within both Kadet party and Progressive Bloc.[26]

When Paléologue enquired if the new session of the Duma would cause trouble, Milyukov contentedly answered 'No, nothing serious. But certain things will have to be said from the tribune, otherwise we should lose all our influence over our constituents and they would go over to the extremists.' This opinion, so reminiscent of Milyukov's 'safety-valve' tactics in July 1915, was hardly expressed before wider developments put intolerable pressure on his consensus of restraint. The public organisations put up an unsolicited campaign of support for a more militant Duma line. Rodzyanko received a message from the UZ assuring him that 'in the decisive battle of the State Duma for the institution of a government capable of uniting all the living forces of the country and carrying our nation to victory, "Zemstvo Russia" will stand united with the people's representatives.' A similar resolution from the UT stressed that 'the decisive hour has arrived – delay is intolerable and all efforts must be bent for the establishment of a government which in union with the people will lead the country to victory.' Although Milyukov could still dominate the parliamentary scene, he was at the mercy of the broadening, militant opposition movement in the capitals.[27]

This outside pressure was insistent enough to fragment the Progressive Bloc at its most fragile. State Council delegates within the Bloc, led by Gurko, sympathised with the general line of a Bloc Declaration drafted by Milyukov but refused to countenance an accusation of treason which he intended to level at Sturmer. The misgivings of the Council combined with trepidation about the Duma session now only two days away to prompt a dramatic protest from the right wing of the Bloc. On 31 October, in fear of provoking the dissolution of the Fourth Duma, Shulgin roundly condemned Milyukov for inciting rather than expressing popular grievance: 'Now the Kadets are introducing a proposal to base agreement on the principle of active struggle with the government ... but we are not prepared to go to the barricades on that basis. The Duma must be the safety-valve for letting off steam, not for making steam.' While the right wing found Milyukov's line suicidally provocative, the left wing considered his decision to concentrate fire on the person of Sturmer irresponsible and cowardly. Efremov's exasperation could not be contained: 'The Declaration is weak and feeble. I cannot be silent any longer. Are we agreed that we must do more, accepting the necessity of further struggle with the government than just against a "personal regime"? We fear that the Zemstvo-Octobrists do not accept even the necessity for attack ... Today I have seen that disagreement is deeper than I realised, it is a fundamental split in the Bloc.' Despite soothing reassurances from Milyukov and Shidlovsky, Efremov could not be mollified: 'the decision of the Progressists is not to subscribe to the Declaration and therefore to quit the Progressive Bloc.'[28]

Efremov's bombshell rocked the Bloc on the very evening prior to the opening of the Duma session. Although the decision of Efremov (so often cavalier about political niceties) was by no means unanimous even among Progressists, and a fraction 'rump' led by Count A.A. Orlov-Davydov refused to quit the Bloc, the repercussions could hardly have been more disturbing. The Bloc was living up to the worst fears of its participants that since June the moderate parliamentary coalition had been inoperable. The Bloc entered the new session with fewer adherents and more unity problems than ever before. The options available to the unenviable Milyukov were all intimidating. To refrain from attacking the government would satisfy the right wing of the Bloc at the expense of estranging the Progressists, very possibly splitting the Kadet party and losing his party leadership, not to mention once again disillusioning the expectant nation. To lead an onslaught on the government might save his personal position as party leader, unite the Kadets, reincorporate the Progressists into the Bloc and revive the drooping national prestige of the Duma; but it had the disadvantages of being personally repugnant, almost certainly prompting the defection of the right wing of the Bloc, and very likely setting the government irrevocably against extending the Fourth Duma. In practice Milyukov chose a compromise course, accepting the necessity for at very least a gesture of attack on the government but deliberately restricting his campaign to a personal vendetta against the man who by now had lost all support both within the Duma and the government.[29]

The first day of the Duma session on 1 November 1916 was electric with anticipation. Informed of developments within the Bloc by Okhrana reporters and their undercover agent P.N. Krupensky, the ministers prudently departed after Rodzyanko's ceremonial opening speech. Following Shidlovsky's formal reading of the Bloc Declaration, Milyukov rose to speak. His speech was not marked by great political insight, striking oratory or cogent argument but there was no doubt of the impact of this *succès de scandale*. Milyukov exploited the ignorance of the presiding officer, S.T. Varun-Sekret, who neither knew German nor appreciated the illegality of employing languages other than Russian in the Duma, to quote passages from the *Neue Freie Presse* describing the baneful influence of the Tsaritsa on Russian politics. He followed this with an elaborate catalogue of accusations against Sturmer, hesitating after each charge to enquire rhetorically 'Is this stupidity or treason?'. Finally he attempted to cover himself against future legal redress by remarking: 'Does it matter practically speaking whether we are dealing with stupidity or treason? ... the government persists in claiming that organising the country means organising a revolution and deliberately prefers chaos and disorganisation. Is this stupidity or treason? Choose either: the result is the same.' Despite claims in the speech that proof of treason was to hand, Milyukov was never willing (or indeed able) to produce it. Milyukov's academic instinct constrained him to claim conclusive evidence for his accusation but in reality the professional historian's respect for rules of evidence had succumbed completely to the exigencies of politics. Given the dilemma of the Russian moderates at this time, the target for Milyukov's attack and the evidence for his sensational assertions had become secondary considerations. Milyukov's speech of 1 November was determined not by the guilt or incompetence of Sturmer but the complex predicament of the Progressive Bloc in the developing revolutionary climate of Russia in late 1916.[30]

The government was thrown on to the defensive. Sturmer asked his colleagues for authorisation to prosecute Milyukov as a political criminal but the other ministers, anxious for a return to calm, persuaded him to sue for slander instead. The passivity of the ministers under fire only encouraged a Bloc onslaught. The Duma expected philippics from the demagogues of the Left (and Kerensky and N. S. Chkheidze predictably attacked on the first occasion) but what alarmed the government was the mobilisation of the moderate Right in the campaign. The right wing of the Bloc was relieved that although Milyukov's speech had expressed criticism of the premier in unprecedented language, it had made no demands for constitutional – let alone unconstitutional – warfare on the tsarist establishment. Immensely comforted by the narrow focus of Milyukov's attack, the moderate Right in the Duma responded gratefully to his tactic of converting a would-be revolution into a witch-hunt. Shulgin poured abuse on the head of Sturmer: 'A man without convictions, ready for anything, who understands nothing about state affairs ... we will fight his administration until it goes. On the home front is the Duma, which watches, listens, finds out and, when necessary, speaks out.' Maklakov too added his considerable talents to the denunciation of the Sturmer administration: 'This cabinet without a programme, ministers without opinions, without faith in one another, without mutual respect, without even tokens of solidarity. The sum of it all is the current administration of Sturmer ... which paralyses and enfeebles the strength of all Russia.'[31] Acutely embarrassed by the personal nature of the campaign and appalled at the broad spectrum of attack, Sturmer reported to the Tsar that there was no alternative but immediate prorogation of the Duma. In declining health, personally distressed and without resource for the future, Sturmer was at the end of his political usefulness. On 8 November Nicholas wearily agreed to his removal: 'I have been thinking of old Sturmer. He, as you rightly say, acts as a red flag not only to the Duma but to the whole country alas. I hear this from all sides; nobody believes in him and everyone is angry because we stand up for him ... He is coming here tomorrow and I will give him leave for the present.'[32]

Sturmer's downfall was accounted a personal triumph by the delighted Progressive Bloc. As Milyukov subsequently related: 'The first impression from the dismissal of Sturmer was that this was a complete victory for the Duma. It seemed as if, in effect, this was the first step towards ministerial responsibility in that an individual, having received a harsh judgement, was dismissed.' The Octobrist Kapnist was even more hopeful: 'the principle has been established that in practice ministers who do not enjoy the confidence of the majority of the Duma and do not respect this majority will be unable to stay in power.' With this latest 'proof' of the moral authority of the national assembly, the self-regard of the moderates received a much-needed fillip. Milyukov made a triumphant return to ascendancy over the moderate camp. An Okhrana report observed that 'the hero of the hour is Milyukov; there is no doubt that his popularity in the Duma, Bloc and his own fraction has reached its zenith.' Though some Progressists were still sulking in isolation, there seemed every ground for hope that they could be enticed back into a Bloc which had miraculously survived the greatest test to its integrity so far. Similarly, although Milyukov's speech did not draw the left Kadets unconditionally back into line, his enhanced authority did arrest the rebel developments of 1916 and halt the leftward drift of the Kadet minority. The Kadet majority was infused with a new breezy self-confidence: 'The Kadets are persuaded that the government cannot refuse the demands of the Progressive Bloc ... they have attained incredible political influence over the last few weeks, their opinions are believed and they are aided by the restlessness in society. Milyukov has become the regular hero of the day.'[33]

Outside the traditional confines of politics, the echoes of the speech reverberated until the February Revolution itself. The charge of treason levelled at Sturmer (and, by some interpretations, implicitly at the Tsaritsa) lent Milyukov's speech enormous notoriety. Despite tight official censorship which struck out all mention of the speech in the press, the news quickly spread from the capitals to the provinces. Although Rodzyanko dared not authorise the publication of a complete stenographic record of the speech, pirated versions (often with scandalous additions) were typewritten and mimeographed by the thousand to satisfy a public eager to learn the worst. The name of Milyukov overnight acquired an aura of charisma. Milyukov was to remark with pride some years later that his speech was a turning-point: 'A blister filled with pus had burst and the basic evil, which was known to everyone but had awaited public exposure, had now been pin-pointed ... My speech acquired the reputation of a storm-signal for revolution. Such was not my intention but the prevailing mood in the country served as a megaphone for my words.' But the new popular following magically acquired by the Bloc was born of a misunderstanding. As Milyukov admitted by his phrase 'such was not my intention', his speech was taken far more seriously than had ever been intended by its author. Milyukov was even to claim that his own answer to the rhetorical question 'Stupidity or Treason?' was the former, but the country jumped to the more sensational conclusion. What had been essentially an improvised tactical response to the immediate predicament of the moderates was taken by the public at large as the final break between the Duma and tsarist government. To the politically unsophisticated wider circles of Russian society, Milyukov's speech confirmed the irrevocable breakdown of the *union sacrée* and constituted what came to be known as the 'Storm-signal of Revolution'. True to Shulgin's earlier misgivings, what had been intended 'to let off steam' had the effect of 'making steam'.[34]

Milyukov's speech was destined to take pride of place in Duma, and particularly Kadet, hagiography. After the February Revolution, when the Kadets were embarrassed by their tactics of restraint during the greater part of the Third and Fourth Dumas and sensitive about refurbishing their revolutionary image, the tag 'Storm-signal' was retrospectively attached to the speech of 1 November 1916. The all-important exigencies of the moment were conveniently forgotten and the speech portrayed as a deliberate and conscious advance in the offensive against tsarism. In the scramble for a place in the history of the fall of tsarism, Kadet apologists and historians queued to legitimise the revolutionary pedigree of the party by claiming the November speech as 'the beginning of the revolution'.[35]

With the fall of Sturmer came the reconstitution of the Council of Ministers. Ever sensitive to the claims of the Duma on his prerogatives, Nicholas insisted that 'while these changes are in progress the Duma will be prorogued for about eight days otherwise they would say it was being done under pressure from them'. Despite the transparent motive for the Duma break, all the changes made were calculated to weaken the resolve of the militants, offer hope to the moderates and appease the Duma: Sturmer was replaced by the moderate Trepov and the incompetent Count A.A. Bobrinsky was succeeded as Minister of Agriculture by A.A. Rittikh. Two of the most despised ministers had been removed to placate the Duma and their replacements specially selected to avoid giving offence. There was even a campaign to remove the third Duma *bête noire* within the government. The move was only possible because of the Tsar's growing doubts: 'I am sorry for Protopopov – he is a good man but he jumps from one idea to another and cannot make up his mind on anything. It is risky to leave the Ministry of Internal Affairs in the hands of such a man in these times.' Divining the political breeze, Trepov made the removal of Protopopov a condition of his premiership at his initial audience with the Tsar. Nicholas's agreement elicited a torrent of protest from Alexandra who, rightly judging that her husband's independence of mind ran in direct proportion to his distance from her side, packed for the Stavka at once. One of her letters before departure illustrates her despair at the threat to her plans for Protopopov's dictatorship: 'Put off Trepov until we have met ... I am but a woman fighting for her Master and Child, only don't pull away the sticks upon which I have found it possible to rest ... only when you tell Trepov you won't change Protopopov, don't for goodness' sake mention my name – it must be your wise wish.' Alexandra arrived at the Stavka on 13 November and remained until early December. There is evidence from Nicholas himself to suggest that the stay was not a very pleasant one: 'Yes, these days spent together were difficult but only thanks to you have I spent them more or less calmly. You were so strong and steadfast – I admire you more than I can say. Forgive me if I was moody and unrestrained.' Alexandra naturally had her way and, at Trepov's second audience with Nicholas, Protopopov's dismissal and Trepov's own subsequent offer of resignation were refused. In a rare attempt at joint action, Trepov appealed to the Duma President to use his influence to oust Protopopov but a visit by Rodzyanko to the Stavka proved no more fruitful than Trepov's own. In spite of his estrangement from the Duma, the Council of Ministers and the Tsar himself, Protopopov was retained. The new authority in government

1 Public and private faces of the Russian monarchy: an official study of the Tsar in 1915 (*left*) and a family snapshot of Nicholas and Alexandra at Livadia in 1914 (*below*)
(Both reproduced by permission of the Mansell Collection)

2 The Tsar and ministers, mid-1915: (*from left, standing*) Sazonov, Krivoshein, Bark, General Yanushkevich, General Polivanov and Shakhovskoi; (*sitting*) Grand Duke Nikolai, Nicholas II, Goremykin and Frederiks (Reproduced by kind permission from Robert Wilton, *Russia's Agony* (Edward Arnold, London 1918), p.26)

3 Leading servants of Nicholas II over the last year of tsarism: Protopopov (*right*), Sturmer (*below left*) and General Alexeyev (*below right*) (Radio Times Hulton Picture Library)

4 The Tauride Palace in Petrograd, seat of the State Duma: exterior view of the main building (*below,* reproduced by kind permission from Harold Williams, *Russia of the Russians* (Pitman, London 1914), p. 72) and the Presidential tribune in the debating chamber (*left,* reproduced by permission of the Mansell Collection)

5 Parliamentary leaders of the Russian moderate parties: Milyukov (*right*), Konovalov (*below left*) and Rodzyanko (*below right*)
(The photographs of Milyukov and Rodzyanko reproduced by kind permission from Stinton Jones, *Russia in Revolution* (Herbert Jenkins, London 1917), p. 212 and p. 1; Konovalov from Radio Times Hulton Picture Library)

6 February 1917: the first Petrograd demonstrations on Znamenskaya Square (*above,* Radio Times Hulton Picture Library) and the Tauride Palace besieged by republican insurgents (*below,* reproduced by kind permission from Stinton Jones, *Russia in Revolution* (Herbert Jenkins, London 1917), p. 256)

7 The first issue of the broadsheet *Izvestia,* the only printed source of news in Petrograd during the February Revolution. (Reproduced by kind permission from Stinton Jones, *Russia in Revolution,* (Herbert Jenkins, London 1917), p.140)

8 Political personalities spotlighted by the February Revolution: Prince Lvov (*right,* Radio Times Hulton Picture Library), Guchkov (*below left,* reproduced by kind permission from Harold Williams, *Russia of the Russians* (London, Pitman 1914) p. 84, and Kerensky (*below right,* reproduced by permission of the Mansell Collection)

which could resist all other factors combined was the Tsaritsa.[36]

Even without a clean sweep of leading reactionaries in the cabinet, the new administration offered olive branches which were difficult for the Bloc to resist. Trepov took care to foster good relations with the Duma, holding exploratory courtesy talks with Rodzyanko, soliciting his advice on a replacement for Protopopov and inviting him to join the cabinet campaign for his removal. On the first day of the reconvened Duma session (on 19 November) Trepov turned his seductive arts upon the more susceptible of the moderates: the promise of a review of agricultural price-pegging set out to woo the landowning Octobrists; official disclosure of the diplomatic agreement guaranteeing Russian acquisition of the Dardanelles at the end of the war was intended to dispel rumours of a separate peace and recommend the new administration to all patriots; and the new premier's long-held opinions favouring the extension of the current Duma went straight to the heart of moderate self-interest. There could be no denying that once again a 'soft line' towards the Duma possessed the government.[37]

The Duma was faced with the familiar issue of what attitude to take to a new administration. Was it to treat the Trepov cabinet as a new government without responsibility for the misdeeds of its predecessor; or as merely 'a re-seating of the musicians' in which nothing fundamental was altered? The response to the dilemma varied widely. The Duma Left decided to press the attack: the Mensheviks and Trudoviks jointly announced their future boycott of the government and on 19 November refused to allow the premier to speak, had to be forcibly ejected from the chamber and were excluded from the next eight Duma sittings in punishment.[38] On the right wing, the first day of the reconvened session was equally traumatic, with the dogged loyalty of the conservative rank-and-file suffering a double shock. The Trepov declaration revising agricultural price-pegging incensed peasant deputies for whose electorates a price freeze might mean the difference between survival and starvation. The peasant deputies condemned the declaration as a dishonourable ploy by the new administration to ingratiate itself with the Progressive Bloc at the expense of traditional loyal support. Peasant disgust at being taken for granted was topped by astonishment at the public defection of the most famous leader of the Right. In a speech which rivalled that of Milyukov in impact, V.M. Purishkevich categorically condemned the government of Sturmer and Protopopov, and demanded the immediate banishment of Rasputin and all other 'dark forces' from Russian political life.[39]

While antagonism towards the government continued on the Duma Left and erupted dramatically on the Right, it faltered in the moderate camp. Bloc uncertainty about tactics was in no sense resolved by the success of the 'Storm-signal' and the moderates were far from unanimous about how to exploit their famous victory. When the Ministers for War and the Navy, D.S. Shuvayev and Grigorovich decided to make an appeal to the Duma on 4 November, their visit was greeted rapturously by the Bloc. The element of misunderstanding which converted a government reconnaissance mission into an acclaimed Duma triumph – Milyukov exultantly claimed that 'the ministers for War and the Navy have taken their stand on the side of the Duma and the nation' – demonstrates the relief with which the Bloc welcomed the slightest sign of concession from the government.[40] At the first Bloc meeting after his speech, Milyukov prudently attempted to place recent events in some perspective: 'I would not call the substitution of Trepov and Protopopov for Sturmer a great event but ... under the influence of the feeling of mortal danger, which we have pointed out here, the country is rousing itself.' Most of his Bloc colleagues favoured postponing any decisions about future policy until the formation of the new administration. In Moscow the local Kadets, more militant yet more realistic than in Petrograd, recovered from the intoxication of victory early to an awareness that the success of the 'Storm-signal' owed more to fortuitous timing and popular misunderstanding than moderate strength. The Okhrana described a meeting of Moscow Kadets as,

> clearly showing utter perplexity at finding solutions, complete recognition of their own impotence and awareness of the power of the government. None of the Kadets believes that the government will meet the demands of the Bloc *in full* and in the last analysis, the whole question for the Kadets is who should replace Sturmer ... In their private conversations, the Kadets demonstrate a strong inclination to compromise ... The Kadets talk of the possibility of a 'Society Cabinet' only in their official statements and in their private discussions are reconciling themselves to a partial renovation of the present cabinet.

While a Bloc meeting on 11 November stipulated government acceptance of the entire Bloc Declaration, the Moscow Kadets were already pre-empting the issue. Both in commitment to attack and resignation to compromise, Petrograd now followed Moscow. On 13 November, the Petrograd and Moscow Kadet Committees supported collaboration with Trepov, demonstrating that the level of Kadet self-assurance in Petrograd was dropping to that of Moscow. The Okhrana noted of the Petrograd meeting, 'even the representative of the left wing of the Kadets Rodichev supported businesslike cooperation ... [and] in general, yesterday's meeting of the Kadets has shown that their spirits are starting to fall.' At the next Bloc meeting, the continuing slump in morale was expressed in a debate on the efficacy of a Duma boycott should the government prove intransigent. The nine-day recess worked to the advantage of the government: Trepov spun out the recess until the fall in moderate morale made practical a working relationship with his administration.[41]

The spirit of 'Storm-signal' which infected the extremes of Left and Right evaporated amongst the Duma moderates within the month. Two of the three principal targets for Duma hostility had been toppled, so with the worst features of the Sturmer regime purged and Trepov personally sympathetic to an extended Fourth Duma, the great majority of Octobrists and Bloc right-wingers had no desire to advance further. With his parliamentary authority re-established and the threat of disintegration to the Bloc and Kadet party reduced, Milyukov returned to the politics of restraint which his instincts had long favoured. Internal divisions among the moderates sabotaged hopes of a sustained offensive, for factional squabbles afflicted the Bloc the moment that tension dipped. At a Duma sitting on 29 November, the land interest accused industry of exorbitant profits: the Zemstvo-Octobrist V.I. Stempkovsky claimed that the meteoric rise in turnover of Konovalov's textile combine could only be described as war profiteering. The antipathy of landowner and peasant, already heightened by the price-pegging issue, was brought to fever pitch by an Octobrist volost zemstvo bill which the peasant deputies saw as a cover for landed exploitation of the peasant. The effect of the squabbles was two-fold: the propertied moderates were marked off from the extremes of Left and Right on the basis of self-interest; and the energies of the Bloc were diverted from the wider conflict between Duma and government. It also emerged that national notoriety was no guarantee of practical support by Russian society. When, for example, Protopopov provocatively banned congresses of the public organisations scheduled for 5 November, the executive of the UZ (later supported grudgingly by the UT) meekly resolved 'under no circumstances to operate by illegal means nor under any circumstances to assemble a congress by revolutionary means'. Despite earlier brave words, the leaders of the public organisations were still not prepared to follow the Bloc into battle, even had the Bloc wished to lead.[42]

Fear now dominated the moderates. Fear of a separate peace and the international humiliation of Russia was a major talking-point by autumn 1916. Fear of the masses was more acute than ever with the leftward sweep of public opinion outside the Duma. The Vyborg complex was as potent as ever, afflicting the entire moderate camp: even after the gratifying success of Milyukov's 'Stupidity or Treason' speech, the moderates could not muster the self-confidence to confront the government decisively. They may have been right: after Protopopov issued an MVD circular to provincial governors on 10 November requesting impressions of the impact of speech, answering reports sanguinely suggested that nationwide interest was obsessive but transitory. A more pressing fear was of the dissolution of the Duma. Although the removal of Sturmer meant the expulsion of the most committed advocate of a Fifth Duma, many Bloc right-wingers suspected that the speech attacking the premier had sealed the fate of the current Duma. What would become of the moderate parties without the Duma as their 'city of refuge'? A series of Okhrana reports illustrates mounting moderate concern. 'Just now the Kadets fear not only the dissolution of the Duma but that the war may finish without their decisive vote ... What will become of the "Party of the People's Freedom" if it has no influence on the affairs on the people? With all the dexterity of a conjuror, Milyukov is trying to throw all the blame on to the government.' By December, the deputies were concerned for their personal safety:

> At present, anxiety about the fate of the State Duma pervades the Progressive Bloc and particularly the fate of individual deputies belonging to the left wing. The prospect of dissolution is particularly menacing to the Bloc, for in the event of such an act of suppression, the deputies would be deprived of their parliamentary immunity and the whole left wing of the Bloc, including the Kadets, would be entirely in the power of the government.

Even more terrifying, the emergence of revolution by December 1916 as a universally-acknowledged threat had the Kadets, Octobrists and Progressists, all with substantial stakes in the maintenance of public order and stable government, trembling for their interests and investments. The Okhrana had no doubt that in the last resort the moderates would ally with the government on any terms to avert revolution: 'The Kadets quite literally contemplate a revolution with feelings of horror and panic. This dread is so great that if there was only the tiniest possibility of agreement with the government, if the government offered the slightest concession, the Kadets would run to meet her with joy.'[43]

For the moderates to rise from the depths of morale in June 1916 to the heights of self-assurance five months later was a transformation too rapid to be real. The 'Storm-signal', a tactical response to the political dilemma of the ailing Progressive Bloc rather than a deliberate decision to confront the government, had entirely spent its force by the end of November, without providing answers to any of the problems afflicting the moderates. The moderate Right reverted with relief to the traditional Bloc policy of restraint. Having briefly lent expression to the welling discontent of the nation, the moderate Left fell prey to familiar doubts and fears. Milyukov's 'Storm-signal' enjoyed considerable (though exaggerated) success as a palliative for chronic internal ailments and as a temporary anti-depressant but within a month its effects had worn off and the moderates had relapsed.

6 On the Eve

In a Russia increasingly vulnerable to political extremism of both the left and right varieties, the moderate course was weakening rapidly. The Tsar still resisted the reactionary urgings of his wife but his surrender was expected daily. The Okhrana discerned two rival groups locked in conflict at court: the Nicholas group 'advocating the immediate necessity of meeting the wishes recently expressed in both legislative chambers' and the Alexandra group which 'categorically opposes any change in the course of politics and stands by an earlier conception of government'. That Nicholas favoured a measure of trust in the Duma is indicated in a letter of 13 December: 'he [Trepov] unfolded his plan concerning the Duma – to prorogue it on December 17th and reassemble it on January 19th, so as to show them and the whole country that in spite of all they have said, the government wish to work together.' However, little faith could be placed on the word of a monarch whose very next letter betrayed an ugly cynicism: 'It is unpleasant to speak to a man one does not like and does not trust like Trepov. But first of all, it is necessary to find a substitute for him and then kick him out – after he has done the dirty work. I mean to make him resign after he has closed the Duma. Let all the responsibility and all the difficulties fall on his shoulders.' Although Trepov was a force for moderation within the government, pressing persistently for the removal of Protopopov and the evolution of some working relationship with the Duma, his days as premier were numbered.[1]

The Progressive Bloc returned to the defeatist mood of early 1916. In the course of December the policy of restraint which followed the 'Storm-signal' degenerated into abject servility towards the government. Unwilling to prejudice the chances of the Fourth Duma at least running its full term, the furthest the Bloc would go was to warn the government of the risks it was running. A speech of Milyukov on 16 December was typical: 'The air is full of electricity and one feels the approach of a thunderstorm. No one can tell where or when the first thunderclap will occur but in order that the storm should not break in a form which we do not desire, we must in conjunction with the nation at large try to prevent the storm itself.' Six weeks after raising the 'Storm-signal', Milyukov had completely changed his tune! The Menshevik M.I. Skobelev spoke for many in accusing the Bloc of listening only to the government, not to the Russian people. The end of the Duma session made little impression on the listless moderates: prorogation was accepted so meekly by the Duma on 16 December that a disgusted Konovalov termed it a 'self-dissolution'. The newly-arrived British agent Samuel Hoare remarked that 'the deputies themselves, impotent and irresponsible, were obviously disillusioned and embittered by the hopelessness of their position. The Duma had in fact become the kind of assembly that a country can get on neither with nor without. Out of touch with reality, cold-shouldered by authority, it was eking out a precarious and often purposeless existence.'[2]

The state of Kadet morale may be judged by the fact that instructions to deputies for the recess were to register the mood of the country, with any possibility of action reserved for the reconvened session. At the last Kadet meeting of the year, a joint Moscow and Petrograd Committee session on 21 December, Shingarev produced a familiar tired line of argument: 'Retain full self-control and restraint ... For the time being there is only one course open to us – the path of parliamentary struggle within legal parliamentary limits. Only when this path is completely exhausted, then and only then will we adopt new and unparliamentary methods of warfare.' Milyukov sought relief from the gloom of the capitals and his downcast party by spending the vacation in the Crimea. Even the Okhrana seems to have been affected by the depths to which Kadet morale had sunk: 'greater disillusionment, greater perplexity than that which currently permeates the Kadets would be hard to imagine; of the exultant spirit which precipitated the fall of Sturmer, there remains not a trace.'[3]

There were some crumbs of comfort. Two unlikely recruits for the moderate cause emerged from within the bounds of 'official Russia' over the last weeks of 1916. What Sturmer had called the growing 'unreliability' of the State Council was most dramatically expressed on 24 November, when resolutions were passed demanding 'the decisive removal from governmental affairs of hidden unresponsible forces' (by 105 votes to 23) and 'the formation of a truly working government, united by a well-defined programme, relying on the confidence and goodwill of the country and consequently capable of collaboration with the legislative institutions' (by 94 votes to 34). Almost simultaneously a congress of nobility from over thirty provinces convening in Petrograd presented a petition to the Tsar attacking the 'dark powers' and pleading for a government 'enjoying popular confidence, capable of joint labour with the legislative institutions yet responsible only to the Monarch'. As Hoare remarked, 'this resolution is the more remarkable from the fact that in the decrees prohibiting meetings, a particular exception was made in favour of the United Council of the Nobility, on the ground that its deliberations were certain to give support to the Government.' With two traditional bastions of conservatism publicly adopting policies associated with the Progressive Bloc, the isolation of the court and government became even more pronounced and the moderate camp sported some strange bedfellows.[4]

The moderates undoubtedly contributed to the political polarisation of the last months of tsarist Russia. By being the only public institution to refuse to respond to the leftward sweep of public opinion, the Progressive Bloc did gain unexpected recruits like the State Council and Congress of Nobility but at the price of alienating its traditional support. As the Bloc welcomed new supporters from the Right, it was losing past supporters to the Left. The most striking example is the estrangement of the public organisations. Under fire from the MVD and angry over a new ban on congresses, the public organisations directed a succession of appeals to the Bloc. Despite the efforts of Chelnokov, the UT was becoming more radical than ever before: 'The Union of Towns calls upon the Duma to do its duty and remain in session until the principal task – the setting up of a responsible ministry – is accomplished.' The WICs made a similar plea: 'Only a responsible government united with the people and with their aid can guide the country out of the cul-de-sac into which the old regime has led us.' The leadership of the more moderate UZ was under pressure too. A campaign by 'Third Element' militants in the UT to ally with their counterparts in the UZ for direct action was only prevented by Lvov threatening to dismiss any UZ personnel involved. Even so, while avoiding any suggestion of unconstitutional action, Lvov felt constrained to complain in the strongest terms.[5] However the Bloc declined to respond, even obligingly banning all open Duma discussion of the appeals at Protopopov's request. It was left to Kerensky and Konovalov to defy both the MVD and the Bloc by reading the appeals in Duma sitting. The public organisations' collapsing confidence in the Bloc found expression in the diatribe of Konovalov on 16 December: 'Let the battle be fought to the finish. Let there be no concessions or compromises on the way ... There is no wavering in the country. Let there be no reservations in the Duma.' The complaisance of the Duma moderates was undermining both traditional support and their recently-acquired popular following: the public organisations were starting the process of transition from a moderate political factor linked to the Duma Bloc to a militant force allied with the Duma Left; the 'Storm-signal' recruits could only interpret the Bloc's conduct as cowardice or complicity and pledged their allegiance and support to the Left.[6]

The moderates' passivity also made a contribution to the reactionary drift of the government. Recognition of the collapse of the constitutional course engendered a rash of right-wing conspiracies.

The political desperation which had induced Purishkevich to make his speech of 19 November now impelled him to join with the dynastic duo Prince Felix Yusupov and Grand Duke Dmitrii Pavlovich in the most famous of plots. The grisly *grand guignol* which took place on the night of 16–17 December is too well known to need retelling. The political effect of the murder of Rasputin was to accentuate the prevailing reactionary complexion of the government. Nicholas returned from the Stavka to console his distraught wife and, whether he privately welcomed the murder or not, Rasputin's death kept him at Alexandra's side and under her influence until 22 February, the very eve of revolution.[7] Protopopov had already acquired exceptional powers (through a new Police Act effected under Clause 87) and demonstrated his administrative vigour by employing them to institute regular pre-publication censorship in the capitals. He was rewarded by being confirmed as Minister of Interior, ending the probationary nature of the appointment under which he had laboured since September. An extensive cabinet reshuffle, destined to be the last in tsarist history, removed Makarov, Ignatiev and Shuvayev from the Council of Ministers. Finally, at the instigation of Alexandra, Nicholas interviewed an unsuspecting Prince Nikolai Golitsyn, president of the Committee for Aid to Russian Prisoners-of-War, with a view to replacing Trepov. Though Golitsyn frantically pleaded every disadvantage from ill-health to crass ignorance, he was formally appointed premier on 27 December. With the few remaining moderates expelled, the Council of Ministers was left to reactionaries, conscripts and incompetents.[8]

A campaign was launched to bridle the insubordination of the legislative institutions. The State Council, a comparatively easy target, was disciplined over the course of late December: MVD pressure filtered off moderate candidates to the elected curiae; punctilious care was taken in the selection of reactionaries to the nominated half of the Council; and the operation was completed according to the promptings of Alexandra with the appointment of 'strong-minded Shcheglovitov' as new President of the Council.[9] There was every indication that the Duma would soon come under fire. Although the murder of Rasputin had taken place during the recess and there could be no immediate repercussions on a Duma session, the timing of the assassination – literally within hours of prorogation – threw suspicion on the Duma. The Christmas recess was an ideal opportunity to determine the fate of the Fourth Duma in its absence. The constitutional armoury was threatening enough: the Tsar enjoyed the rights of prorogation, legislation (through Clause 87) and dissolution. But greater danger threatened from outside the rubric of the Fundamental Laws. Protopopov, an increasingly unstable personality, had abandoned his earlier soft line and was setting his face more and more sternly against the Duma. A persuasive end-of-year report by his Director of Police, General P.G. Kurlov, pressing for the abolition of the State Duma and the turning-back of the constitutional clock to before 1905, impressed Protopopov profoundly. Personal pique was added to political expediency when Protopopov was openly snubbed by Rodzyanko at a New Year reception at the Winter Palace.[10] Active preparations for the demise of the Fourth Duma were begun by the MVD. Protopopov ordered increased surveillance over all leading political personalities in the capital by the Okhrana. The army detachment responsible for guarding the Tauride Palace during Duma sessions was for the first time ever retained throughout the recess, inviting the sinister interpretation that a military *coup d'état* was in the offing. At the first cabinet meeting of 1917 on 3 January, Protopopov's proposal to dissolve the Fourth Duma at once was only narrowly defeated in favour of Golitsyn's preference for postponement of the Duma until February. Nikolai Maklakov was brought out of retirement to plan the elections to the Fifth Duma and was soon reporting enthusiastically on the progress of his schemes. Finally, Golitsyn secured from Nicholas three signed but undated ukases: one for prorogation *sine die*, another for prorogation until the end of the war and the last for the dissolution of the Fourth Duma. With this arsenal of paper and practical power, the cabinet leaders Golitsyn and Protopopov were invested with total control over the fate of the Duma.[11]

The polarisation of Russia stretched the moderates grotesquely, resulting in a reaction to the emergency more varied and fragmented with each passing month. The most spirited and adventurous response was the palace revolution plot of Guchkov. Together with his political and personal friends Krivoshein and Polivanov, Guchkov had committed himself unreservedly to the attempt at reconciliation between state and society in mid-1915. With the defeat and subsequent collapse of the Progressive Bloc, Guchkov, the former leader of the Octobrist fraction, despaired of the Duma as an agency of political progress. His motive for participation in a plot was similar to that of Purishkevich: constitutional methods were impotent in the face of the political emergency, which must therefore be resolved by unconstitutional direct action. But while Purishkevich's plot, though bloody, was strictly limited to removing a pernicious influence on the Tsar, Guchkov (whom Trotsky perhaps admiringly called 'a liberal with spurs') came to the painful conclusion that the monarchy could be saved only by the displacement of the present Sovereign. A conspiracy was mounted attempting to exploit two sets of Guchkov's contacts, the masonic and the military. In autumn 1916 Guchkov sounded out some masonic colleagues, probably including Nekrasov and Konovalov, but found their firmly republican tenets made them unreceptive to plans to save the monarchy.[12] On the military side, while many senior army officers were sympathetic to a coup, very few were prepared to take action themselves. In the words of General A.M. Krymov in January 1917, the prevailing mood in the officer corps was that 'if you decide on this extreme course, we will support you'. Guchkov's plan on the ground came to depend on the dedication of a clique of young cavalry officers headed by Prince D.L. Vyazemsky and the putative support of Krymov and possibly General Alexeyev. Bad luck and medical misadventure served to prolong and postpone commitment to a definite coup. At the moment that an embryonic plan to kidnap the Tsar from the royal train was emerging, illness struck down its principals. By no means recovered from his near-fatal heart attack late the previous year, Guchkov was forced to spend from October until the end of 1916 undergoing medical treatment at the remote Caucasian spa of Kislovodsk and was not at hand to inspire the plans to which he was clearly indispensable. Alexeyev too was compelled by overwork to take extended sick-leave from the Stavka from November until mid-February 1917. As reported by the Okhrana, Guchkov was still confident enough to drop a broad hint to an Octobrist Central Committee meeting on 30 December: 'Guchkov's statement was in the most gloomy strain, almost of complete despair of finding any solution with the present fragmented state of society forces and parties, but through all his pessimism Guchkov stressed the possibility of an unexpected solution to the deadlock in the near future, outside the scope and efforts of society.' The judgement that fed this confidence – that there was still time – proved misplaced. The postponed plot hung fire until it was overtaken by the greater revolution.[13]

Although rejecting involvement in the Guchkov coup, the left Kadets and Progressists were not opposed to illegal action. Unrepentant about secession from the Bloc, Efremov explained 'we have not subordinated ourselves to the discipline or orders of an over-cautious general but instead have formed a detachment and advanced to a forward position, hoping thereby to draw the entire army after us.' Initially the strategy seemed successful. The Progressist deputies lost to the Kadets by withdrawal from the Bloc, the Orlov-Davydov group, were numerically compensated by new left Kadet recruits to the Progressist camp. Once it became apparent that the 'Stupidity or Treason' speech had been more a tactical ploy than a declaration of principle, the left Kadets of Nekrasov and Adzhemov associated closely with the Progressists to negotiate with the Left: 'considering the tactics of the Progressive Bloc mistaken and having lost faith in their leaders, the left Kadets and various Progressists, while not yet decided to join the Social Democrats and Social Revolutionaries, are very close to their point of view.' Free from the constraints imposed by membership of the Bloc, the group professed no confidence in the Trepov administration – *plus ça change, plus c'est la même chose* was Efremov's comment – and demanded a government responsible to the Duma. On 16 November Efremov released a nine-page defence of his policy which concluded 'for us Progressists, standing for battle with the regime, the position is clear – the fight with the government has only just begun.' Konovalov expressed the new spirit in his Duma speeches when he defied the authority of both the MVD and Bloc to announce the new militancy of the public organisations. Progressist direct action was as its most articulate at a meeting on 3 January 1917, which resolved that in the event of the Duma being dissolved, its membership would reconvene in Moscow at a villa placed at its disposal by Konovalov and Ryabushinsky. From Moscow, the heart of the Russian war effort, the Russian parliament would appeal to the country for support against the isolated government in Petrograd.[14]

The militant course soon collapsed. As early as 15 November an angry Progressist Central Committee categorically condemned Efremov's withdrawal from the Bloc, claiming that the fraction had undermined the moderate offensive and consigned the party to political oblivion. Only days later the precarious compact with the Duma Left failed its first (and only) test: when the Mensheviks and Trudoviks confidently obstructed the Duma sitting of 19 November, the Progressists and left Kadets voted for their explusion from the chamber. Although they subsequently pleaded with Rodzyanko for lenient treatment, the Progressists vividly demonstrated that they were moderate rebels rather than recruits to the Left. Just as worrying, at the elections to the Kadet fraction bureau in late November, Nekrasov was voted out as vice-president and replaced by the official Kadet K.K. Chernosvitov. Far from indulgently keeping the door ajar for the left Kadets, Milyukov seemed determined to slam the door in their faces. The Moscow resolution of 3 January prompted a crisis in the left moderate camp. The Progressist majority in the Central Committee and fraction were alarmed by the prospect of what it called 'another Vyborg' and drifted back towards association with the Bloc. Desperate to forestall this move, a Moscow meeting held on 19 January demanded illegal action to bring down the government and an ultimatum on the first day of the new Duma session. Konovalov sneered at Kadet tactics of restraint: 'an impotent Duma is an object of mockery on the part of the government and worse than no Duma at all in the eyes of the people.' But despite the efforts of Konovalov and Ryabushinsky, by late January 1917 the Duma Progressists and left Kadets had largely abandoned their militant stance of autumn 1916. To most, the act of withdrawal from the Bloc now appeared not as the loosening of intolerable restraints but ill-advised estrangement from the coordinating executive of the moderate opposition movement.

Whilst flirting discreetly with the extra-constitutional schemes of Guchkov, Ryabushinsky and Konovalov, the Progressist-left Kadet camp could not long resist the companionship of the Progressive Bloc or the moral authority of Milyukov.[15]

At the other extreme of the moderate spectrum, the most passive response to the emergency came from those who relied on constitutional pressure alone, the Zemstvo-Octobrists. The morale of the Octobrists was now very low, their political initiative slight and in so far as they followed any coherent philosophy, it was still the hopeless 'mad chauffeur' parable of Maklakov. Fatalistically rejecting direct action, the fraction rested all its hopes on Rodzyanko's Duma office and its accompanying privilege of access to the Tsar. More than aware of his responsibility, Rodzyanko made a succession of constitutional approaches to Nicholas. With rumours of MVD preparations for the Fifth Duma (including the employment of S.E. Kryzhanovsky, the architect of the 3 June electoral laws) reaching the moderates, Rodzyanko made a last appeal for the extension of the Fourth Duma. Even the reactionary Shcheglovitov, alarmed at the left landslide in recent Moscow municipal elections, was convinced that a Fifth Duma could not be more Right than the Fourth and openly advocated extension. *Russkia Vedomosti* reported that the MVD had issued a circular to provincial governors asking whether elections would benefit the Right; the majority of replies would hazard no opinion (pointing out that the bulk of the electorate was at the front), a minority was convinced of a victory for the Left, and not one predicted any advantage to the Right. Although it was to the mutual benefit of the government and almost the entire Fourth Duma to retain the existing Duma, the decision went against Rodzyanko. The flawed political judgement of Alexandra and Protopopov gratuitously deprived tsarism of a last compact against revolution.[16]

Despite the almost casual rejection of his petition, Rodzyanko did not overstep his official functions. When General Krymov met Bloc leaders to assure them that 'the mood in the army is such that everybody would greet the news of a revolution with joy', Rodzyanko indignantly protested: 'I will never support a revolution. I have sworn an oath of loyalty. I must ask you not to discuss such matters in my house ... Palace revolutions are not the affair of the legislative chambers and I have neither the desire nor the means to incite the populace against the Tsar.' But he was sufficiently alarmed to pull no punches at his next audience with Nicholas:

The nation realises that you have banished from the government all those in whom the Duma and people trusted, and replaced them by unworthy and incompetent men ... It is an open secret that the Tsaritsa issues orders without your knowledge, that the Ministers report to her on matters of state, and that by her wish those whom she views with disfavour lose their posts ... To save your family, Your Majesty should find some way of preventing the Tsaritsa from exercising any influence on politics.

Though affected by this straight talking, Nicholas had been persuaded by the many warnings delivered on earlier occasions that Rodzyanko made a habit of crying wolf to enhance his self-importance. What was to emerge as Rodzyanko's last chance was his audience on 10 February. Despite a reception which Rodzyanko described as 'less indifferent than downright brusque', the Duma President presented a detailed report on the dangers of the current situation. Nicholas set his face against the warning from the start, tetchily demanding to know 'since Protopopov was your vice-president in the Duma, why he no longer pleases you' and coolly refusing to credit the emergency outlined by Rodzyanko: 'my information contradicts this completely ... if the Duma allows itself unrestrained outbursts like last time, it will be dissolved.' Rodzyanko was trapped by his own political morality: his advice rejected and his constitutional resources exhausted, he found himself at an *impasse*. With Rodzyanko's failure, the once-powerful Octobrists folded their hands and resigned themselves to the worst.[17]

In the pole position in the moderate camp, the Kadets were caught between their political fears and their constitutional scruples. The prevailing Kadet mood was demonstrated at a Moscow meeting on 7 January 1917. Kizevetter regretted that 'there is a very dangerous feeling of indifference towards the Duma [and] no one at present can rely on the mass support of society.' A feeling of inescapable doom possessed Kokoshkin: 'we are confronted by great danger, we stand before the unknown and unexpected; around us the gloom is thickening and we know not what lies two steps ahead.' Many Kadets were convinced with Shingarev that the opportunity for compromise had gone:

> I fear that even if our crazy government is prepared to concede, even if it concedes a government composed of the most reliable men, it will not be enough. The mood has already passed over our heads and is to the left of the Progressive Bloc. We have to recognise that we cannot satisfy that mood, we cannot restrain it. The country is listening to the Left, not to us. It is too late.

The collapsing nerve of the Kadet party was noted by the Okhrana: 'notwithstanding a whole series of conferences first in Moscow and more recently in Petrograd, the Kadets not only cannot agree about tactics for the future but demonstrate the very sharpest differences of opinion.' As Maklakov showed, the Kadet leadership still favoured restraint: 'The revolutionary path of struggle is inevitable. The only question is when to start the fight ... As long as all parliamentary resources are not exhausted, the Kadets consider this moment has still not arrived. Perhaps the moment is very, very near but none the less there is no sense in forcing events.' On the eve of revolution, the Kadet consensus was to play safe and refuse to be drawn across constitutional bounds.[18]

This is not to say that the Kadets were not seeking a way out of their dilemma. One possibility was to induce some other less fastidious political force to do the dirty work from which the Kadets would benefit. There was a moral double standard in the Kadet and Octobrist attitude. Both Rodzyanko and Maklakov knew in advance of the Yusupov plot and offered all the blessing that their constitutional principles would allow. The Kadets and Octobrists knew about the Guchkov plot and in their hearts must have prayed for its success. Milyukov may have had this in mind when he wrote in a *Rech* editorial on 12 December 1916 that 'the public demands which have so far been directed exclusively at the Duma should also turn to other factors which might influence the course of political events.'[19] To this scheme there was the objection that whoever took the fatal step might well cull greater advantage than those who waited. Under pressure from Guchkov's projected coup, the only alternative was to discover a previously unexploited political lever which would leave the constitutional principles of the Kadets and Octobrists unsullied. The sole salient force which might serve was foreign intervention as posed by the imminent Allied Military Conference.

At first the Kadets were uncertain how to turn the Petrograd Conference to their advantage. Indeed on 10 January the Kadet fraction unsolicitedly resolved that 'in view of the fact that Allied delegations will be visiting Russia and that the duty of the Kadet party is to support the continuation of the war to a successful conclusion, it is decided to refrain from any provocative speeches, even within the budget commission.' The ensuing restlessness of the party and the realisation that the conference was the only foreseeable answer to their dilemma forced the abandonment of this throwback to the self-censorship of the *union sacrée*. By late January the Okhrana reported that 'the Kadets are placing all their hopes to the most significant degree on the Allies, and in particular the English who ... (while preferably not interfering in the internal affairs of Russia) will make representations to the Russian government concerning "a softening of the internal line of policy".' Although the stratagem had proved unsuccessful on its last application in 1906, with all other avenues explored, the Kadets were compelled by desperation to launch an appeal for foreign intercession.[20]

The Military Conference, the first on the Eastern front since the outbreak of war, ran from 16 to 31 January 1917 (with a subsequent week for ceremonial functions). Over that period a succession of veiled or overt approaches were made to the delegates by moderate leaders. Lord Milner, the head of the British delegation, was soon swamped with information. Struve, now a renegade on the Kadet right, spoke for all the moderates when, in the first of two letters, he asserted that 'at present all well-intentioned and politically-educated persons have only one wish: that the Crown should not commit the irrevocable and absolutely unjustifiable act of dissolving the State Duma on the pretext that its mandate has expired and new elections must be held.' Rodzyanko told Milner in confidence that the majority of the Duma deputies would refuse to disperse in the event of dissolution. At a reception arranged by the Duma (from which the ministers were specifically excluded), the delegates were left with no illusions about the position of the moderates in Russia.[21]

Elements outside the Duma were more practical. At a banquet for the visitors at the Moscow Merchants' Club, its president Ryabushinsky candidly considered Allied loans to Russia: 'it would be expedient if the administrative direction of these sums were under the appointed central control of a commission of the State Duma and our public organisations, in which event purely English control over the sums would become unnecessary.' Two days later, after a striking prediction that there would be a revolution within three weeks, Lvov made a similar proposition to Milner: 'the Allies should only grant their future supplies on condition that they were used, or some of them, by organisations in which the Allies had confidence, such as the Unions presided over by himself and Chelnokoff respectively.'[22] The affinity of these two proposals to the trend of Kadet thought is unmistakable. Milyukov personally made approaches to Milner and his French counterpart Gaston Doumergue. To Milner, Milyukov insisted 'that the storm was approaching, that if at the last hour the dynasty would not consent to compromise, its fall was inevitable'. To Doumergue, Milyukov protested that 'we have exhausted all our patience ... if we do not act soon, the masses will no longer listen to us.' There is no record of Milyukov suggesting anything as specific as Lvov and Ryabushinsky but conversation must surely have touched upon their proposals. On the basis of his recent visits to western Europe, Milyukov could not have been sanguine about the approaches to the Allied delegates and it is more than likely that he regarded foreign intercession as the longest of long shots by January 1917. He rested content allowing others to take the risks, in the knowledge that he could claim authorship of the policy in the unlikely event of its success.[23]

At all events, the various approaches failed. By postponing the reconvening of the Duma from 12 January to 14 February, the government planned to avoid exhibiting any political washing to its foreign guests. As Lloyd George related, 'the Duma was to meet in a week after the close of the conference. The delegation asked permission to remain in Russia to witness the meeting. A government official intimated to them that if they stayed, the assembling of the Duma would be put off another fortnight.' The visitors had not expected to have politics thrust in their military faces and took the line that their delegated authority allowed them no competence outside military issues. Bemused but courteous, they listened to the overtures of the Russian moderates and prudently vouchsafed no reply. Towards the end of his stay, Milner presented Nicholas with an interim report of his findings which not only restricted itself to purely military matters but was quick to stress that 'there can be no question of interference in the affairs of the Russian military authorities'. As Hoare pointed out, the delegates were not up to their task: 'The Allies were mistaken in sending such a mission at all; the members of the mission were equally mistaken in almost all their conclusions about the Russian front and the state of Russia.' To the huge relief of the tsarist government, the foreign visitors from a blend of diplomacy and ignorance refrained from any embarrassing attempt to influence the internal political course of Russia.[24]

While the moderates (and most of the government) hardly dared breathe for fear of precipitating the supreme crisis, Protopopov blundered on with his erratic stick-and-carrot policy towards society. On 20 January he antagonised the proletariat of Petrograd and Moscow by arresting and imprisoning the entire workers' group of the Central WIC. In exasperation, Golitsyn demanded to know why the arrests could not at least have been postponed until after the Allied delegates left the country. His representations had some effect on the almost unhinged Protopopov, who in a gesture of apology to his cabinet colleagues agreed to suspend police operations for the duration of the Military Conference. In a last attempt to win over the moderates, Protopopov transparently offered to double the pay of Duma deputies (to 700 roubles a month), but although deputies had been agitating for months for an increase to offset the meteoric rise in the cost of living, they had no choice but indignantly to reject this most blatant bid to buy them off. On 8 February, the very day that the Allied delegation left Russia, the Petrograd Military District was placed under the martial jurisdiction of General S.S. Khabalov. The next day Khabalov imposed a ban on all meetings, private and public, in Petrograd. With the new Duma session scheduled for the fourteenth, it was naïve to interpret the latest moves as anything but plans for the immediate suppression of the Duma and any popular movement which might seek to defend it.[25]

With the elimination of the possibility of foreign intervention, now so patently a policy of clutching at a straw, the moderates were left with the stark alternative: either a constitutionalism rendered impotent by social forces released by the war or an opportunism which shrugged off traditional parliamentary constraints. They had little hesitation in choosing the former course. Obsessively self-interested, the Duma moderates were pitiable in their anxiety to avoid giving offence. Their only hope for the Duma rested on preventing the government finding any pretext for dissolution, which meant the sedation of all opposition inside and outside the Duma. Shortly after the arrest of the WIC workers' group, Konovalov and Guchkov held a protest meeting at which Milyukov was invited to speak. In a statement which astounded organisers and audience, Milyukov not only refused to add his voice to the protests but condemned the 'interference' of the workers in a political contest in which 'only the State Duma can dictate the conditions of struggle with the government'. Fear of the government combined with jealousy for the Duma's monopoly of politics in Milyukov's demand that the proletariat mind its own business and refrain from political action. At a Moscow Kadet meeting on 4 February, Milyukov encountered such criticism that his nerve showed signs of cracking. The Okhrana believed 'Milyukov wishes to rid himself of the responsibility for a possible false step and its possible repercussions ... the theme constantly recurring in all his conversation is the danger of taking a wrong decision "for which it will be necessary to answer before History and the whole civilised world".'[26] For once intimidated by Moscow and left Kadet antagonism, Milyukov conceded that 'the new session will be a direct continuation of the glorious November days'; but official Kadet policy over the next fortnight only too plainly contradicted this assurance. At a Central Committee meeting only two days later, the crypto-Octobrism of the Kadets was summed up in the sentiments of that former radical Rodichev: 'the absolute necessity is to liberate the Tsar and Tsaritsa from the "prison" of the clique which is concealing from them the menacing mood of the entire country and directing the government towards the abyss.'[27] Milyukov was so terrified of MVD provocation that on 9 February, with the blessing of Rodzyanko, he authorised a statement in the press appealing for calm and opposing any demonstrations to greet the Duma opening. The unfortunate appearance of the appeal next to Khabalov's warnings against civil unrest in many newspapers did nothing to disabuse the workers and the Left of the conviction that the moderates were playing the government's game. Next day, Milyukov's editorial in *Rech* blamed the demonstrations of the fourteenth in advance on Okhrana provocation, arguing that it was still not too late to cheat the government of its design. A last emergency measure proposed by a hurriedly-convened Kadet Central Committee was a direct appeal to the Tsar, a recourse rejected by Milyukov (significantly enough) on its unconstitutional grounds. When 14 February dawned, a last appeal by Rodzyanko to the workers to stay away proved unnecessary: the giant demonstrations feared by the Duma did not materialise. The desperate braking influence of the moderates on the Petrograd labour movement achieved its immediate objective; but at the price of destroying what little sympathy still existed between them.[28]

The Duma session brought no change in the craven policy of the moderates. The unprecedentedly dispirited atmosphere was admitted by Rodzyanko: 'the mood in the Duma was languid ... the impotence of the Duma was felt everywhere. The Duma maintained its traditional stance and did not precipitate an open break with the government. The Duma had only one weapon – the spoken word'. Milyukov greeted the new session with the statement 'our only deeds are our words', a claim so unintentionally self-revelatory that he felt obliged to amend it in Duma sitting on 15 February to 'the word and the vote are for the time being our only weapons'. The Left was infuriated by what it regarded as the moral cowardice of the moderates: in a letter to Lenin, the local Bolshevik A.G. Shlyapnikov reported in disgust that 'the liberals and particularly Milyukov behave like scoundrels towards the revolutionary movement.'[29] Kerensky had a field day. In a speech on the fifteenth he singled out the Tsaritsa for attack, going so far as to demand the immediate overthrow of the 'tyrants'. Only Rodzyanko's discreet censorship of the published Duma proceedings and the determination of Golitsyn to avoid taking offence wherever possible (braving Alexandra's demand that Kerensky be hanged) saved the Duma from prompt dissolution as a seditious assembly. Kerensky also vented his spleen on the moderates:

> The historic task of the Russian people at the present time is the overthrow of this medieval regime but you wish to fight only 'by legal means' ... You consider your duty done once you have concluded your diagnosis of the ills of the country. I say to you that your speeches on the necessity of calm at all costs are either the naïve sentiments of superficial thinkers or just an excuse to avoid the real fight, just a pretext to stay safely in your warm armchairs ... You don't want to listen to anybody but yourselves but soon you will have to listen, for if you do not hear the warning voices, you will encounter the harsh facts.

Kerensky's pitiless indictment of the bankruptcy of moderate politics has not been substantially revised to this day.[30]

On the very brink of revolution, the disintegration of the moderates reached its climax. The Octobrists' subordination within the Progressive Bloc had always been offensive to their *amour propre* and when Guchkov advised the Octobrist Central Committee on 30 December 1916 'not to allow the Kadet party complete primacy in the current political struggle but be sure to attract to yourself the greatest attention',the Duma Octobrists were roused to a last spasm of activity. An Okhrana report of 18 February gleefully noted Kadet fears for the future of the Bloc: 'at the moment, according to Chelnokov, the Octobrists are expressing dissatisfaction about the over-dictatorial manner of Milyukov, who is leading the Bloc according to his own whims and forcing his decisions on them.' If resentment of Milyukov's domination provided the element of 'push' about Octobrist initiative, the possibility of a new compact with the government provided an element of 'pull'. The Okhrana tapped a Petrograd-Moscow telephone call from Shingarev to Kishkin on 17 February: 'Shingarev definitely corroborated that serious rifts exist in the Bloc and heroic efforts will be needed to keep the Octobrists from their wish to move to meet the government.' Though later embarrassment that they were negotiating a political bargain with tsarism only days away from the February Revolution had the effect of suppressing almost all Octobrist evidence on this episode, rumours that Golitsyn was seeking allies in the Duma (and had already promised a ministerial post to the Nationalist leader Balashev) all too easily detached the Octobrists from the Bloc in a last desperate bid for government favour. Worn down by the war of nerves, at the moment of crisis the Octobrists in the Duma abandoned pretensions to independence and threw themselves on the mercy of the government. With the defection of its largest fraction, the Progressive Bloc was finished.[31]

The Russian moderates made a sorry spectacle on the eve of the February Revolution. Within the government, the prevailing reactionary salient fostered by Alexandra and Protopopov had eliminated almost all ministerial personalities and bureaucratic cadres sympathetic to a moderate course and the MVD was poised to effect a final solution to the Duma problem. In the country at large, the leftward surge of public opinion had left the moderates behind, accentuating the isolation and declining national memberships of the Kadet, Octobrist and Progressist parties. The wider support created by the 'Storm-signal' had been quickly dissipated by the moderates' relapse into self-interested restraint. Inside the Duma, the most the crumbling Progressive Bloc would publicly adopt was the policy of 'the word and the vote', the prerogative of a strictly consultative assembly and the weakest brand of constitutionalism. In his memoirs, Milyukov tries to leave the impression that formal contingency plans for an autocracy-eroding regency had been formulated before the Revolution:

It was clear to everyone that it was not the business of the Duma to arrange a coup. It was extremely important however to define the role of the Duma once the coup would be arranged. The bloc started with the assumption that given the coup, Nicholas II would be removed from the throne one way or the other. The bloc agreed on transferring the authority of the monarch to the legal heir Alexei under the regency of the Grand Duke Mikhail Alexandrovitch until Alexei reached maturity. The Grand Duke's gentle character and the young age of the heir seemed to be the best guarantee of a transition to a constitutional system.

Without independent corroboration, this assertion seems very suspect. The available evidence suggests rather that the most the Bloc would contemplate behind its public facade of scrupulous constitutionalism was general speculation, which by now represented the only consensus between the left-orientated moderates, desperately but unconvincingly demanding direct action, and the right-orientated moderates, fatalistically settling for parliamentary expression alone. Although, in the words of the Okhrana, 'the majority of high society agreed with the legality of palace revolutions and murders', the Duma leaders declined to take the initiative and responsibility for a bold unconstitutional stroke. As Maklakov remarked, on the possibility of a dynastic revolution by the Grand Dukes, 'they want the Duma to put the match to the powder; in other words, they are expecting of us what we are expecting of them.'[32] Finally, the health of the Progressive Bloc was on the point of total breakdown: a leftward haemorrhage of membership had for some time threatened a lingering death by anaemia; and at the eleventh hour, the defection of the Octobrists rendered collapse and political decomposition irrevocable. When asked what could possibly save them now, Shingarev gloomily answered 'only a miracle'.[33] In February 1917 the paradox was consummate: although the moderates unanimously abhorred revolution, only the intervention of a revolutionary *deus ex machina* could prevent the immediate annihilation of the moderate course in Russia.

7 The Reluctant Revolutionaries

It was a sudden, unpremeditated upsurge of the Petrograd labour movement, the product of intolerable local economic and social pressures, which precipitated the supreme crisis. The introduction of flour and bread rationing in Moscow on 20 February led to rumours of deficiencies, then panic shortages and finally food riots in Petrograd. On 22 February the management of the Putilov works, the largest employer in Petrograd, ordered a lock-out of their protesting 40,000 staff. The next day, workers from some fifty industrial plants came out in sympathy with the *Putilovtsy*, using the pretext of International Women's Day to throng the city centre and organise a general strike. Whether the government's jittery nerves made it over-react to the situation or the disturbances were taken by Protopopov as a convenient excuse for implementing a scheme of provocation and suppression, there was no doubt of the gravity with which latest developments were viewed. At 2 p.m. on the twenty-third, the administration of Petrograd was transferred from the city police chief A.P. Balk to General Khabalov. The menace implicit in this transfer seemed unequivocal when Khabalov ordered the closure of shops and offices, a night curfew, the halting of the city transport services and the introduction of cavalry units to reinforce the police. The scene was set for a showdown between the proletariat of the capital and the government.[1]

Trotsky's opinion that 'the higher the leaders, the further they lagged behind' is especially valid regarding the moderates, whose reaction to the events of the day was strangely muted. Mansyrev recalled that on the 23rd 'neither amongst the broad Duma groups nor among society in general was any special significance attached' to the local emergency. While casual conversation inevitably touched on the situation, the deputies attending the Duma sitting that day gave no indication that the subject would be tabled for formal debate. The attention of the Duma moderates was fixed on the supply crisis and the current negotiations between Agriculture Minister Rittikh and Shingarev over the fixing of bread prices. The furthest the Bloc was prepared to go in acknowledging the local emergency was a motion put up by Milyukov: 'The government should take immediate steps to provide food for the population of the capital and other cities and towns; the workers employed in factories of the defence industry should be supplied with food immediately; town administrators and public bodies should be enlisted straight away in the distribution of food, and food committees should be set up.' It was left to Kerensky to introduce the amendment that 'the jobless workers from the Putilov works should be taken back and the factory resume operations immediately'. Although prepared to accept this amendment, the Bloc reiterated its policy of avoiding any pretext for reprisals against the Duma and declined to exploit the situation outside the Tauride Palace.[2]

On the next day, Friday 24 February, the social crisis worsened. Assurances of the adequacy of flour and bread supplies posted overnight throughout Petrograd had no success in calming the tense atmosphere. Khabalov added infantry detachments to the cavalry which had reinforced the police the previous day, employing the cavalry and infantry regiments to patrol the streets as a show of overwhelming force while the police took action. Although Znamenskaya Square, the principal congregating-point for demonstrators, was forcibly cleared by mounted police, the attitude of the attendant troops was by no means certain. The infantry regiments stationed to divide the city with picket lines were newly conscripted and made little effort to conceal their sympathy with the crowds; the cavalry regiments whose loyalty in the barracks had been unquestioned wavered in the face of confrontation with the people.

The mood of the Duma on 24 February heralded not an alliance of moderates and proletariat against the government but an attempt at collaboration with the government to tackle what they both declared to be the basic problem. The great stumbling-block to cooperation remained Protopopov. The Duma published its challenge by passing an emergency bill to transfer the entire administration of supply in the capital to the UZ, UT and Petrograd city duma. Protopopov naturally responded with a flat refusal to surrender any jurisdiction. A way out of the apparent *impasse* was only possible because of the split in the cabinet between the reactionary Protopopov group and the more moderate Golitsyn group. Golitsyn had long been convinced of the necessity of removing Protopopov from the MVD but his pleas to Nicholas and Alexandra had been rejected. The initiative for negotiation came from Rodzyanko, who breached the discipline of the moribund Progressive Bloc to give expression to the traditional and recently-revived Octobrist policy of expedient alliance with the government. When Rodzyanko approached Golitsyn on the morning of 24 February with a request to effect the transfer of supply forcibly, the premier was prepared to listen in order both to tackle the local crisis more effectively and to secure the dismissal of Protopopov. As ever, the government was amenable to the moderates only when it suited ministerial politics. An emergency conference was agreed by Golitsyn and Rodzyanko for that very evening. The attendance was significant: for the government were Golitsyn himself, Rittikh, M. A. Belyayev (Minister of War), Grigorovich, Shakhovskoi and E.B. Kriger-Voinovsky (Minister of Communications); for the Duma came Rodzyanko, Nekrasov (in his capacity as Vice-President) and Dmitryukov (as Duma Secretary); and for the State Council were Shcheglovitov (President) and V.N. Dietrich (Vice-President). The presence of six ministers demonstrated a practical element of official goodwill towards society and Rodzyanko went so far as to commit not just himself or the Octobrists but the State Duma to the principle of collaboration with the government. However the conference also brought to a head the fatal schizophrenia in the cabinet between the Golitsyn group favouring cooperation with the Duma (most of whom took care to attend the conference) and the Protopopov group proposing the suppression of the Duma along with the Petrograd disturbances. Protopopov personally declared he was too busy to attend the conference, which not surprisingly went against him in his absence: the Duma, Council and ministerial delegates 'unanimously voted to transfer food supply in Petrograd immediately to the jurisdiction of the Petrograd municipal administration'.[3]

Even at this juncture, when the moderates were actively or tacitly cooperating with the government for a return to normal rather than leading the workers to the barricades, neither Duma nor government appreciated the full extent of the emergency or the speed at which events were moving. The joint decision over the transfer was accompanied by an almost leisurely optimism that once the matter was settled, the danger was past: 'It was noted that the Petrograd municipal administration did not have a suitable organisation at its disposal for this purpose ... [therefore] as soon as the Petrograd municipal administration, in conjunction with the Duma municipal affairs commission, is able to set up a suitable organisation, the whole matter of supplying food to Petrograd will be placed under its jurisdiction.' At a moment when time was at a premium, supply was transferred to an agency still to be created and the formalities of the transfer entrusted to the notoriously slow Duma bureaucracy. The government and Duma were alike in failing to recognise that an important political concession which satisfied them neither answered the practical needs of the hungry citizen nor made any impact on the developing crisis in the capital. At this moment of closer company, the government and moderates revealed identical estrangement from the mass of the people.[4]

The morning of Saturday 25 February again saw the anonymous, almost instinctive march of the workers to the city centre, ignoring press (including Kadet) assurances that ample stocks of bread and flour were available and in defiance of punitive raids by the police in the industrial suburbs. By late morning Petrograd was once more occupied by the workers, who were encouraged to suffer the increasingly vicious actions of the police by the growing sympathy of military units. At 3 p.m. came the first clear evidence that the obedience of the army could not be relied on: on Znamenskaya Square a mounted police officer was shot down by a 'stray' Cossack bullet while leading a charge on the crowd. Alarmed by the incident, Khabalov threatened the strikers (by now numbering 250,000) with conscription to the front line unless they reported back to work by the 28th, but this three-day ultimatum had the opposite effect to that intended, encouraging the workers to further efforts in the time remaining before sanctions were imposed.

The impact of these developments on the moderates was still relatively slight: the Duma rested content with passing a motion demanding the expediting of the transfer of supply. But a row occurred when Rodzyanko proposed that the next Duma sitting be set for the morning of the 28th. The Left complained shrilly that events were moving so quickly that a three-day break was criminal neglect of the Duma's duty. The Kadets now demonstrated their influence: after a fraction meeting which voted for bringing the next Duma sitting forward one day to the 27th, the Kadet vote secured a majority within the *senioren konvent*. Irritated that his proposal be rejected and his recent understanding with Golitsyn jeopardised, Rodzyanko conceded but insisted that the next sitting be in closed session. A difference was emerging between Octobrist and Kadet tactics: while the Octobrists had committed themselves almost unreservedly to the government, the Kadets were hedging their political bets and waiting on events.[5]

Despite the Duma's careful restraint and well-advertised constitutionalism, its supporters within the government came under sustained fire. Even the ostensibly trivial bargaining over the date and form of the next sitting suggested to some ministers that the Bloc might be shifting towards the side of the insurgents. At a Council meeting on the evening of 25 February, Protopopov's personal and political antagonism towards Golitsyn came across strongly with his threat 'to arrest your Rodzyanko and dissolve the Duma'. Despite general distaste for Protopopov, more and more ministers were coming to agree that the Golitsyn policy of *rapprochement* was not helpful in the current crisis. Golitsyn did secure agreement to defer the decision on the future of the Duma for twenty-four hours, employing the time to commission Rittikh and Foreign Minister N.N. Pokrovsky to confer with Bloc leaders, but his policy of *ad hoc* alliance with Rodzyanko was near to collapse. In the meantime, a firmer line against the insurgents was agreed. Towards the end of the meeting Khabalov was summoned to the telegraph to receive the curt response of the Tsar (who had been at the Stavka since 23 February) to his account of the disturbances: 'I order that the disorders in the capital be stopped tomorrow; such disorders are impermissible during this difficult time of war with Germany and Austria.' After informing the Council, Khabalov issued instructions that the sabre and *nagaika* were to be abandoned in favour of the rifle and machine-gun. In the course of the night of 25–6 February, the Okhrana effected a series of raids in the Petrograd suburbs which netted some one hundred revolutionaries and by almost all accounts was completely successful in decapitating the parties and organisations of the Left.[6]

The precise effect of the Okhrana sweep on the events of 26 February is difficult to assess. Both Belyayev and Alexandra sent premature 'all clear' telegrams to the Stavka at about 11 a.m. but the day was a Sunday, with the workers sleeping late before setting off for the city centre. By early afternoon the crowds matched those of the previous day. Despite Rodzyanko's plea to use fire-hoses rather than bullets against the insurgents, the troops received orders to shoot wherever necessary. The principal confrontation of the day was again on Znamenskaya Square but, on the order to fire, the Volynsky regiment laid down its arms, forcing the police to take sole responsibility for the ensuing fusillade which claimed forty lives. Although the immediate objective was achieved and the crowd forcibly dispersed, the insubordination of the Volynsky regiment augured badly for the government. This development was taken a stage further when part of the Pavlovsky regiment mutinied, not only refusing to fire on the crowd but turning their rifles on the police instead. The trend was ominous: the sympathy of the soldiers for the insurgents was expressing itself in increasing committment to their side.

When the Council of Ministers reconvened on the evening of the 26th to determine the fate of the Duma, the situation required the nicest judgement. Some evidence pointed to the weakness of the government position. The insubordination of the Volynsky and Pavlovsky regiments brought home to the cabinet its dependance on army loyalty, which could no longer be relied on for offensive operations. An Okhrana report on the afternoon of 26 February suggested that 'the government is without support from anybody ... Bourgeois circles insist on a change of government and stress continuing the war to a successful conclusion but the workers advance the slogan "Bread, down with the government and down with the war" ... At present, everything depends on the line taken by the armed forces.' However it was still possible to interpret developments as moving in the direction the government desired. The lapses of detachments of two regiments did not necessarily imply the disloyalty of the remainder and indeed the mutiny of the Pavlovsky company had been dealt with very ably by the Preobrazhensky regiment. The actions of the workers on Sunday, their day off, could not be taken as typical and the demands of their families could well send them back to work early in the coming week. Most telling of all, there was substantial evidence for believing that the local labour movement had reached its peak and would now subside. The most important cogs in the left organisations had been removed by the Okhrana and the disturbances could not be expected to continue leaderless. Trotsky later admitted that the 26th was the turning-point at which all the local revolutionary parties (Bolsheviks included) were for abandoning the struggle for the time being. The campaign to restore law and order over the course of the 26th encountered such little resistance that, as the Menshevik N.N. Sukhanov conceded, 'it might well have seemed that tsarism had again won the throw and that the movement was going to be suppressed'. On the crucial night of decision, it was possible to argue that it was necessary only to weather a storm which was already moderating.[7]

With the social and political balance so delicate, the government's relations with the Duma were of vital importance, but the negotiations between Rittikh and Pokrovsky and the Duma are still shrouded in mystery. Who did the ministers contact and what was the point of their discussions? Neither question has been satisfactorily answered for few of the participants have cared to divulge any significant details. Nekrasov seems to have demanded a constitutionally-responsible government. Milyukov mentions merely that he was contacted together with Maklakov and the Octobrist Savich, but 'I do not remember at all what they actually spoke about with me.' This forgetfulness of Milyukov, so consistently linked with embarrassing issues, is more than suspicious. Shulgin recalls that there was a Bloc meeting on 26 February, which he condemns for its failure to take a firm line against the government; he may also have had this occasion in mind when he remarks that 'the feeling of the closeness of revolution was so terrifying that through the eleventh hour the Kadets became even softer.' It is probably significant that most individuals known to have been contacted were right moderates susceptible to government intimidation. Maklakov in particular gave an impression of Bloc complaisance with his well-known view that the Duma should be prorogued only to allow time for the formation of a ministry of confidence. But whatever the details of the discussions, Rittikh and Pokrovsky returned to the Council of Ministers with impressions favouring a hard line towards the Duma.[8]

The cabinet debated the situation from 9 p.m. until shortly after midnight. Protopopov's argument that this was no time for concession as the crisis was already receding won the grudging agreement of a majority of the Council. News of the weak line of the

Duma moderates convinced all that no danger could spring from prorogation (and little from dissolution). To Protopopov, prorogation automatically suspended the transfer of supply away from the MVD; to this extent, Protopopov may have seen the prorogation of the Duma less as an assault on the national assembly than as a defence of his own position. Acceding reluctantly to the prevailing opinion but exercising his prerogative as Chairman, Golitsyn opted not for dissolution but prorogation 'until a date not later than April 1917', completing a blank shortly after midnight. At 2 a.m. Golitsyn informed the Tsar by telegram of what had been done in his name, and shortly afterwards despatched the formal decree of prorogation to the Senate, from where it would pass to the Duma President. The deed was done: although the decision for prorogation was only a minor cabinet reverse for Golitsyn and in no sense a total surrender to Protopopov, the triumph of Protopopov's optimistic view of the crisis was to draw the Duma reluctantly into the insurrection against the government.[9]

The news of prorogation spread quickly and by early morning on Monday 27 February agitated deputies were thronging the Tauride Palace. A meeting of the bureau of the Progressive Bloc predictably oscillated between despair and ambition for, as Shulgin remarked, 'Not everybody understood their impotence. Some believed that now was the moment when we could do something, now that the masses had crossed into "action". And what did they propose? Sitting at their cosy green velvet-covered tables, they thought that the bureau of the Progressive Bloc could manage insurgent Russia as it had managed the fractions of the Duma.' When the *konvent* convened in mid-morning, it was still difficult to assess the local situation. The Council of Ministers had made its decision at what appeared to be the turning-point of the disturbances; within twelve hours the moderates had little more information upon which to base the most far-reaching judgement in the career of the Duma.[10]

The prorogation issue split the *konvent*. The inclination of the right camp was to accept prorogation if it was accompanied by the establishment of a ministry of confidence. Maklakov's plan for a ministry headed by Alexeyev was the most concrete version, though in retrospect it is hard to dispel the image of the moderate Right attempting to pass off moral cowardice as self-sacrifice. Following the retaliatory proposal of the extreme Left for an official Duma sitting in defiance of the prorogation decree, the Kadets once again demonstrated their pivotal authority and came up with a compromise formula. It was decided neither to disperse nor to defy the prorogation decree but convert the official closed sitting scheduled for that afternoon into a meeting of deputies in their private capacities. Kerensky was to condemn this compromise as disastrous for the future authority of the Duma:

The Council [of Elders – *senioren konvent*] overruled our proposal, deciding that the Duma convene in 'unofficial session' ... Politically and psychologically this meant there was to be a private meeting of a group of private individuals ... This refusal to continue in session formally was perhaps the greatest mistake of the Duma. It meant committing suicide at the very moment when its authority was supreme in the country and it might have played a decisive and fruitful part had it acted differently ... The Imperial Duma wrote its own death warrant at the moment of the revolutionary renaissance of the people.

But on that morning the concern of the moderates lay, as ever, less with their relationship with the people than with the government. The direction in which events were moving was still a matter for conjecture rather than informed judgement and the Bloc was not prepared to gamble away the future by adding its signature to a movement which might be crushed the next day. In their conviction that the Duma had too much to lose to put itself at risk, the moderates would only gamble on a certainty.[11]

By early afternoon there was incontrovertible evidence that the position of the government in the capital was becoming untenable. Despite the arrests of local revolutionary leaders, the workers' movement continued under its own impetus and the almost apolitical militancy of its sub-elites. At noon, the Okhrana Headquarters were occupied and sacked by a mob probably led by agents anxious to detroy evidence of their complicity. Most significantly, army regiments started to commit themselves unreservedly to the insurgents: in the early hours of 27 February, the Volynsky regiment voted to join the insurrection, followed over the course of the morning by the Litovsky, Preobrazhensky and Pavlovsky regiments. The Duma was now secure against any attempt to enforce the prorogation decree by military action. The selection of the Tauride Palace as the seat of the State Duma had been largely governed by the fact that the site was entirely surrounded by regimental barracks. The location, designed in 1905–6 to facilitate a military coup, now worked to the advantage of the Duma.

Just before the start of the unofficial sitting, a company of the Preobrazhensky regiment arrived to defend the Duma, the first of many military units to offer their services. The response of the deputies was far from effusive: few except the Left welcomed the self-appointment of a guard committed to revolution which presumably expected the same of the Duma it came to defend. Following the soldiers came a horde of insurgents whom the Duma dared not refuse and who rapidly occupied all but a few rooms of the Tauride Palace. Chernov was to note with satisfaction that the failure of the Duma to go to the Revolution had brought the Revolution to the

Duma. The close presence of their revolutionary guard and their equally uninvited and undesirable guests assaulted the drawing-room sensibilities of the deputies almost beyond endurance. Shulgin recalled the experience with a shudder:

> I remember the moment when the blackish-grey sediment, pressing at the doors like a never-ceasing flood, drowned the Duma ... From the first moment of that inundation, repulsion filled my soul ... I felt helpless. Something dangerous, terrifying and abominable had been unleashed which threatened all of us alike. Even the old fighters in our midst shared in the common wave of fear then sweeping over us, as we sat together huddled in a vain attempt to draw courage and support from each other.

The invasion of the Duma quite literally brought home to the deputies the difficulty of maintaining a moderate line in a revolutionary context.[12]

Despite growing revolutionary pressure, the moderates still steered a cautious and legalistic course. Rodzyanko continued his constitutional role by informing the Tsar of developments and proposing political solutions. On the evening of the 26th he sent a warning telegram: 'It is necessary that some person who enjoys the confidence of the country be entrusted at once with the formation of a new government. There must be no delay. Any procrastination is tantamount to death.' Just prior to the unofficial sitting on the 27th, Rodzyanko made another appeal:

> The session of the State Duma has been suspended until April by Your Majesty's ukase. The last bulwark of order has been eliminated ... Cancel Your imperial ukase and order the reconvening of the legislative chambers. Make these measures known without delay through an imperial manifesto. Sire, do not delay ... the hour which will decide the fate of Yourself and of the homeland has come. Tomorrow it may be too late.

Unfortunately, Rodzyanko's telegram arrived in the wake of two unduly optimistic messages from Alexandra and Belyayev, eliciting from Nicholas the legendary remark that 'fat Rodzyanko has sent me some nonsense which I won't even bother to answer'. Notwithstanding Nicholas's scorn, it cannot be denied that Rodzyanko had a realistic perception of the emergency and performed his constitutional duty as Duma President as long as practicable.[13]

The unofficial sitting which began at 2.30 p.m. reflected the loyalist constitutional stand of Rodzyanko. Shulgin noted that the popular occupation of the Duma had the effect of uniting the moderate camp: 'even enemies of many years standing suddenly felt that there was something equally dangerous, ominous and repulsive to them all – the street mob.' Mansyrev witnessed the Duma's total lack of composure: 'There was complete confusion amongst the Duma deputies. Almost everybody had expected revolution but now that it had actually erupted, no one was prepared for it, not even our Duma socialists ... everyone felt complete unpreparedness for any action and the total absence of any plan.' For over an hour the future of the Duma was debated. The Left now declared itself prepared to accept an interim constituent assembly formed of deputies from all four Dumas – in the calculation that the radical majorities of the first two Dumas would outvote the conservative majorities of the last two. A surprisingly right-wing proposal from Nekrasov that power should be invested in a popular 'responsible dictator' like General Polivanov or Alexeyev not only angered the Left but found little support among the moderates, who were hoping for a compromise plan which offered the Duma protection against possible government reprisals. Characteristically, it was Milyukov who judged the consensus accurately and proposed a course which combined opportunism with circumspection:

> I proposed to wait awhile until the character of the disturbances became clearer and in the meantime to create a temporary committee of Duma members 'for restoring order and maintaining contact with various persons and organisations'. This awkward formula had the advantage of meeting the problem of the moment without determining anything for the future. Limiting itself to the minimum, it created a working body but did not lead the Duma members into criminal action.

Despite the protests of the Left, Milyukov's formula was the only motion with a sufficiently low common denominator of content to permit a clear majority. The unofficial sitting commissioned the *konvent* to elect a 'Provisional Committee' at once.[14]

The membership list for the Provisional Committee was complete by 4 p.m. There were no surprises. As Shulgin said, 'in essence it was the bureau of the Progressive Bloc with the addition of Kerensky and Chkheidze.' But while the Committee invited representation from further left than the confines of the Bloc, its overall balance was at least as far right as that of the Bloc. The party composition of the Committee was four Octobrists (Rodzyanko, Dmitryukov, Shidlovsky and B.A. Engelhardt), two Kadets (Milyukov and Nekrasov), two Progressists (Konovalov and Rzhevsky), one Progressive Nationalist (Shulgin), one Centre (Vladimir Lvov), one Trudovik (Kerensky) and one Menshevik (Chkheidze). The essentially counter-revolutionary nature of the Committee was symbolised by its Octobrist hegemony. Moreover the Committee, headed informally by Rodzyanko, took great care to disclaim any official Duma status. The moderate leaders were still living in the shadow of their defeat of 1915: too close identification between Duma and Bloc had on that occasion led to punishment falling on both. Such a double reprisal must be avoided in 1917. Should the worse come to the worst, the Provisional Committee would be represented as the unofficial executive of a private conference. The Duma itself had to be protected, with the authority to disavow any actions of the Provisional Committee.[15]

The circumspection of the Duma leaders disappointed and then angered the insurgents. Sukhanov expressed typical revolutionary misgivings about the role of the moderates:

> Power had to go to the bourgeoisie but was there any chance that they would take it? … Would they, after calculating all the difficulties of their position, accept power from the hands of the revolution? Or would they prefer to disassociate themselves from the revolution which had just begun and destroy the movement in alliance with the tsarist faction? Or would they finally decide to destroy the movement by their 'neutrality' – by abandoning it to its own devices and mass impulses that would lead to anarchy?

In the late afternoon of 27 February, it seemed that the last course of neutrality was being favoured: the name of the Committee was 'as cautious and reluctant an appellation as ever assumed by any revolutionary body'; both the Committee and the unofficial sitting which fathered it were meticulously distinguished from the Duma and *konvent* in official bulletins; and details of the Committee and its composition were deliberately withheld until midnight (by which time the sweep of events made mock of any vestigial policy of restraint).[16]

Even these superficially unremarkable developments would have been unlikely without the atmosphere of revolution which pervaded the Tauride Palace and, most particularly, the emergence of a rival to the Duma Committee. It seems that the decision to follow the pattern of 1905 and call a Soviet was made at Menshevik initiative on 25 February. The proletariat of the industrial suburbs responded enthusiastically to the invitation to elect delegates, invading the Duma on the afternoon of the 27th to demand accommodation for the Soviet. At 3 p.m., while the Duma unofficial sitting was in session, Rodzyanko grudgingly allocated room 13 to the leaders of the insurgents, admitting the most unwelcome house-guest so far into the Tauride Palace. The existence of a rival for authority over the revolution operating within the same building undoubtedly spurred the Provisional Committee to greater activity and responsibility over the next twelve hours. As the *konvent* elected the Provisional Committee, it knew that the interim Executive Committee of the Petrograd Soviet was conducting its founding session only just out of earshot.[17]

The evening of 27 February saw a last attempt by Rodzyanko to stabilise the deteriorating situation. When, earlier that afternoon, Shcheglovitov had been brought forcibly to the Duma by a group of insurgents, Rodzyanko and the moderates were acutely embarrassed by the problem with which the revolution had confronted them. As Kerensky testified, 'the deputies were greatly distressed and the moderates urged Rodzianko to have him [Shcheglovitov] released since, as the president of a legislative body, he enjoyed personal immunity ... I saw Rodzianko greet him amiably and invite him into his office as a "guest".' Kerensky seized the initiative and histrionically arrested Shcheglovitov in the name of the revolution, daring Rodzyanko to contradict him before the thronged hall but 'everyone fell back, and Rodzianko and his friends, somewhat embarrassed, returned to their rooms'. The citizens' arrest of Shcheglovitov convinced Rodzyanko of the declining moral authority of the moderates over the insurgents and the necessity of full cooperation with Golitsyn to save the local situation. Both despatched telegrams to the Tsar describing the emergency and proposing identical solutions: early in the evening, Rodzyanko beseeched Nicholas 'immediately to call on a person in whom the whole country can have confidence and who would be charged to form a government having the confidence of the population'; almost simultaneously, Golitsyn, P. L. Bark (Minister of Finance) and Pokrovsky jointly petitioned the Tsar 'to dismiss us at once and nominate a person enjoying the confidence of the Sovereign who will not arouse the mistrust of wide sectors of society'.[18]

At a meeting of the Council of Ministers the same evening, Golitsyn announced that he could see no future for his administration. The man so consistently portrayed as a colourless nonentity was at his most impressive in taking the decision to disband the cabinet. Protopopov was intimidated into resignation, pathetically muttering 'now there is nothing left for me but to shoot myself'. By further insisting that this individual 'act of self-sacrifice' must be accompanied by the collective resignation of the entire cabinet, Golitsyn went far beyond his delegated powers as Chairman of the Council of Ministers. In acceding to outside pressure, preferring his own counsel, urging a renovated cabinet and then promoting collective resignation in order to force the Tsar's hand, Golitsyn was himself making a revolutionary departure and invading the imperial prerogative. The fact of revolution drew a revolutionary response from the Tsar's own government. Golitsyn attempted to cover himself in part against accusations of *lèse-majesté* by persuading Rodzyanko to arrange for the attendance of Grand Duke Michael at the meeting. Long well-connected in grand-ducal circles, Rodzyanko had already asked Michael to come to Petrograd from Gatchina so that a representative of the Romanov dynasty could be at hand as a rallying-point for loyalist forces. On arriving in Petrograd late in the afternoon of the 27th, the Grand Duke was conducted at once to the Mariinsky Palace to lend Golitsyn greater courage and stature by his presence. It is doubtful whether Golitsyn would have gone so far had it not been for the attendance of one regarded by many moderates as the future Regent.[19]

Following the Council of Ministers, an equally historic meeting took place. The leaders of the government and Duma jointly appealed to Michael to save the military and political situation in the capital. In the words of Rodzyanko, 'he should assume on his own initiative the dictatorship of the city of Petrograd, compel the personnel of the government to tender their resignations and demand by telegraph, by direct wire from His Majesty the Emperor, a manifesto regarding the formation of a responsible cabinet.' By the time that Rodzyanko published this account (1922), the embarrassment of admitting any collusion with tsarism had induced Rodzyanko to play down the combined nature of the meeting but the testimony of Golitsyn to the Investigatory Commission of the Provisional Government in April 1917 was that 'both Rodzyanko and I beseeched Mikhail Alexandrovich to take the regency and immediately release us, that is, the ministers'. Even if Nicholas could not appreciate the exigencies of the moment, the heads of both government and Duma were prepared to compromise their oaths of loyalty to save the dynasty in spite of itself. Their common enterprise broke down over the irresolution of the Grand Duke. Following the account of Rodzyanko, 'the indecision of the Grand Duke Mikhail Alexandrovich contributed to the favourable moment being lost. Instead of taking active measures and gathering around himself the units of the Petrograd garrison whose discipline was not yet shattered, the Grand Duke started to negotiate by direct wire with the Emperor.' Fearing to assume the responsibility of 'usurping' the authority of the Tsar, however locally and temporarily, Michael refused to make a decision until he had received permission from his brother.[20]

Throughout the evening of 27 February power drained away from the government. At 5 p.m. the Winter Palace was occupied by the Pavlovsky regiment. At 7.30 p.m., with only the Semyenovsky and Izmailovsky regiments still loyal, Belyayev requested immediate external reinforcements from the Stavka. By 10 p.m. the remaining loyal troops commanded by Khabalov and his chief-of-staff M.I. Zankevich were besieged in the Admiralty building, with numbers so small and morale so uncertain as to preclude any possibility of regrouping and counter-attack. Shortly before midnight, Khabalov despatched a telegram to the Tsar belatedly confessing that he could not restore order. Its authority and self-assurance intimately linked with the fortunes of the military, the government became inoperative: at 11.30 p.m. Golitsyn and his cabinet resigned, dispersing within the hour without waiting to hear the Tsar's response. As the Council of Ministers surrendered power (and the Tsar refused to accept its resignation), local authority in Petrograd fell to whoever was willing to take it. The power vacuum could not be expected to last very long and, as Kerensky recalled, the insurgents instinctively turned to the Duma: 'from every direction people approached us for instructions and advice. The Provisional Committee, which had only just been formed, was compelled to act as an executive power. We were like the general staff of an army during war operations.' The local collapse of tsarist government increased the painful pressure on the Duma moderates to abandon restraint and assume power in the capital.[21]

Three factors finally compelled the Provisional Committee to commit itself. A joint meeting of leaders of the UZ, UT, WIC and Petrograd municipal duma the same evening 'unanimously welcomed the resolution of the State Duma not to disperse and its decision to take power into its hands'. In point of fact, neither of these statements was accurate at the time. Conceivably the public organisations were genuinely misinformed of the exact state of Duma affairs. For example, it is true that the only printed source of news for the period 27 February to 4 March, the broadsheet *Izvestia*, featured an over-sensational coverage of what it called the 'dissolution' of the Duma. It is also undeniable that the scrupulous distinction between the Duma and the new Committee drawn by Rodzyanko in official communiqués was blithely disregarded by *Izvestia* and the vast majority of insurgents. But it is also likely that the mass if not the leadership of the public organisations was convinced of the necessity of adding their weight to the revolutionary movement: with the process of politicisation complete, the UZ, UT and WIC deliberately issued a premature statement to stampede the Provisional Committee into action. Whatever the real circumstances of their public announcement, the endorsement of the public organisations to revolution must have weighed heavily with the members of the Duma Committee.[22]

At the Stavka, Nicholas's ignorance of the extent of the emergency in Petrograd had the effect of postponing a response until events had progressed too far for an unrevolutionary solution. At a discussion with his advisers in the early evening of the 27th, Nicholas was impressed by the argument of V.N. Voyeikov that the disorders were being exaggerated by Rodzyanko and could be met by military action alone. Alexeyev was unable to put up a persuasive counter-argument through illness (and soon retired to bed with a high fever). Nicholas had been as influenced by the events of 1915 as the moderates, drawing the lesson that only decisive action was needed to dissolve a crisis. By 9 p.m. he had decided to reject concession and to despatch General N.I. Ivanov to restore order in the capital. By the time that Grand Duke Michael succeeded in contacting Nicholas over the telegraph at 10.30 p.m., a policy of repression had been adopted and he was told none too courteously to keep out of high politics. Golitsyn's submission of the resignation of the Council of Ministers was answered by a testy insistence on the restoration of order and the curt judgement that 'changes in the composition of the ministers are inadmissable in these circumstances'. The recalcitrance of Nicholas (like the cabinet and Duma before him having to make momentous decisions on the basis of inadequate information) brought the dynastic schemes of Rodzyanko to nothing and presented the Duma with a stark choice: either the people or the Tsar.[23]

Finally, as the Provisional Committee temporised in an agony of indecision, its putative rival was fast developing in stature. As Kerensky said, 'the formation of the Soviet earlier in the day was regarded as a critical event since there was now a danger that, unless we formed a provisional government at once, the Soviet would declare itself the supreme authority of the Revolution.' In retrospect, it would seem that the Soviet was by no means as eager to aspire to total authority over the revolution as at first appeared but to the jealous moderates the threat was real enough. From 9 p.m. ran the first plenary session of the Petrograd Soviet, which though both chaotic and unproductive thoroughly alarmed the Duma. Just as the simultaneous meetings of the Soviet Executive Committee and the Duma *konvent* on the afternoon of 27 February spurred on the creation of the Provisional Committee, so the plenary Soviet in the evening helped to force the Committee through its next (and most far-reaching) decision.[24]

By late evening, every member of the Provisional Committee except Rodzyanko had been converted to the revolution. As the most cautious of the moderates, Rodzyanko openly and hysterically lamented: 'I do not wish to rebel. I am no insurgent. I did not make and do not wish to make a revolution. If it has been made, it is because people did not heed us. I am no revolutionary. I don't want to go against the Supreme Authority ... What shall I do? Step aside? Wash my hands of it? What shall I do?' even Shulgin, nominally more right-wing than Rodzyanko, urged him: 'Take power. The position is plain. If we don't, others will.' Rodzyanko hung on for the result of Michael's appeal to Nicholas before committing himself irrevocably. With all practical and constitutional alternatives eliminated, Rodzyanko was compelled either to follow his Duma colleagues or 'step aside' into oblivion. At midnight on 27–8 February Rodzyanko gave his assent to the Provisional Committee taking power. In an attempt to keep the tide of revolution in check and retain power for himself and the Octobrists, Rodzyanko priced his agreement as an undertaking that 'all members of the Committee unconditionally and blindly subordinate themselves to my command', a stiff demand which still gained the acquiescence of all but Kerensky. The newly-elected Soviet Executive Committee was summoned and within an hour the two executives had produced a working agreement by which the Soviet agreed to subordinate itself to the Duma Committee. Before the Committee broke up to allow its exhausted members some sleep at 2 a.m., it published the first carefully-worded announcement of its momentous decision:

> Under the difficult conditions of internal chaos brought about by the measures of the old regime, the Provisional Committee of the State Duma has found itself compelled to take the responsibility for restoring national and public order. Conscious of the vast responsibility it has assumed by this decision, the Committee expresses its assurance that the population and army will assist in the difficult task of forming a new government that will correspond with the desires of the population and will be capable of commanding its confidence.

Despite being the most reluctant of revolutionaries, Rodzyanko retained authority as the 'dictator' of the Duma Provisional Committee.[25]

Over the next twenty-four hours, the remaining vestiges of tsarist government in Petrograd disappeared. The Mariinsky Palace was occupied and the ex-ministers either hid out or, anticipating a worse fate at the hands of the mob, surrendered themselves to the Duma. General Zankevich, trapped with a small body of troops still dwindling through desertion, telegraphed the Stavka that he was evacuating the Admiralty to return to barracks. With the withdrawal of the Izmailovsky, the last loyal regiment, the final redoubt of tsarism in revolutionary Petrograd was abandoned. As the authority of the government evaporated, that of the Duma and Soviet rushed to take its place. Engelhardt was commissioned to organise the Duma Committee's assumption of power in Petrograd. The committee appointed some two dozen 'commissars' (a term antedating Bolshevik usage) from the membership of the Progressive Bloc to effect the takeover of the tsarist ministries. After seizing the Ministry of Transport, the Progressist commissar A.A. Bublikov issued a general telegram which informed the entire Empire that the Duma had taken power in Russia. Grandiose claims notwithstanding, by that evening the authority of the Duma Committee in collaboration with the Soviet had entirely replaced that of the Tsar in the imperial capital.[26]

Tuesday 28 February witnessed the first attempts of the Tsar and Duma to come to terms. Having indignantly refused the resignation of a cabinet which (unknown to him) no longer existed, Nicholas decided to return to the capital: at 5 a.m. the imperial train left Mogilev, thereby exposing its passenger to infinitely greater stress and danger than at the Stavka. A full thirty-eight hours were to elapse before the diverted train eventually came to rest, a period throughout which Nicholas was almost completely *incommunicado*. The Tsar was out of touch with the capital and could neither learn of events nor effectively respond to them. To quote Nicolas de Basily, who was at the Stavka at the time, 'misfortune had willed that there was no longer any means of communicating with the Emperor at a time when he alone could make the necessary decisions to put to an end to the anarchy.' Nicholas saw little reason to hurry his decisions in transit, unaware that while 'he was still reckoning in days and weeks, the revolution was keeping its count in minutes'. It was under these disorientating circumstances that the Tsar was called upon to make the most critical decisions of his reign.[27]

By the evening of the 28th, Rodzyanko was concerned to stabilise the situation before the revolution threatened the dynasty, and telegraphed the Tsar to request a meeting at Bologoe or Dno the next day. Rodzyanko had persuaded the Grand Dukes Paul, Cyril and Michael to put their signatures to a manifesto conceding more responsible government and now intended to employ the manifesto in a personal confrontation with Nicholas. But Rodzyanko never kept his appointment. Sukhanov (and also Chernov) claimed that Rodzyanko was forcibly prevented from meeting the Tsar by the suspicious Soviet:

> Rodzianko must not be allowed to see the Tsar. We still don't know the intentions of the leading groups of the bourgeoisie, the Progressive Bloc and Duma Committee, and no one can vouch for them ... If the Tsar has any power on his side – which again we don't know – then the 'revolutionary' Duma which 'stands for the people' will certainly side with the Tsar against the revolution ... We must not create the possibility of the formation of a counter-revolutionary force – what the Tsar would not be strong enough to do alone, he will easily be able to do with the help of the Duma and Rodzianko.

Shulgin recalled a conversation with Rodzyanko on the evening of the same day (1 March) when the Duma President complained,

This morning I was to have left for the Stavka to meet the Emperor to submit to his Majesty the only possible solution – abdication. But those scoundrels found out about it and just as I was about to set off told me the train would not be allowed to leave … They said they would not let me go alone but I must take Chkheidze … who was to be accompanied by a battalion of 'revolutionary soldiers'. Who knows what outrages they would have committed there.[28]

But although at least three contemporary accounts indicate either that Rodzyanko was physically prevented from keeping his appointment or only permitted under conditions which he considered unacceptable, other historians (notably Katkov and Hasegawa) contend that the restraint imposed by the Soviet was minimal and that Rodzyanko employed the Soviet as a convenient bugaboo to cover his reluctance to leave Petrograd. It is probably fair to suggest that while Rodzyanko did encounter resistance from the Soviet, his principal reason for not going was concern for his authority over the Revolution. In a later telegraph conversation with General N.V. Ruzsky, Rodzyanko claimed that 'the unbridled passions of the popular masses must not be left without my personal control because I am still the only one who is trusted and whose orders are carried out.' If Rodzyanko had set off for Bologoe on the morning of 1 March, he would have missed the arrival of Prince Lvov (a projected new premier) that afternoon and the meeting of the Duma Committee to finalise the manifesto and composition of the Provisional Government scheduled for that evening. Rodzyanko must have been aware that his self-appointment as dictator of the Revolution was universally resented and nowhere more than amongst his moderate colleagues. To abandon the capital at such a time, on no matter how important a mission, was to invite a coup in his absence. Rodzyanko simply did not dare turn his back on political developments to spend days chasing the Tsar over the disorganised railways of north-western Russia. Nicholas had put himself at an enormous disadvantage by consigning his throne to a railway carriage; Rodzyanko had no intention of making the same mistake.[29]

Informed of Soviet control of the rail route to Petrograd, Nicholas decided to travel across country to the headquarters of the Northern Front at Pskov, which was the nearest place with direct telegraph connections to both the Stavka and the revolutionary capital. By the time that Nicholas finally reached Pskov at 7 p.m. on 1 March, the Northern Front commander General Ruzsky knew more of events in Petrograd than the Tsar. Rodzyanko had informed all army commanders through Alexeyev of the Duma takeover and convinced the Stavka of the success of the revolution. Because of the personal unavailability of Rodzyanko, it fell to the embarrassed Ruzsky to negotiate between the Revolution and the Tsar. Assured by Alexeyev and Rodzyanko that political concessions were essential to calm the revolutionary excesses which threatened the war effort, Ruzsky spent the better part of the evening of 1 March attempting to persuade Nicholas to concede, but without success. A chance remark to Ruzsky's adjutant – 'perhaps we should call on Krivoshein' – reveals just how out of touch Nicholas was. The turning-point in Ruzsky's campaign was the arrival at 11 p.m. of a telegram from Alexeyev:

> The ever-increasing danger of anarchy spreading all over the country, of the further disintegration of the army and the impossibility of continuing the war under present conditions urgently demand the immediate publication of an imperial act which could still have a calming effect, and this is possible only by calling a responsible ministry and charging the President of the State Duma to form it. The news which reaches us gives us reason to hope that members of the Duma under the leadership of Rodzyanko are still in a position to stop the general disintegration and that it would be possible to work with them, but the loss of every hour reduces our last chance to preserve or restore order.

The message prompted another long discussion with Ruzsky from which the pressed soldier-diplomat eventually emerged victorious. In the early hours of 2 March, intimidated by what one tsarist apologist has called Alexeyev's 'deluge of tendentious and distorted information', the Russian Sovereign fatalistically agreed to surrender his prerogatives in government in favour of the legislative assemblies.[30]

However, even this most fundamental of constitutional concessions conspicuously failed to satisfy the political needs of the moment. Rodzyanko had exploited his monopoly of communication with the Stavka to present an impression which was in keeping with his ambitions as dictator of the revolution but not with the true state of affairs. Alexeyev and Ruzsky were led to believe that Rodzyanko could control the situation if armed with the political weapons which only they could secure. In fact, the mood in the capital had already outdistanced the constitutionalism of Rodzyanko: the abdication of Nicholas had secured almost universal agreement and the principal issue was fast becoming the future of the monarchy. Even as the Tsar reached Pskov, the Duma Committee in Petrograd was meeting to complete its 'Manifesto of the Provisional Government' and agree on the removal of Nicholas as Tsar. When the Duma Committee met the Soviet Executive Committee to discuss joint signature of the Manifesto, the overwhelmingly republican Soviet insisted that 'the Provisional Government must not take any steps to predetermine the future form of government'. The Duma Committee, largely monarchist by persuasion, defended 'the Romanov dynasty and monarchy, with Alexis as Tsar and Michael as Regent'. According to Sukhanov, a tired Milyukov 'made some "liberal advances" to us, pointing out that the Romanovs could no longer be dangerous, and that Nicholas was unacceptable to him too and must be removed. He naïvely tried to convince us of the acceptability to the democracy of the arrangement, saying of his candidates that "one was a sick child, the other a thoroughly stupid man".' Hours of desultory debate produced an interim formula which was only tolerated because it was by now 4 a.m. (on 2 March) and the wording was equally disagreeable to both sides. This tired stalemate over the future of the monarchy also symbolised the final failure of Rodzyanko's dynastic designs and, at one remove, his own imminent fall from power. The anachronistic grand-ducal manifesto organised by Rodzyanko was handed over to Milyukov (significantly enough) for suppression. It was little wonder that by now, in the words of the Duma President's assistant N. Ivanov, 'Rodzyanko did not look like a triumphant triumvir on the revolution's chariot but rather a pitiful coachman who had lost the reins.'[31]

Although arriving too late for the meeting, Guchkov was acutely disturbed by colleagues' accounts of the accelerating trend towards republicanism. After conferring with Milyukov and the despondent Rodzyanko, Guchkov came to the conclusion that only swift and decisive action could forestall complete disaster:

> In this chaos we must above all think of saving the monarchy. Without the monarchy, Russia cannot live. But evidently, the present Emperor must not reign any longer ... If that is so, how can we calmly and indifferently await the moment when the revolutionary rabble destroys the monarchy? This will inevitably happen if we let the initiative slip from our hands ... Therefore we must act quickly and secretly, without asking, without taking advice ... we must confront them with an accomplished fact. We must give Russia a new monarch.

Since Rodzyanko had failed to make the journey to meet the Tsar, Guchkov decided he must go to prevent a slide into revolutionary chaos. With luck, the revolutionary aspect of recent events might be camouflaged: 'I knew that if he abdicated into our hands, there would be so-to-speak *no revolution*. The Emperor would abdicate of his own free will, power would pass to a regent, who would appoint a new government. The Imperial Duma, which had submitted to the ukase of dissolution and had taken power only because the old ministers had fled, would transfer power to the new government. Juridically speaking, there would be no revolution.' In effect, Guchkov intended his mission to effect the same limited palace revolution which he had been planning before the Petrograd insurrection. He could leave the capital secure in the knowledge that the composition of the Provisional Government had been finalised and, come what may, he would be Minister of War. He had everything to gain by his dramatic mission to Pskov and, unlike Rodzyanko the previous day, nothing to lose. Accompanied by Shulgin, Guchkov slipped away from Petrograd, requisitioning the train reserved for Rodzyanko. Neither knew that very early that morning the Tsar had rendered a revolution inevitable even in law.[32]

On the same morning of 2 March, a pleased Ruzsky reported his success to Rodzyanko: 'His Majesty, meeting the general desire of the legislative bodies and the people, has expressed his final decision and has authorised me to inform you that he has decided to grant a ministry responsible to the legislative bodies and charges you with the formation of the cabinet.' Although welcoming Nicholas's conciliatory attitude, Rodzyanko could not conceal that events in Petrograd had passed the point at which such a concession could stem the revolution. Having come directly from witnessing the fierce republicanism of the Soviet, 'with an aching heart' Rodzyanko replied that 'hatred of the dynasty has reached extreme limits ... and threatening demands for abdication in favour of the son, under the regency of Michael Alexandrovich, have become a very definite demand ... Unfortunately the manifesto has come too late.' By mid-morning Alexeyev had received details of the conversation from Ruzsky and decided to launch a High Command campaign for abdication. Alexeyev telegraphed to Ruzsky his 'deep conviction that there is no alternative and abdication should take place ... it is very painful for me to say but there is no other solution.' At 11 a.m. Alexeyev issued a circular to all front commanders: 'the war may be continued until a victorious end only provided demands regarding the abdication from the throne in favour of the son and under the regency of Mikhail Alexandrovich are satisfied. Apparently the situation permits no other solution and every minute of further hesitation would only increase the claims.' The appeal of war necessity elicited a prompt and favourable response from all commanders (including Grand Duke Nikolai). Alexeyev concluded the flood of telegrams to Pskov urging abdication with his own personal appeal at 2.30 p.m.: 'Involvement by the army in internal affairs would mean the inevitable end of the war, Russia's shame and disintegration. Your Imperial Majesty loves Russia dearly and for the sake of her integrity, independence and victory, You must deign to make the decision.'[33]

The campaign brought an unexpectedly easy victory: within minutes of receiving the Alexeyev telegram, the Tsar had agreed to abdicate. Alone in Pskov after a nightmare two-day train journey,

Nicholas felt – and to a lesser extent actually was – isolated from his resources, especially his autocratic inspiration Alexandra. His incidental visit to Pskov reinforced his appreciation of the overwhelming importance of the war effort, as his ready acquiescence to Alexeyev over the granting of responsible government and the abdication itself suggests. Nicholas found abdication infinitely easier than granting a constitution: shortly *before* the arrival of the generals' telegrams, he confided to Ruzsky that on mature consideration he was inclined to abdicate rather than surrender the principle of autocracy. By abdicating, Nicholas may have hoped to wipe out the constitutional concessions of his reign and bequeath an uncompromised autocracy to his successor. Self-sacrifice was always attractive to Nicholas, a man of limited gifts drawn to the idea of martyrdom for a cause. Although his strict sense of conscience and duty prevented him ever seeking abdication, Nicholas appreciated that it furnished a political and personal escape. By the time the generals' telegrams arrived, Nicholas had already made up his mind. In the absence of any Duma envoy, Nicholas authorised transmission of telegrams of abdication to the capital and the Stavka; but at just this moment Ruzsky heard on the telegraph from Rodzyanko that Guchkov and Shulgin were on their way to Pskov. During the seven-hour wait for the delegates' train to arrive, Nicholas considered not so much the inevitability or otherwise of abdication as the future of the dynasty. At 3 p.m. he consulted the imperial physician Dr Fedorov about the health of the Tsarevich and brooded on his pessimistic diagnosis for the rest of the day. Fresh news that his endlessly suffering son had developed measles with complications only fortified his emerging decision. By the time that Guchkov and Shulgin arrived at 10 p.m., Nicholas had decided to abdicate in favour of Grand Duke Michael rather than inflict the crown on his twelve-year-old invalid son.[34]

Guchkov had come prepared for an acrimonious encounter and launched into a set speech despite the embarrassment of Shulgin and (unknown to him) the willingness of the Tsar to abdicate. Determined to play his part to the full at the risk of arrest or even execution, and unaware that he was breaking down an open door, Guchkov tentatively approached the subject of abdication just as Ruzsky, arriving late at the audience, told Shulgin that the matter was already decided. After listening to Guchkov's superfluous peroration with only minor signs of impatience, Nicholas delivered his bombshell: 'I have made the decision to abdicate from the throne. Until three o'clock today I had thought to abdicate in favour of my son Alexei but now I have changed my mind in favour of my brother Michael.' The Duma emissaries' amazement on discovering Nicholas's compliant attitude reflected the speed at which events were moving: when they left Petrograd, not only had the Tsar not been approached over abdication but they had not even heard the news of his granting a constitution.[35]

For the first time in the revolutionary crisis Nicholas was *au fait* with the latest political developments and had an advantage over the Duma delegates. As a result Guchkov and Shulgin overlooked various implications of the abdication, notably that Nicholas was flagrantly contravening the Succession Laws of 1797. In general, the deal which the Soviet had feared Rodzyanko would make with the Tsar was concluded by Guchkov and Shulgin. Lenin was to declare that 'a handful of landowners and capitalists, with Guchkov and Milyukov at their head, wanted to deceive the will and ambitions of the vast majority and conclude a bargain with the declining monarchy in order to support and save it.' Although, as usual, Lenin pitched his conspiracy theory a little high, it is clear that the Tsar and the leaders of the moderate Right negotiated in Pskov to preserve, or at least lend the advantage to, a traditional monarchist system of government. An abdication document was formally signed to satisfy Guchkov and Shulgin, who were of course opposed only to Nicholas's tenancy of the throne and vigorously supported both monarchy and Romanov dynasty. The nearest the document came to determining the future government of Russia was the sentence: 'We bequeath it to our brother to direct the forces of the state in full and inviolable union with the representatives of the people in the legislative institutions on the basis of principles which will be established by them.' The delegates were finally concerned to concoct an unchallengeable juridical link between the government of Nicholas II and the new regime. As finalised just prior to departure from Petrograd, Prince Lvov was to be premier, a welcome surprise to Nicholas who had always thought of Rodzyanko, and Grand Duke Nikolai was to be restored as Commander-in-Chief. Nicholas signed documents to this effect, thoughtfully backdated to 3 p.m. the same day (the time of his decision to abdicate and well before the arrival of the Duma delegates) to forestall any accusation of duress or forcible dethronement. Nicholas's last act as Tsar was to bolster the legal fiction that the revolutionary Provisional Government was the direct heir and sole beneficiary of the tsarist government.[36]

At 2 a.m. on 3 March Guchkov and Shulgin began the one hundred and sixty mile trip back to Petrograd, leaving Nicholas to return to the Stavka in distress later the same day. Flushed by relief and self-congratulation after their unexpectedly easy victory, they were confident that the document they flourished at every stopping-place en route was the political blueprint for the future. They were not to know that events in the capital had moved so fast in their absence that the carefully-phrased moderate manifesto with which they returned already stood no chance of general acceptance.

On the afternoon of 2 March, Milyukov had typically and perhaps unnecessarily announced the as yet unpublished Manifesto of the Provisional Government to the crowds thronging the Tauride Palace. His remarks on the collapse of tsarism, though less than truthful about the Duma role, were greeted rapturously and even the details of the composition of an overwhelmingly moderate cabinet received a fair measure of approval. With a show of modesty, Milyukov proclaimed: 'We were chosen by the Revolution. It was our good fortune that at the moment when it was impossible to wait any longer, a small group of men was at hand whose political past was sufficiently known to the people, and against whom there could be no hint of those objections that brought about the downfall of the old regime.' Milyukov attempted to leave the matter with this early exercise in historical revisionism but was prevented from withdrawing by loud challenges on the future of the Romanov dynasty. Milyukov had no alternative but to broach this most explosive of political issues:

You ask about the dynasty. I know beforehand that my answer will not satisfy all of you but I will tell it to you. The old despot who brought Russia to the brink of ruin will either voluntarily renounce the throne or be deposed. (Applause) Power will be transferred to a regent, Grand Duke Michael Alexandrovich. (Prolonged bursts of indignation, exclamations of 'Long Live the Republic' and 'Down with the Dynasty'. Weak applause drowned by fresh bursts of indignation.) The heir will be Alexei. (Cries of 'This is the old dynasty.') Yes, ladies and gentlemen, this is the old dynasty, which perhaps you don't like and perhaps I don't like either. But who we like is beside the point right now. We cannot leave the question of the form of government unanswered and undecided. We can visualise it as a parliamentary, constitutional monarchy.

Popular antagonism towards the monarchy was rendering the policy of the moderates more and more dangerous. The dilemma was either to defend the Romanov monarchy and risk the revolution turning on its moderate 'leadership' or follow the prevalent trend by condemning the monarchy and risk the hazards of a country at war without formal or legal authority. Milyukov was relying on Guchkov to come to an arrangement with the Tsar which could be presented to the Revolution as an acceptable *fait accompli*. The announcement of Guchkov as Minister of War that afternoon had provoked noisy complaint from the mob but elicited a most interesting defence from Milyukov: 'A.I. Guchkov was my political enemy throughout the life of the Duma but now we are political friends. I am an old professor accustomed to reading lectures but Guchkov is a man of action. At this moment, while I speak to you in this hall, Guchkov is on the streets of the capital organising our victory.' Guchkov was indeed taking action though (as Milyukov knew) in Pskov, not Petrograd. The exigencies of the revolutionary situation had forced Milyukov and Guchkov into the same camp, with Guchkov negotiating in the field while Milyukov covered for him in the capital.[37]

For the remainder of 2 March Milyukov lay low as he waited for news from Pskov. At a meeting of the Duma Committee and Soviet Executive Committee that evening, Sukhanov pointed out that Milyukov's 'attempts to thrust the Romanovs upon us ... would not help the monarchist cause but at best destroy the prestige of his own cabinet'. The moderate leader wearily put up little resistance: 'Milyukov listened and seemed to acknowledge that we were right. He too had experienced the day's events ... but however risky this gamble on the monarchy may have been, it was still indispensable to Milyukov and Guchkov: a gamble on the monarchy was still less risky than a gamble on bourgeois statemanship *without* the monarchy.' In the face of a Soviet argument that a constituent assembly would abolish the monarchy, Milyukov could only stoically argue that 'the Constituent Assembly may decide as it pleases. If it pronounces against the monarchy, then I shall be able to go, but at the moment I cannot.' Later, Milyukov experienced a more distasteful encounter with the anti-monarchism of the insurgents:

> I saw Rodzyanko trotting towards me accompanied by a handful of officers smelling of liquor. In a halting voice he repeated their words, that after my statement about the dynasty, they could not return to their soldiers. They demanded that I take back my words. Of course I could not take them back but, seeing the behaviour of Rodzyanko who knew very well that I had spoken not only in my own name but in the name of the bloc, I agreed to annouce that I was expressing my own personal opinion.

The revolutionary mood was moving so irrevocably against the retention of the Romanovs that, in the words of Chernov, 'the majority of the Progressive Bloc felt that the only thing left was to beat an orderly retreat.'[38]

At 2.30 a.m. on 3 March a telegram from Guchkov and Shulgin reached the Tauride Palace and the moderates hurriedly convened to discuss the implications of the abdication. All but Milyukov accepted, however reluctantly, that the revolution had passed by Grand Duke Michael. With all his dislike of Rodzyanko, Milyukov had not expected him to desert the royalist banner and found himself having to plead the cause of monarchy alone. Rodzyanko gloomily telegraphed Ruzsky to hold the publication of the abdication manifesto until the dynastic situation became clearer:

> It is with great difficulty that we managed to retain the

revolutionary movement within more or less tolerable limits but the situation is still far from settled and a civil war is quite possible. Perhaps they would reconcile themselves to the regency of the Grand Duke and the accession of the Tsarevich but his accession as Emperor would be completely unacceptable ... we would lose all authority and no one would remain to appease popular unrest.

Although Rodzyanko insisted that 'the return of the dynasty is not excluded', the most expedient way for the moderates 'to beat an orderly retreat' was to induce the man at the centre of the crisis to decide in their interests. If Michael accepted the crown, the moderates would be compelled either to follow him into personal danger and political oblivion or abandon their proclaimed principles in the interests of self-preservation. Everything hinged on the attitude of the Grand Duke. At 6 a.m. Kerensky phoned Michael to arrange a meeting for that same morning. All the moderates except Milyukov agreed to press for the Grand Duke's refusal and elected Rodzyanko and Lvov as spokesmen. This transparent attempt to muzzle Milyukov and present the majority viewpoint as unanimous was caustically challenged by the Kadet leader (a past master at such tactics), who raised such a fuss that it was agreed to allow the spokesmen for the two opposing arguments – Milyukov and Kerensky – to debate before the Grand Duke.[39]

The members of the Provisional Government began to assemble at Michael's temporary residence on the Millionaya at 10 a.m. The first to arrive were those advocating refusal of the crown – Kerensky, Lvov and Rodzyanko – who may have hoped to steal a march on Milyukov by forcing the crucial decision from Michael before his reinforcements arrived. Guchkov and Shulgin returned to Petrograd at just this time, blissfully unaware of the radical change in attitude towards the monarchy in their absence. Although Milyukov managed to telephone a warning to Shulgin, Guchkov grandly announced the accession of Tsar Michael to the station workers and was only with difficulty rescued from an angry mob. Milyukov's policy at the meeting with Michael was to ensure that the proceedings lasted long enough for Guchkov and Shulgin to cross town from the Warsaw Station to support his case. As arranged, Kerensky initiated the debate but naturally kept his arguments uncharacteristically brief. Milyukov rose to counter the majority view at length, earning his protagonist's complaint that 'Milyukov was stalling for time – to the obvious embarrassment of the Grand Duke'. While the accusation of deliberate prevarication was of course justified, Milyukov was genuinely carried away by the fear that Michael would be pressured into an irreversible error: 'I showed that in order to strengthen the new order, a strong governmental authority was needed and that it can only be strong when it relies on the symbol of authority to which the masses are accustomed. The monarchy serves as just such a symbol. The Provisional Government by itself, without the support of this symbol, will simply not survive until the opening of the Constituent Assembly.' It was with enormous relief that at 11.30 a.m., at the end of his speech, Milyukov greeted the arrival of Guchkov and Shulgin. The presence of comparable support for and against Michael's acceptance now threw the meeting wide open and 'in spite of our agreement, a whole torrent of speeches poured forth.'[40]

Milyukov's relief was misplaced. The Duma emissaries had been profoundly shocked by their experiences and though their political philosophies bound them to the chariot-wheels of tsarism, they were starting to feel that the monarchy simply could not survive in the present revolutionary climate. Although they did not go so far as Rodzyanko, both Guchkov and Shulgin were suffering a new crisis of confidence. When he finally brought himself to express an opinion, Guchkov suggested that the regency of Michael might be more feasible than his accession to the throne. Milyukov's bearing switched from guarded confidence to near-despair as he realised that the support for which he had waited was proving unexpectedly feeble. Shocked that Guchkov should lend his support so 'weakly and lifelessly' and Shulgin remain completely dumb, 'Milyukov seemed unwilling or unable to stop talking. This man, usually so polite and self-controlled, would not let anybody else speak, interrupted those who tried to answer him, cut off Rodzyanko, Kerensky, everyone ... White as a sheet, his face bluish-grey from lack of sleep, completely hoarse from making speeches in barracks and at street meetings, he croaked and wheezed.' After some two hours of debate, the speeches stuttered to a close. The Grand Duke (who had made no comment) begged leave to think alone for a few minutes, then returned to ask Rodzyanko and Lvov to accompany him. It was natural that Michael should turn to Rodzyanko, for this combination had been seeking dynastic solutions to the crisis since the first hours of the Revolution. As throughout the Third and Fourth Dumas, it was the Octobrist vote which proved crucial to the political balance. Ironically, it was the voice of Rodzyanko, a monarchist who could not envisage tsarism in the context of revolutionary 1917, which decided the issue: 'It was quite clear to us that the Grand Duke would have reigned only a few hours. This would have led to colossal bloodshed in the capital, which would have degenerated into general civil war ... The Grand Duke asked me outright whether I could guarantee his life if he acceded to the throne and I had to answer in the negative.' For the second time in a week Michael declined the responsibilities of Tsar. To the unconcealed delight of Kerensky and Konovalov and the despair of Milyukov and Guchkov, the Grand Duke announced his decision to refuse the crown offered by his brother.[41]

The legal niceties were concluded with almost indecent haste. Nekrasov had actually come to the meeting with a draft refusal and the afternoon was spent with Nabokov, Shulgin and the state lawyer B.E. Nolde drawing up the definitive document. The message of the act of renunciation was clear:

> I have taken a firm decision to assume the Supreme Power only in the event that such is the will of our great people, upon whom it devolves by a general vote through their representatives in a Constituent Assembly ... I ask all citizens of the Russian state to pay allegiance to the Provisional Government, which has come into being at the initiative of the State Duma and which is endowed with full power until such time as the Constituent Assembly ... , by its decision on the form of government, expresses the will of the people.

By the evening of 3 March 1917, the initial process of revolution was complete: the tsarist government had collapsed, the monarchy had abdicated (ostensibly to await the judgement of the people), and their authority had been transferred to the new Provisional Government.[42]

The rivalry for leadership of the parliamentary moderates which had been such an obsessive feature of the wartime Duma continued relentlessly through the February Revolution. The revolutionary upsurge which dictated the formation of the Duma Provisional Committee and its development into the Provisional Government also prompted a qualitative evolution from the Octobrist control of the former to Kadet hegemony of the latter. The intermediate 'parity phase' was the period of the commissars: of the twenty-eight commissars named by *Izvestia*, ten were Kadets, nine Octobrists, seven Progressists and two Centrists. The Kadet takeover was first expressed in the composition of a twenty-man Tauride Palace Commission established on 1 March to run the 'citadel of the Revolution': excluding the eight technical staff, nine of its twelve members were Kadet deputies, and not one was Octobrist.[43] The writing was on the wall for the Octobrists. At the personal level, the shift meant the declining authority of Rodzyanko and the rising power of Milyukov. Rodzyanko's position deteriorated because the anonymous developments of the revolutionary crisis were compounded by his own failings. He alienated his moderate colleagues by his determination to claim dictatorship over the revolution. His exaggerated claims first deceived and then infuriated the army High Command. In a circular to army commanders on 3 March, Alexeyev expressed the belief that 'there is no frankness or sincerity in the communications of Rodzyanko' and he was soon bitterly reproaching himself for allowing Rodzyanko to dupe him: 'I can never forgive myself for believing in the sincerity of certain persons and for following their advice by sending the army-group commanders the telegram concerning the Emperor's abdication.' But for all his bombast, Rodzyanko demonstrated clear incapacity to live up to his own inflated claims. Milyukov was to accuse him of political cowardice, notably in the incident with the drunken officers on 2 March and at the meeting with Grand Duke Michael on 3 March. Transparently irresolute once his various dynastic schemes had collapsed, Rodzyanko made many more enemies than decisions. Duma politicians, soldiers and insurgents alike resented the magisterial tones and mocked the increasing political irrelevance of the self-appointed dictator of the Revolution.[44]

Conversely, despite his notable defeat over Michael's acceptance of the crown, Milyukov was the only moderate leader to retain and enhance his political stature through the hectic and exhausting days of the February Revolution. His parliamentary opponents could not match his nerve and stamina. The Progressists Efremov and Konovalov had no thought of independent action over this period and shamelessly indicated Milyukov when asked their opinion of any action to be taken. The left Kadets split on the first day of revolution: Nekrasov opted for a military dictatorship while a group led by Adzhemov demanded the Duma take power at once. Sukhanov was in no doubt of Milyukov's predominance:

> Milyukov was at this time the central figure, the spirit and backbone of all bourgeois political circles ... Without him all bourgeois and Duma circles would at that moment have constituted a chaotic mass and without him there would have been no bourgeois policy at all in the first period of the revolution. This was how his role was evaluated by everyone, independently of party, and how he himself evaluated it ... I always considered this fateful man to be head and shoulders above all his colleagues in the Progressive Bloc.[45]

Milyukov fostered the general spirit of resentment towards Rodzyanko in a campaign to exclude his rival from the Provisional Government. It was possible to argue that for Rodzyanko, a Zemstvo-Octobrist, to become the premier of the revolutionary Provisional Government would in any case have been unrepresentative and undiplomatic. At the same time, Rodzyanko's ambitions and formidable *amour propre* would not permit him to accept a lessser position. When the membership list was finally published on 3 March, it was Prince Lvov who headed the new government. Lvov's premiership had certain advantages: representing 'society Russia' and the patriotic war effort, his leadership was calculated to reassure Russia's Allies and dispose them towards early diplomatic recognition of the Provisional Government; as a right Kadet, his position in the party spectrum made him an acceptable centre of the coalition in power; and his distaste for party politics both suggested a departure from the sordid politickings of the pre-revolutionary period and intimated to Milyukov that he would represent no threat to his own domination of the cabinet. Lvov's campaign for the premiership was conducted, almost despite the candidate, by Milyukov and the Kadets. Lvov made no efforts to press his candidacy and indeed only bothered to turn up at the Tauride Palace on the afternoon of 1 March. For Milyukov, the overriding concern was not the promotion of Lvov but the exclusion of Rodzyanko.[46]

Milyukov made sure that Rodzyanko was unable to make political capital out of his presidencies of the Duma and Provisional Committee. At first Rodzyanko may not have fully comprehended his political ruin. Chernov mockingly detailed Rodzyanko's conception of his future role:

> The fact that the Government preferred to do without him was to him an added excuse for imagining that he had been placed *above* the Government ... Rodzyanko became confirmed in his pose and psychology of 'progenitor' ... This Government was merely a ministry which might resign; then power would revert to its original source, to the Provisional Committee, and to its President Rodzyanko. According to this idea, the members of the Provisional Committee were actually kinds of 'sovereign-rulers'.

If Rodzyanko believed this in early March, he was soon smartly disabused. Milyukov attacked with all the formidable legalism he could muster. At a Kadet Central Committee meeting late on 3 March it was resolved that 'the Provisional Committee of the Duma be kept in an inactive state'. Rodzyanko forlornly described his defeat in his memoirs: 'The project of the President of the State Duma was that the Duma would be the bearer of supreme authority and the body to which the Provisional Government would be responsible. This plan was resolutely opposed primarily by the leaders of the Kadet party who simply did not want an operative Duma so they could employ complete power themselves.' As Chernov remarked, 'unfortunately for Rodzianko, Prince Lvov, Kerensky and the others immediately turned their backs on the institution which had created their government, or rather tossed it aside like a ladder – once useful but now in the way.' As ever, Rodzyanko was trapped by constitutional forms. The President of the Duma proved unable to prolong his political authority through or after the Revolution, and was instead excluded from the Provisional Government into prestigious impotence.[47]

Milyukov was not of course undermining one would-be dictator of the Revolution out of political altruism, he was after that power for himself. When appealing so hysterically for the retention of the monarchy on 3 March, Milyukov emphasised the necessity of a symbol or axis of traditional authority to stabilise the revolutionary situation; otherwise the Provisional Government 'will turn out to be a fragile boat which will sink in the ocean of mass disturbances'. So upset was Milyukov about Michael's refusal that he decided to quit the new government and was only dissuaded by a Kadet deputation led by Nabokov and Vinaver. Yet after the double abdication, there remained only one such axis of authority acceptable to a broad spectrum of society – the Duma. Even the Kadet Central Committee had a majority supporting the constitutional responsibility of the Provisional Government to the Duma but Milyukov now insisted that 'the convening of the Duma would be pointless since its composition was so bourgeois that it would attract attacks from extreme elements bent on its overthrow ... [and] given the current state of the country, the government needed to command absolute plenitude of power including legislation.' Milyukov's drive for power involved the political exclusion of his principal rival for authority over the Revolution and the suspension of the only elected national assembly available until the convening of the Constituent Assembly.[48]

In the long term, Milyukov's victory was to benefit him not at all. In his obsession to exclude Rodzyanko from the premiership, Milyukov was too quick to settle on the first alternative candidate who seemed malleable. Lvov proved a broken reed over subsequent months and a source of perpetual regret to Milyukov. In later years Milyukov admitted that 'during the formation of the Provisional Government, I spent twenty-four hours ... pushing Prince G.E. Lvov against the candidacy of M.V. Rodzyanko, and now I believe I made a big mistake: Rodzyanko would have been more suitable.' Similarly, by asserting the complete independence of the Provisional Government from external control or jurisdiction, Milyukov promoted an executive more constitutionally unresponsible than that of the last tsar and contributed to the seepage of political ballast which was to allow the new ship of state to drift into the power of the Left. Milyukov had coined the phrase 'fragile boat' to describe the Provisional Government but he rejected every means of increasing its seaworthiness in order to retain command. The decision was not only selfish but short-sighted: when the 'fragile boat' foundered, a significant proportion of the responsibility and blame was directly Milyukov's.[49]

But for the moment the power was Milyukov's. To lend credibility to the concept of collective leadership, the heads of all three moderate parties received cabinet office. Milyukov became Foreign Minister, a post 'long intended for me both by the public and by my comrades'.

Konovalov was an automatic choice as Minister of Trade and Industry. Guchkov became Minister of War and, when no other suitable candidate could be found, Minister for the Navy too. However Guchkov's position among the most right-wing of the ministers offered little chance of effectively challenging Milyukov, while the likelihood of the Revolution shifting further left augured the forcible removal of Guchkov from the government in the near future. His political self-confidence had been shaken, the Octobrist Union was in tatters, like Milyukov he seriously considered resigning from the Provisional Government after Michael's refusal of the crown, and his listless defeatist attitude was in marked contrast to the 'Young Turk' of earlier years. Milyukov professed great disappointment in Guchkov: 'I had hoped to find an ally in him but ... he kept to the sidelines and did not often participate in cabinet sessions ... This is partly explained by his ill-health but the weakening of his will must be explained mainly by his pessimism over what had happened ... I considered that it was still possible to fight but he did not support me in the struggle.' On the basis of personality, there could be no doubt that the leadership of the Provisional Government was Kadet.[50]

The composition and complexion of the Provisional Government were a tribute to the expertise of a politician adept at leading from behind. Although the ministers, like the commissars they replaced, were selected almost entirely from the Progressive Bloc, politics dictated some surprising omissions. Both a party leader and one of the four commissars to the Ministry of Interior, Efremov still failed to secure a ministerial portfolio (for the Interior was already reserved for Lvov). Thus both great rivals to Milyukov in the years preceding 1917, Rodzyanko and Efremov, failed to make the Provisional Government. Bublikov, whose enterprise in seizing the Ministry of Transport initiated the 'commissar phase', was compelled to hand over to the political appointment Nekrasov. Even the Kadets had to make sacrifices. Although the Kadet party, so rich in the legal profession, confidently expected to appoint the Minister of Justice, both Maklakov (already one of three Justice commissars) and Nabokov were squeezed out of the cabinet (and were expected to rest content with the posts of, respectively, ambassador to France and head of the government chancellery). The tactical need to mollify the Soviet by concessions to the Left was admitted at a very early stage even by the right-winger Shulgin: 'If power is thrust on us, we must seek support by enlarging the Progressive Bloc to the left. I would invite Kerensky as Minister of Justice, let us say ... Right now this post has no importance but we must snatch its leaders from the revolution. Among them Kerensky is really the only one ... It is much better to have him with us than against us.' In the event both leaders of the Duma Left were offered posts and although Chkheidze refused the Ministry of Labour on principle, Kerensky decided to accept the Ministry of Justice.[51]

There were unexpected appearances in the cabinet as well as surprise absences, particularly the appointment of M.I. Tereshchenko as Minister of Finance. Indeed so bizarre was the choice of this obscure sugar millionaire from the Ukraine that the clandestine influence of freemasonry has been advanced as the only explanation. It does seem likely that an original masonic *troika* of Kerensky, Nekrasov and Tereshchenko had such recruitment success over the course of 1916 that by the time of the February Revolution Lvov, Konovalov and Guchkov, as well as the founder-members (together with other prominent moderates like Maklakov and Efremov) shared a masonic allegiance. Milyukov and his Kadet circle were firmly, even militantly, anti-masonic, indignantly refusing offers of membership. On this basis a dangerous schism existed within the Provisional Government from the outset between the Milyukov 'establishment' and the masonic 'opposition'. Elaborate secrecy surrounding the topic means that there are conspicuously more questions than answers about the masonic role. On the one hand, masonic influence is so sensational an example of the conspiracy theory in history that its importance may well have been exaggerated. The ostensible lack of Okhrana coverage (though a suspiciously complete lacuna) would also suggest a minor role for freemasonry. At the same time, masonic testimony is still awaiting publication. In 1956, for example, Kerensky and E.D. Kuskova entrusted detailed accounts of masonic activities to their literary executors with strict instructions not to release the manuscripts for thirty years. Until this and similar evidence is forthcoming, one of the most tantalising aspects of the Russian Revolution must remain a topic for speculation.[52]

In early March 1917 nothing could dim Milyukov's triumph. The range of the Provisional Government ran from the Trudoviks to the Centrists, with the right Kadet position constituting the political axis. Of the twelve ministers in the cabinet, four were to the left of the Milyukov Kadets – Kerensky, Konovalov, Nekrasov and Tereshchenko – and three were to the right – Guchkov, Godnev and Vladimir Lvov. Moreover the five right Kadets – Milyukov, George Lvov, Shingarev, Rodichev and the editor of *Russkia Vedomosti*, A.A. Manuilov – occupied a commanding role through numerical strength. In competition, the Progressists could muster only two (Konovalov and Tereshchenko), the Octobrists two (Guchkov and Godnev), and there was one each for the Trudoviks (Kerensky), left Kadets (Nekrasov) and Centre (Vladimir Lvov). In the course of the formation of the Provisional Government, Milyukov had engineered a cabinet of which he personally was the only pivot.

In the space of a single breathless week, from Friday 24 February to Friday 3 March 1917, more had been achieved politically and constitutionally than during the entire Duma period. The arid intervening years between 1905 and 1917 when principles were held in abeyance and compromise for survival had been the hallmark of the moderates were over. The politics of restraint adopted by the moderate majority over the last years of tsarist harassment and intimidation had fortuitously paid off. The Kadet leadership of the moderates which had evolved over the course of the war was confirmed and strengthened in the character and composition of the new revolutionary government. Although the February Revolution was a classic case of 'Those behind cried "Forward" and those before cried "Back!"', the most reluctant of revolutionaries had none the less muddled through. Hopes for the future of Russia ran high as the Provisional Government, the moderates in power, faced the challenge of revolution.

8 Epilogue

The intimidating confrontation of tsarism and revolution in early twentieth-century Russia briefly created a parliamentary no-man's land where the political moderates learned to contrive a precarious existence. Menaced by the Red revolution of the country and the Black revolution of the Tsar, the moderate course depended ultimately on the range and quality of its national support. Despite understandable moderate diffidence on the subject, the Okhrana provides irrefutable testimony of the numerical and organisational weakness of the moderate parties. The Progressists were more a parliamentary pressure-group than a genuine national movement. The Octobrists, shocked by their schism of late 1913, abandoned politics en masse for service in the war effort. Every party congress or conference provided more evidence of the persistent debilitating decline in the moderates' provincial membership and public role. Even the Kadet party, relatively the most healthy of the moderates, could at best survive only in the cities and towns, compromising a 'Kadet Archipelago' within the Russian Empire; at worst, the party was effectively reduced to the confines of Petrograd and Moscow. Although precise figures about party membership are impossible to acquire, it seems reasonable to hazard that active support for the moderate parties was down to a few thousand by the eve of the February Revolution.[1]

This national collapse was to a large extent not the fault of the moderates themselves. Sustained Okhrana persecution and harassment undoubtedly contributed to falling membership. More alarmingly still, political concern on the part of broad sectors of the populace evaporated so quickly that after 1914 Bublikov could remark that,

> What interest was still retained in politics bore a purely sporting character. The public observed with complete political impassivity, though not without curiosity ... The State Duma definitely enjoyed no support in the country. The government could dissolve it whenever it wished and in the country not even the suggestion of protest was heard ... Every party life declined – and not because it was being killed off by police persecution but because interest in them had fallen away.[2]

If the parties of the Right, heavily subsidised and supported by the government, were unable to retain their membership, it was little wonder that the politically and financially vulnerable moderates suffered so grievously. The experience of the Duma period seemed to confirm the jeremiads of the pessimists among the moderates: Russian society was insufficiently mature and politically sophisticated to sustain a constitutional order over any extended period, particularly under fire from traditional authority.

The response of the moderates to the decline of what had in 1905–6 been projected as a 'Third Course' between tsarism and revolution polarised into mutually incompatible approaches. The left wing pursued a more radical, even militant, policy towards tsarism to win converts for the moderate cause. Unfortunately, these recruitment drives directed at the peasantry, proletariat and parties of the Left typically encountered either impenetrable political indifference or ideological commitments already too deep-rooted to contest. As a result, the few recruitment successes chalked up by the left moderates were almost exclusively at the expense of other moderates. The Kadets proved the most uninhibited political cannibals, for example in feeding off the corpse of Octobrism after late 1913 (although the Progressists also fared well). The limitations of what amounted to an exercise in 'poaching' are self-evident: the moderates only indulged in competing for their own supporters because they had no success in expanding that support; unable to break out of traditional confines, the moderate parties were reduced to squabbling over the diminishing territory they still held.

Unhappy about the left direction of recruitment but perversely cheered by its failures, the right wing of the moderates protested to the point of threatening a partition of the moderate camp. Though less than beneficial to an already beleaguered movement, the differences of opinion were less damaging than at first appears. Throughout the almost continuous dialogue of the left and right wings (often expressed through the traditional rivalry of Moscow and Petrograd), the moderates' high level of toleration ensured that irrevocable schism was averted. Moreover, almost every Russian party experienced some level of debate between left-orientated militants and more right-orientated moderates: over the period 1914–17 all three moderate parties (not to mention the Nationalists and Rights) underwent the experience. To this extent, the Social-Democratic record was not so much unique as precocious: the career of every Russian party featured some individual version of the Bolshevik-Menshevik schism.

Given the impracticality of the manoeuvres of the left, it was the right wing which dominated the policies of the moderate camp. The Vyborg complex disposed the majority of moderates to shun revolution from below in favour of reform from above. By 1914 the moderates were convinced that while a democratic relationship with the country was a desirable luxury, a healthy understanding with the government was a stark necessity. Right into the February Revolution, the moderates repeatedly asked themselves 'Who will win?'. With the answer always the same, it was only responsible for moderates, out of self-interest and for the long-term survival of the Duma, to accommodate themselves to the Tsar, if necessary at the expense of the nation. Though their supporters outside the Duma (and even more so the wider public) agitated for more vigorous opposition to tsarism, the moderates within the Duma settled for a policy of at very least *détente* with the government. From 1914 to 1917 the moderates were campaigning not for revolution, not even for fundamental reform, but for the maintenance of the political and constitutional *status quo*.

The Progressive Bloc was the institutional manifestation of this right-moderate philosophy. The Bloc represented a moderate offer to tsarism to broaden its support and appeal for the political and military benefit of the war effort. The Bloc Programme of August 1915, pre-dating the October Manifesto in the modesty of its political demands, disappointed and angered the recently-activated wider political movement. The Bloc's resounding failure in September 1915, which seemed to remove any grounds for the survival of this fragile moderate consensus, must be seen not only as the most critical episode in wartime relations between government and Duma but as a turning-point in the Kadet drive for power. Milyukov's policy of winning the respect and eventual political acquiescence of the government by the impressive unanimity of the moderate Bloc combined a concept of civic responsibility with a large measure of Kadet self-interest. The large number of varied participants in the Bloc blurred party principles at a time when Milyukov was attempting to cover himself against the forthright criticism of the Progressists and the Kadet left wing. Moreover, by not admitting the Duma right wing, the Bloc constituted a more left-orientated institution than the Duma as a whole: the exclusion of all Right deputies and most Nationalists had the effect of drawing the axis of the Bloc some 65 places to the left of the Duma axis (see diagram, p.15). Milyukov was the champion of the Progressive Bloc in defeat, keeping the Bloc alive as a Kadet device to secure leadership of the Duma by offsetting the natural Octobrist hegemony. But the retention of the Bloc for the eighteen months after August 1915 had a high price. To the left moderates, Octobrist membership of the Bloc was paid for by the adoption of a quasi-Octobrist policy. In Chernov's judicious phrase, 'the law of all opposition blocs is that ... they adopt the programme of the least oppositional party in the bloc'. Milyukov's Bloc shackled the frustrated Progressists and left Kadets to the conservative Zemstvo-Octobrists and Progressive Nationalists. As a result, Bloc action was readily sacrificed to unanimity, reducing the official utterances and policies of the moderates to an abysmally low level. At a time when the moderates should have spoken out constructively, notably during early 1916, they were gagged by the Bloc Right. This deafening silence, variously interpreted outside the Duma as cowardice or complicity, alienated existing support (notably the public organisations) and first dismayed and then exasperated wider public opinion.[3]

The right-moderate philosophy prevailed despite the lack of any evidence that the responsible behavior of the Bloc was winning over the government. Revolution was becoming a recurrent nightmare and as early as August 1915 Sazonov could remark that 'if everything is arranged decently and an opening offered, the Cadets will be the first to come to an agreement. Miliukov is a thorough-going bourgeois and dreads a social revolution worst of all. The majority of the Cadets are trembling for their capital.' Confronted by a bald choice between tsarism and revolution, the moderates had no hesitation in preferring the former.[4] At a less apocalyptic level, the moderates relied on the government to protect their political position. Government manipulation of the elections to the Third Duma in 1907 had falsified the complexion of the Duma to the disadvantage of the left moderates; ten years later, public opinion had moved so far left that a democratic vote would deprive the moderate camp of both its numerical strength and pivotal position in the Duma. Today's moderates would be tomorrow's right wing. The Okhrana believed that the Kadets, for example, were too far Right to retain any of their four seats in Moscow in any Fifth Duma elections (and three of these had only been captured from the Octobrists in 1912).[5] Over ten years the change in the position of the Duma had been dramatic: in 1906 the First Duma had been a society 'city of refuge' against the tsarist *revanche*; by 1916 the Fourth Duma had become a tsarist 'city of refuge' for the moderates against oppositional society. With the Tsar now their sole protection against political ruin, the moderates' only resort in the increasingly volatile social situation was to persuade the government by good behaviour to turn the Fourth Duma into a Russian 'Long Parliament'. Their last card was that, given the trend of public opinion (which even the gerrymandering ingenuity of Nikolai Maklakov would be tested to pervert), the Fourth Duma was the most amenable national assembly the government was likely to get. In the forlorn hope that the government might settle for an extension of the Fourth Duma rather than risk either a Fifth Duma or the provocative suppression of the Duma altogether, the moderates' counsel of despair was reliance on this perverse community of self-interest with tsarism.

Unfortunately for the moderates, it was tragically plain that they needed tsarism far more than tsarism needed them. With an effective monopoly of legislation, full executive authority and declared ambitions for financial independence, the government could and did operate during the war with minimal recourse to the Duma. The bureaucracy shunned the Duma as a recruiting-ground for government personnel: of the forty-three ministerial incumbents over the five years before 1917, only two (Alexei Khvostov and Protopopov) were taken from the Duma. 'Fraternisation' between moderates in government and society was impermissible since Stolypin's decrees of 1906 and 1908. Unofficial contacts between the Duma and the government that did periodically occur were at ministerial initiative and invariably designed for cabinet or bureaucratic advantage. The purge of moderate elements within the bureaucracy was relentless: civil service cadres sympathetic to the moderates were removed and personalities benevolent towards the Duma disappeared from the Council of Ministers. In relations with the Duma, the government never lost the upper hand. Kept well-informed by the Okhrana, the government knew that the moderate cause in general and the Progressive Bloc in particular was a political confidence-trick, a hopeful exercise in sustained bluff. Armed with superior political intelligence, the tsarist establishment was always in control, cynically appreciating that the moderates were prisoners of their past triumphs and tragedies. Octobrist policy was still dominated by the ambition to return to the golden age of privilege in the early Third Duma; the Kadets were obsessed by a determination to avoid another Vyborg fiasco. With this in mind, the government dangled the 'carrot' of alliance before the Octobrists and brandished the 'stick' of dissolution at the Kadets whenever crisis loomed. Through the period 1914–17 this government ploy proved a reliable, almost foolproof means of bringing the moderates and therefore the Duma to heel. The relationship between the moderates and tsarism was of necessity on the part of the moderates but expediency, convenience or even charity on the government side.

By comparison with the irresistible, almost supra-human dynamism of war and revolution, the contribution of the moderates could at best be tactical. While the forces of tsarism and revolution were still massing, unable or unwilling to precipitate the final confrontation, the moderates could still tip the balance. Having lost all credibility as a third force in Russian political life, the moderates fell back on a policy of 'trimming' against the greater danger. When tsarism was on the offensive, the moderates headed the defensive response of wider society. When the country's mood was threatening and the government appeared hard-pressed, the moderates exerted their influence to restrain the opposition movement. Thus, at different times, the moderates made contributions both to protecting the revolution from tsarism and to saving tsarism from revolution.

In practice, the ambivalent trimming policy of the moderates, invariably motivated by healthy self-interest, benefited no one. The mounting irritation of the government and nation became directed at the moderate-ruled Duma, which seemed intent on promoting the postponement of the inevitable dénouement purely in the interests of its own prestige and authority. By late 1916 both principal protagonists (for quite opposite reasons) had lost confidence in the Duma moderates, and the value of the existing national assembly to either side was seriously in doubt. 'Moderates' in their principles and position in the party spectrum, the Kadets, Octobrists and Progressists pursued a policy of attempting to 'moderate' the increasingly explosive relationship between the country and its government. In so doing, they drew the fire of both sides. Trapped between tsarism and revolution, the dilemma of the Russian moderates became a predicament admitting no constructive solution.

By early 1917 the moderates were dwarfed by the looming confrontation between tsarism and revolution. The obsessive party politics of the moderates over the last years of tsarism were to a degree a morale-boosting exercise to conceal both from others and themselves the unpalatable truth that they were at the mercy of external factors outside their control. Within the Bloc and Kadet party, Milyukov spent infinitely more time and energy on the routine maintenance of morale than facing the near-insoluble fundamental issues of the day. By February 1917 the moderates in Russia had become as isolated and fatalistic – and as far from assuming state power – as any émigré revolutionary colony in Paris or Geneva. Partly by external constraint (of which the Okhrana's confinement of 'politics' to the Tauride Palace was the most overt feature), partly from their own lack of resources, the moderates were reduced to the level of political émigrés *within* Russia. In this spectacle of individuals set apart by superior talents from a mediocre society but doomed to ineffectuality by a combination of denied opportunities and personal inadequacies, it is tempting to discern a reincarnation in political form of the traditional phenomenon of the 'superfluous man'.

Pressed into power by a February Revolution which could find no other alternative to tsarism, the moderates enjoyed poor prospects. Even Milyukov, for whom the Provisional Government was his crowning achievement as a politician, exhibited many of the worst faults of the moderate camp. Cruelly spotlighted by the revolutionary challenge was Milyukov's alienation from the 'man in the street'. As Chernov remarked: 'His chief weakness was a complete lack of feeling for popular, mass psychology. He was too much a man of the study, hence a doctrinaire ... He never spoke the language of the people. For him it was a tremendous and alien force.' Milyukov's characteristic of regarding the people as either malleable ignoramuses or an inhuman mob was typical of the moderates as a whole. In 1907 Milyukov had sanctimoniously quoted Gladstone in describing liberalism as 'confidence in the people' and conservatism as 'lack of confidence in the people'. By this loaded definition, the period 1905 to 1917 saw the Kadets shift from a 'liberal' outlook orientated towards mass politics to a 'conservative' psychology geared to elite politics and authority. The estrangement from the people which made such a decisive contribution to the fall of tsarism was no less a feature of the new moderate administration.[6] A related component of Milyukov's leadership was his disorientation outside the parliamentary milieu. The moderates had become seduced by the privilege and prestige afforded by what Chernov called 'that peculiar little world which in Russia more than elsewhere was isolated, protected against the pressure of the street'. It was in the exclusive club environment of the Tauride Palace, artificially maintained and increasingly out of touch with and unrepresentative of the mainstream of political life, that the moderates played out their often almost irrelevant intrigues. Like Nicholas II himself, the moderates seemed designed by nature to function within the framework of an established constitutional monarchy, which did not exist in Russia. In conversation with Vinaver in mid-1917, Kokoshkin admitted 'you and I were born to be parliamentarians but fate always places us in circumstances where the struggle must be waged along different paths. So it was in 1905–6 and so it is again now.' Milyukov hoped in March 1917 that his successful Duma career would serve as a political apprenticeship for the wider world of ministerial office but in practice he proved unable to make the transition from an established quasi-parliamentary regime to the volatile, often chaotic, world of revolution. Again typifying the moderate camp, Milyukov's later performance demonstrated that the Duma, far from being a preparation for higher things, represented the ideal environment for his style of expertise and the practical limit of his considerable but specialised talents.[7]

The moderates could not succeed where the Tsar had failed. The Duma had never been a training-ground for a Government, only for an Opposition, and an 'Opposition of His Majesty' at that. In part the responsibility lay with the tsarist government, for the Stolypin decrees which purged the state apparatus also prevented the moderates gaining the practical experience of administration which they were to need so desperately a decade later. The moderates were with rare exceptions 'men of little deeds' and woefully ignorant of the practical demands and responsibilities of national government. In 1909 Izgoyev had admitted in *Vekhi*: 'we must finally have the courage to confess that the vast majority of members of our State Dumas, with the exception of thirty or forty Kadets and Octobrists, have not shown themselves to possess the knowledge required to undertake the task of governing and reconstructing Russia.' In late 1915 Maklakov was even more pessimistic: 'we do not understand this business, we do not know the technique, and there is now no time to learn.'[8] Although conspicuously the best qualified of the Duma membership, the moderates were still no viable substitute for tsarist government, only potentially a powerful corrective. Fashioned by years in the political wilderness and with all the least attractive features of the 'opposition mentality', the moderates made their worst showing of all in the Provisional Government. Milyukov's 'fragile boat' was conspicuously underpowered and undermanned for the storms of 1917: the demands of central and local government at a time of national emergency predictably proved too burdensome for individuals without the background, training or mass support for this unaccustomed exercise of power. First reluctant and then conservative revolutionaries, the moderates inherited all the problems of tsarism with none of its resources. The February Revolution perversely saved the moderates from political oblivion and generously offered an undeserved last chance in the Provisional Government. Given the magnitude of the challenges of 1917 and the proven limitations of the moderate movement, it could only be another chance to fail.

Notes

CHAPTER 1 INTRODUCTION

1 G.G. Perets, *Tsitadel Russkoi Revolyutsii* (Petrograd, 1917), p.80; *Rech*, 5 March 1917, p.1.
2 The eight Fourth Duma deputies were Milyukov, Kerensky, Nekrasov, Konovalov, Shingarev, Godnev, V.N. Lvov and Rodichev. The two ex-deputies were Prince Lvov (First Duma) and Guchkov (Third Duma). Guchkov and Manuilov were members of the current State Council, the upper house of the Russian legislature from 1906 to 1917. Only Tereshchenko had no past or present membership of either State Duma or State Council.
3 The stenographic records of the Fourth Duma – *Gosudarstvennaya Duma: stenograficheskie otchyety, sozyv 4* (St Petersburg/Petrograd 1913–17) – will be cited hereafter as *Duma*. The following reference conventions will be observed: session (*sessia*) number in Roman numerals; sitting (*zasedanie*) in Arabic numerals, with date in parentheses; and column (*stolbets*) number(s).
4 For examples of condemnation and commiseration, see A. Goulevitch, *Czarism and Revolution* (New York, 1962), pp.238 and 253–5; and Thomas Riha, *A Russian European: Paul Miliukov in Russian Politics* (London, 1969), pp.333–47.
5 Louis Menashe, 'A Liberal with Spurs: Alexander Guchkov, a Russian Bourgeois in Politics', *Russian Review*, vol.xxvi, no.1 (1967), p.42.
6 W.G. Rosenberg, *Liberals in the Russian Revolution: the Constitutional Democratic Party, 1917–1921* (New York, 1974), pp.5–6.
7 Examples of Kadet history include I.V. Gessen, *V Dvukh Vekakh: zhiznennii otchyet* (Berlin, 1937); A.A. Kizevetter, *Na Rubezhe Dvukh Stoletii: vospominania 1881–1914* (Prague, 1929); and of course Milyukov, *Political Memoirs 1905–1917* (Ann Arbor, 1967) and *Histoire de Russie* (Paris, 1933), vol. 3: 'Réformes, Réaction, Révolutions'.
8 The most authoritative Soviet studies of the topic are E.D. Chermensky, 'Borba Klassov i Partii v chetvertom gosudarstvennom dume 1912–17 gg.' (unpublished doctoral thesis, Moscow State University, 1947); V.S. Dyakin, *Russkaya Burzhuazia i Tsarism v gody Pervoi Mirovoi Voiny 1914–17 gg.* (Leningrad, 1967); V.Y. Laverychev, *Po Tu Storonu Barrikad: iz istorii borby moskovskoi burzhuazii s revolyutsei* (Moscow, 1967); and E.N. Burdzhalov, *Vtoraya Russkaya Revolyutsia*, 2 vols (Moscow 1967 and 1971).
9 Soviet archival references will be abbreviated according to the standard conventions: Repository (by initials); fund (*fond*) number, with designation in parentheses; catalogue (*opis*) number in Roman numerals; item or file (*delo*) number in Arabic numerals; and page number(s).

10 TsGIA, 1276 (Council of Ministers), x, 7, pp.1–476 (hereafter *Council*).
11 R.J. Johnson, 'Zagranichnaya Agentura: the tsarist political police in Europe', *Journal of Contemporary History*, vii, 1–2 (1972), pp.221–42.
12 For example, in Ronald Hingley, *The Russian Secret Police* (London, 1970), the otherwise convincing chapter on the period 1908–17 is perversely called 'The Decline and Fall of the Okhrana', a title at odds with the narrative.
13 Hingley, pp.79–115; Johnson, pp.233–7; Norman Cohn, *Warrant for Genocide* (London, 1967), pp.84–137.
14 Alexander Solzhenitsyn, *Gulag Archipelago: Two* (London, 1975), p.10.
15 V.M. Chernov, *The Great Russian Revolution* (New York, 1936), p.448; the files of the tsarist political police, located in TsGAOR, 102 (Department of Police), will be cited as *Okhrana*.

CHAPTER 2 UNION SACRÉE

 1 V.N. Kokovtsov, *Out of My Past: Memoirs* (Stanford, 1935), pp.283 and 418; *Krasnii Arkhiv* (Moscow, 1922–41), xlvii/xlviii, p.43.
 2 V.P. Semennikov (ed.), *Monarkhia pered Krusheniem* (Moscow, 1927), pp.92–5; *Padenie Tsarskogo Rezhima*, Proceedings of the Special Investigatory Commission of the Provisional Government, ed. P.E. Shchegolev (Moscow-Leningrad, 1924–7) in seven volumes (hereafter *Padenie*), vols ii, pp.435–8 (testimony of Shcheglovitov); iii, pp.133–5 and v, pp.193–6 (N. Maklakov); and vi, pp.305–7 and 358–9 (Milyukov).
 3 Balashev's letter of 14 July 1914 is in *Council*, pp.1–2; *Duma*, ii, pp.1 and 3.
 4 P.L. Bark, 'Vospominania', *Vozrozhdenie*, Apr 1965, p.87; *Padenie*, vi, pp.307–8 (Milyukov); the official Kadet account is *Otchyet Partii Narodnoi Svobody: voennie sessii* (Petrograd, 1916), p.10 (hereafter *Kadet*).
 5 K.A. Krivoshein, *A.V. Krivoshein 1857–1921: ego znachenie v istorii Rossii nachala XX veka* (Paris, 1973), pp.148–51 and 210–15.
 6 Krivoshein, pp.152–3, 290 and 219–21; S.I. Shidlovsky, *Vospominania 1861–1922*, 2 vols (Berlin, 1923), ii, p.21; M. Paléologue, *An Ambassador's Memoirs 1914–1917*, 3 vols (London, 1923–5), i, pp.272–3; *Council*, p.4.
 7 *Council*, pp.4 and 9; *Kadet*, p.10; *Padenie*, vi, p.308 (Milyukov).
 8 Statistics computed from index (*ukazatel*) to *Duma* (Petrograd 1915), pp.19–24.
 9 *Utro Rossii*, 20 July 1914, p.1; *Golos Moskvy*, 18 July 1914, p.2; P.N. Miliukov, *Political Memoirs*, p.305; *Duma*, ii, 26 July 1914, p.1.
10 R. Pearson, 'The Russian Moderate Parties in the Fourth State Duma 1912–17', (unpublished PhD thesis, Durham, 1973), pp.91–101 and 127–31; also Krivoshein, p. 148.
11 P.A. Buryshkin, *Moskva Kupecheskaya* (New York, 1954), p.284; G.A. Hosking, *The Russian Constitutional Experiment: Government and Duma 1907–14* (London, 1973), pp.189–95; Laverychev, pp.80–108.
12 *Okhrana*, xv, 27–46, p.2 (Moscow report of 2 June 1914).
13 Riha, *A Russian European*, pp.207–8 and 213–14; Hosking, pp.218–20 and 237–40; V.D. Nabokov, *V.D. Nabokov and the Russian Provisional Government 1917*, ed. V.D. Medlin and S.L. Parsons (New York, 1976), pp.106–8.
14 A.F. Kerensky, *The Kerensky Memoirs: Russia and History's Turning-Point* (London, 1966), pp.128–30; *Kadet*, p.5; Vladimir I. Gurko, *Features and*

Figures of the Past: Government and Opinion in the Reign of Nicholas II (New York, 1958), p.528; Paléologue, i, pp.57–8; P.G. Kurlov, *Konets Tsarisma* (Petrograd, 1923), p.208; Chernov, p.55.

15 *Duma*, ii, 26 July 1914, pp.7–29 *passim*; Paléologue, i, pp.56 and 68–70; Kerensky, pp.132–3; *Kadet*, p.6; V.V. Shulgin, *Dni* (Belgrade, 1925), p.60.

16 Bernard Pares, *Day by Day with the Russian Army* (London, 1915), pp.10–16; Paléologue, i, pp.76–7, 84 and 108; W.E. Gleason, 'The All-Russian Union of Towns and the Politics of Urban Reform in Tsarist Russia', *Russian Review*, xxxv, 3 (July 1976), pp.291–2.

17 *Padenie*, iii, pp.302–4 and 311–12 (Goremykin) and vii, p.118 (Rodzyanko); S.D. Sazonov, *Fateful Years 1909–1916* (London, 1928), p.291; Nicolas II, *Journal Intime de Nicolas II* (Paris, 1934), entry for 19 July 1914.

18 *Padenie*, iii, pp.320–4 (Goremykin).

19 M.V. Rodzyanko, *Krushenie Imperii* (Leningrad, 1926), pp.104–6; *Okhrana*, xv, 27–46b, 1914, p.15 (report of 23 Sep 1914).

20 *Krasnii Arkhiv*, lxiv, pp.31–2 and 35–9; A.S. Badayev, *The Bolsheviks in the Tsarist Duma* (London, 1932), pp.213–17.

21 Badayev, pp.214–21; Okhrana report of 8 Nov 1914 in TsGAOR, 826 (V.F. Dzhunkovsky), i, 212, p.4; Rodzyanko, *Krushenie,* p.107; *Rech,* 6 November 1914, p.2; *Krasnii Arkhiv,* lxiv, pp.46-51

22 *Okhrana*, xv, 27–1914, pp.53–4 (4 Nov 1914); TsGAOR, 6/c, 31, pp.183–4 and 188, quoted in Chermensky, pp.478–80; TsGAOR, 523 (Kadet Party), i, 32, pp.3–12, quoted in Dyakin, p.64.

23 *Okhrana*, 307a–1914, pp.109–114 (22 Aug 1914) and xv, 27–46b, pp.11–12 (29 Aug 1914); *Council*, pp.9–10; *Utro Rossii* and *Russkia Vedomosti* (hereafter RV), 29 Aug 1914, p.1; MVD circular of 2 Sep 1914: *Okhrana*, 27–1914, p.87.

24 *Okhrana*, xv, 27–46b, pp.13–14 (17 Sep 1914) and 16–22 (22 and 24Sep 1914); and xv, 27–1914, pp.34 and 40 (30 Sep and 10 Oct 1914); *Golos Moskvy*, 17 Sep 1914, p.2.

25 *Okhrana*, xv, 27–1914, p.41 (circular); 307a–1914, p.117 (18 Oct 1914); and xv, 27–46b, p.23 (19 Oct 1914).

26 TsGIA, 1274, 547–1914, pp.10–11 and 14–20; also TsGIA, 1282 (MVD Chancellery), i, 732, pp.76–92 cited in Dyakin, p.68.

27 *Okhrana*, xv, 27–46b, 1914, p.37 (30 Nov 1914); *Padenie*, v, p.204 (N. Maklakov), Gleason, p.301.

28 Norman Stone, *The Eastern Front 1914–1917* (London, 1975), pp.66–7 and 145–50; B.A. Engelhardt, 'Vospominania' (unpublished memoirs located in manuscript department of the Lenin Library, Moscow: *Biblioteka imeni V.I. Lenina; rukopisnii otdel*, fund 218), pp.330–3 and 579–80.

29 *Padenie*, vii, p.23 (Shingarev); Paléologue, i, pp.217 and 221–2 and ii, p.21; Sir George Buchanan, *My Mission to Russia*, 2 vols (London, 1923), i, p.219; J. Hanbury-Williams, *The Emperor Nicholas II as I knew Him* (London, 1922), pp.19–20.

30 Paléologue, i, pp.223–4; Buchanan, i, p.219; Sazonov, pp.286–7.

31 TsGAOR, 523 (Kadet Party), i, 32, pp.105–21, cited in Dyakin, p.65.

32 *Okhrana*, xv, 27–46b, p.22 (9 Oct 1914); TsGAOR, 6–c, 32, pp.109–10, quoted in Chermensky, p.485.

33 *Okhrana*, xv, 27–46b, p.44 (3 Jan 1915); *Kadet*, p.11; *Birzhevia Vedomosti* (hereafter BV), 20 Jan 1915, p.4.

34 Engelhardt, pp.598–9; BV, 25 Jan 1915, pp.3 and 8; Dyakin, pp.68–9.

35 *Council*, pp.22, 25 and 29–30; *Padenie*, iii, p.305 (Goremykin).

36 *Council*, pp.19, 31 and 36; *Rech*, 21 Jan 1915, p.1; *Padenie*, vi, pp.309–11 (Milyukov) and vii, pp.21–2 and 27 (Shingarev); *Kadet*, pp.12–13; Bark, 'Vospominania', *Vozrozhdenie*, no.167 (1965), p.83.

37 *Duma*, iii, 2 (27 Jan 1915), pp.61, 54, 46, 50 and 194; and 3, p.281; *Council*, p.40; *Kadet*, p.12.

38 *Kadet*, p.9; TsGAOR, 6–c, 32, p.53 quoted in Chermensky, pp.480–1.

39 *Okhrana*, xvi, 27–46, pp.3–4, 5 and 12; *Krasnii Arkhiv*, lxiv, p.51; Badayev, pp.232–41; BV, 22 Jan 1915, p.3; 21 Feb 1915, p.3; and 15 Mar 1915, p.4; *Kadet*, p.13; TsGAOR, 605 (Rodzyanko), i, 70, p.1.

40 S.O. Zagorsky, *The State Control of Industry in Russia during the War* (Newhaven, 1928), pp.76–7, 82 and 87–8; Stone, pp.150–63 and 196–7; BV, 27 Feb 1915, p.4 and 7; 28 and 29 March 1915, all p.4.

41 Compare the official Kadet account in *Kadet*, pp.13–40 with the official Progressist account of Efremov, which may be located in the fund of P.P. Ryabushinsky (Lenin Library manuscript department, *fond* 260), item 4–10, pp.1–23, or in the Milyukov fund (TsGAOR, 579), item 386, pp.1–23.; also BV, 1 and 2 Apr 1915, both p.3.

42 Pares, *Day to Day*, p.157; Stone, pp.114–16; BV, 15 Feb 1915, p.4; 5 Apr 1915, p.2; and 12 May 1915, p.3.

43 Stone, pp.128–43; Progressist account, pp.2–3; note that Milyukov omits Efremov's role entirely in his own account in *Padenie*, vi, p.312.

44 Zagorsky, pp.76–7, 82 and 87–8; Dyakin, p.74; Stone, pp.160–2 and 195–201.

45 *Kadet*, p.17; Progressist account, p.3; A. Shlyapnikov, *Kanun Semnadtsatogo Goda* (Moscow, 1922–3), pp.99–100; Stone, pp.201–4; M. Philips Price, *My Three Revolutions* (London, 1969), p.36; BV, 28 and 29 May 1915, pp.8 and 3.

46 *Okhrana*, 27–1915, pp.3–6 (14 Apr 1915); 206, p.4 (29 Apr 1915); 307–a, 1915, pp.19 (27 May 1915) and 16 (4 June 1915); BV, 27 and 29 May 1915, pp. 7 and 3; *Padenie*, vi, p.312 (Milyukov).

47 The records of the Vyborg meeting are in *Krasnii Arkhiv*, lvii, pp.85–99 and the proceedings of the Vyborg trial in *Vyborgskii Protsess* (St Petersburg, 1908), pp.1–168; see also V.A. Maklakov, *The First State Duma* (Bloomington, 1964), pp.218–32; M.M. Vinaver, *Istoria Vyborgskogo Vozzvania* (Petrograd, 1917), pp.9–46; A.V. Tyrkova, *Na Putyakh k Svobode* (New York, 1952), pp.301–2 and 361–2; and Miliukov, *Political Memoirs*, pp.98–9.

48 M.O. Gershenson *et al.*, *Vekhi: sbornik statei o russkoi intelligentsii* (Moscow, 1909), p.89; for recent comment, see J. Brooks, 'Vekhi and the Vekhi Dispute', *Survey*, xix, 1(1973), pp.35–6; also P.N. Milyukov, *Vtoraya Duma* (St Petersburg, 1907), p.28.

49 *Krasnii Arkhiv*, lix, pp.110–45; also TsGAOR, 523 (Kadet Party), ii, 39, p.1; *Okhrana*, 307a–1915, p.69 (8 June 1915); and 27–1915, pp.36, 42–4 (17 June 1914) and 51 (undated).

CHAPTER 3 THE PROGRESSIVE BLOC

1 Shulgin, pp.78–9; also *Council*, pp.42–3.

2 Zagorsky, pp.38 and 83–4; BV, 23 Apr 1915, p.3.

3 Rodzyanko, *Krushenie*, pp.113–17; *Kadet*, p.16; *Okhrana*, 307a–1915, p.20 (27 May 1915); TsGIA, 669 (I.S. Klyuzhev), i, 14, p.156; Lenin Library manuscript department, 260 (P.P. Ryabushinsky), iv, 10, p.5.

4 Chermensky, p.495; *Den*, 17 July 1915, p.2; Zagorsky, pp.84–8.

5 Sazonov, pp.283–8; Rodzyanko, *Krushenie*, pp.122–3; Nicholas II, *The Letters of the Tsar to the Tsaritsa 1914–17*, ed. C.E. Vulliamy (London, 1929), p.57(cited hereafter as *Nicholas*).

6 Semennikov, *Monarkhia*, pp.96–7; Rodzyanko, *Krushenie*, pp.121–2; Kurlov, p.177; A.A. Oznobishin, *Vospominania Chlena IV Gosudarstvennoi Dumi* (Paris, 1927), p.211.

7 Rodzyanko, *Krushenie*, p.122; Milyukov, *Political Memoirs*, p.318; Sazonov, pp.284 and 288–9.

8 *Kadet*, p.19; Progressist account, pp.3 and 6; *Okhrana*, 307a–1915, pp.62 and 71–3 (9 and 11 June 1915); TsGIA, 669 (Klyuzhev), 16, p.18 and 18, pp.167–8; *Padenie*, vi, pp.312–14 (Milyukov); BV, 3 to 14 June 1915.

9 Progressist account, pp. 4 and 7–8; *Okhrana*, 307a–1915, p.73 (11 June 1915).

10 TsGAOR, 579 (Milyukov), 695, pp.1–4; TsGIA, 669 (Klyuzhev), 16, p.24; Progressist account, pp.7–9.

11 *Council*, pp.64–5; Rodzyanko, *Krushenie*, p.123; *Kadet*, pp.19–20.

12 B.B. Grave, *Burzhuazia nakanune Fevralskoi Revolyutsii* (Moscow, 1927), pp.6–10; Dyakin, p.76; BV, 26 June 1915, p.3.

13 TsGIA, 1278 (State Duma), v, 447, pp.5–187, cited in Dyakin, pp.90–1; also Shulgin, pp.67–73, and Chermensky, p.521.

14 Progressist account, p.16; *Rech*, 28 July 1915, p.2; *Duma*, iv, 4 (1 Aug 1915), 300–2 and 324; also Dyakin, pp.91 and 94 and Chermensky, p.522.

15 Grave, *Burzhuazia*, pp.19–20; BV, 13 June 1915, p.3; Paléologue, ii, p.27.

16 BV, 16, 21 and 28 June 1915, pp.3, 4 and 8 respectively; Rodzyanko, *Krushenie*, p.123; Progressist account, p.15; *Okhrana*, 27–1915, 50 (undated); TsGAOR, 523 (Kadet Party), i, 32, p.175 cited in Dyakin, p.78.

17 *Den*, 19 July 1915, p.2; Shulgin, p.62; *The Times*, 6 Oct 1915 (n/s), p.6.

18 Paléologue, ii, pp.39–40; *Duma*, iv, 2 (20 July 1915), pp.189–90.

19 Rodzyanko, *Krushenie*, p.126; *Kadet*, pp.23–4; Progressist account, pp.10–13; *Duma*, iv, 1 (19 July 1915), 72 and 90–1, and 2 (20 July 1915), 189–96; Shulgin, p.63; *Okhrana*, 307a–1915, p.145 (17 Aug 1915).

20 Progressist account, pp.13–14; *Kadet*, p.28; *Den*, 22 and 23 July 1915, both p.2.

21 *Duma*, iv, 3 (28 July 1915), 233–6; *Kadet*, p.28; *Okhrana*, 307a–1915, pp.128–31 (undated); *Council*, p.89.

22 *Okhrana*, 307a–1915, pp.134 and 135 (5 and 6 Aug 1915); *Den*, 3, 6 and 21 August 1915, all p.2; *Kadet*, pp.29–30; see also A. Grunt, 'Progressivnii Blok', *Voprosi Istorii*, 1945: 3/4, p.109.

23 Vladimir Gurko, pp.555 and 571–2; *Den*, 14 Aug 1915, p.4.

24 *Padenie*, vi, pp.315–6 (Milyukov); *Den*, 11, 12 and 14 Aug 1915, pp.2, 4 and 3; *Kadet*, pp.29–30 and 35–6; *Okhrana*, 307a–1915, p.135 (undated).

25 *Krasnii Arkhiv*, l/li, pp.122–37; Milyukov's original copy of the Programme is in TsGAOR, 579 (Milyukov), item 385; *Okhrana*, 307a–1915, p.136; Shulgin, p.65; Miliukov, *Political Memoirs*, pp.329–36.

26 *Padenie*, vi, p.318 (Milyukov); *Kadet*, p.28; note Milyukov's attempt to play down the Moscow initiative in *Rech*, 15 Aug 1915, p.4.

27 *Kadet*, p.132; *Den*, 17 and 19 Aug 1915, pp.2 and 1; *Okhrana*, 343, 4, p.28 (17 Aug 1915) cited in Dyakin, pp.104–5.

28 Okhrana report located in TsGAOR, 826 (Dzhunkovsky), i, 212, p.5; *Den*, 22 and 28 Aug 1915, both p.2; also Grave, *Burzhuazia*, pp.22–3.

29 *Den*, 18 Aug 1915, p.4; *Okhrana*, 307a–1915, p.149 (21 Aug 1915).

30 *Krasnii Arkhiv*, l/li, pp.137–8, 145–9 and 159; *Kadet*, pp.32–6; Progressist account, p.9; Vladimir Gurko, pp.572–6; M. Cherniavsky, *Prologue to Revolution* (London, 1967), pp.180–218; *Padenie*, vi, p.317 (Milyukov).

31 Sazonov, p.291; Nicolas II, *Journal Intime*, entry for 20 Sep 1914; Pierre Gilliard, *Thirteen Years at the Russian Court* (London, 1921), p.136; Hanbury-Williams, p.50; Maklakov, 'On the Fall of Tsardom', *Slavonic and East European Review*, xviii, 52, p.76; Countess Kleinmichel, *Memories of a Shipwrecked World* (London, 1923), p.199.

32 Krivoshein, pp.237–8; Paléologue, ii, pp.41, 60 and 77; Vladimir Gurko, pp.555 ff.; M.T. Florinsky, *The End of the Russian Empire* (London, 1961), pp.72–6; Engelhardt, pp.600 and 609; Sazonov, p.290.

33 Cherniavsky, pp.91–4 and 166–7; Sazonov, pp.291–5; Paléologue, ii, p.58; Buchanan, i, p.238; *Padenie*, vii, p.220 (Shcherbatov); V.N. Shakhovskoi, *Sic Transit Gloria Mundi 1893–1917* (Paris, 1952), p.126.

34 Vladimir Gurko, pp.573 and 567–8; Buryshkin, p.319; Paléologue, ii, pp.60–1; George T. Marye, *Nearing the End in Imperial Russia* (Philadelphia, 1930), p.241; Semennikov, *Monarkhia*, pp.267–8 and 270–5; *Padenie*, vii, pp.32–3 (Shingarev); *Den*, 23 Aug 1915, p.4.

35 Okhrana report of 29 Aug 1915 quoted in Grave, *Burzhuazia*, p.29.

36 *Arkhiv Russkoi Revolyutsii*, ed. I.V. Gessen, 21 vols (Berlin, 1922–6), xviii, pp.119–24 (notes of cabinet secretary A.N. Yakhontov); Shidlovsky, ii, pp.37–40; *Padenie*, vi, pp.316–7 (Milyukov); *Den*, 16 Aug 1915, p.1; *Nicholas*, p.78 (letter of 31 Aug 1915).

37 *Krasnii Arkhiv*, l/li, pp.150–4; Rodzyanko, *Krushenie*, pp.132–3; *Council*, p.99; *Duma*, iv, 16 (3 Sep 1915), 1207–8.

38 *Kadet*, pp.39–40; Progressist account, pp.22–3; *Den*, 5 and 7 Sep 1915, pp.3 and 2; *Krasnii Arkhiv*, l/li, pp.154–5; Rodzyanko, *Krushenie*, pp.132–3.

39 Cherniavsky, pp.227 and 235; Sazonov, p.295; Vladimir Gurko, pp.579–80; *Nicholas*, p.89 (letter of 14 Sep 1915).

40 Cherniavsky, p.243; *Padenie*, vii, p.70 (Polivanov); A.N. Naumov, *Iz Utseplevshikh: vospominania*, 2 vols (New York, 1954–5), ii, p.306; *Nicholas*, pp.90 and 91 (16 and 17 Sep 1915); Sazonov, p.295.

41 Okhrana reports of 4, 5, 8 and 29 Sep 1915 quoted in Grave, *Burzhuazia*, pp.30, 40 and 50; TsGAOR, 523 (Kadet Party), i, 32, pp.196–202 cited in Dyakin, p.120; also Chermensky, p.571.

42 *Okhrana*, 343, 345–d, 1915, p.42 and xvi, 27–46, p.39 (5 and 8 Sep 1915); *Den*, 3, 8 and 10 Sep 1915, all pp.1–2; B. Pares (ed.), *Letters of the Tsaritsa to the Tsar 1914–16* (London, 1923), p.135 (letter of 2 Sep 1915), hereafter *Alexandra*; TsGAOR, 523 (Kadet Party), iii, 10, pp.13–14; Okhrana report located in TsGAOR, 627 (B.V. Sturmer), 14, pp.4–5.

43 Okhrana report of 9 Sep 1915 quoted in Grave, *Burzhuazia*, pp.53–4; TsGIA, 669 (Klyuzhev), 17, pp.6–7 and 10–11; Buryshkin, p.190; TsGAOR, 627 (Sturmer), 14, pp.1–6; Gurko, pp.579–81; *Rech*, 30 Sep 1915, p.2.

44 *Nicholas*, p.70 (25 Aug 1915); Naumov, ii, p.36; Gilliard, p.137.

45 *Alexandra*, pp.117, 127, 130 and 131 (letters of 23, 28, 29 and 30 Aug 1915); Krivoshein, pp.239–42; Kerensky, p.140.

46 *Okhrana*, xvi, 27–57, 1915, p.44 (23 Oct 1915).

47 *Den*, 4 Sep 1915, p.3.; Paléologue, ii, pp.72–3; Engelhardt, p.615.

48 J.V. Stalin *et al., The History of the Civil War*, 2 vols (London, 1937), i, p.27.

CHAPTER 4 CRISIS OF CONFIDENCE

1 *Padenie*, iii, p.313 (Goremykin), vi, pp.196 (Markov) and 316 and 319 (Milyukov); *Okhrana*, 307a–1915, pp.150, 153 and 177; *Kadet*, pp.20 and 37–8; *Council*, p.102; *Den*, 16 Sep 1915, p.2.

2 *Padenie*, i, pp.331–2 and 337 (Naumov), iv, pp.276–9 (A.N. Khvostov), and vi, p.319 (Milyukov); *Okhrana*, xvi, 27–57, pp.26 and 138; 27–1915, pp.112–13; 307a–1915, p.173; *Council*, pp.108 and 115; *Den*, 24 Nov 1915, p.1.

3 Semennikov, *Monarkhia*, pp.224–5 and 228–41; *Padenie*, vii, p.26 (Shingarev); S.P. Beletsky, 'Iz vospominanii', *Byloe*, xx (1922), p.199.

4 *Okhrana*, 307a–1915, p.152 (22 Sep 1915); xvi, 27–46, 1915, p.33 (5 Oct 1915); and 27–1915, p.98 (13 Oct 1915); *Rech*, 25 Sep 1915, p.1; TsGAOR, 523 (Kadet Party), iii, 10, pp.11–12.

5 *Okhrana*, 27–1915, pp.26–8 and 44–5; xvi, 27–57, 1915, pp.29–31, 38–41, 59, 66–73, 87–96 and 126–8; 243, 345–d, p.49; and 307a–1915, p.159.

6 TsGAOR, 523 (Kadet Party), iii, 10, pp.11–12; *Okhrana*, xvi, 27–46, 1915, pp.B–8, 33–5, B–12 (8 Nov 1915) and 34–b (15 Nov 1915).

7 TsGAOR, 523 (Kadet Party), iii, 10, pp.11–12 (3 Sep 1915) and 13–14 (5 Oct 1915); *Okhrana*, xvi, 27–46, 1915, pp.22–3 and 33.

8 *Okhrana*, 27–1915, pp.124–6, 169 and 227; xvi, 27–46, 1915, pp.40–1; 69–b (Saratov), p.3; 68 (Samara), p.10; and 32–b (Kiev), p.8.

9 *Krasnii Arkhiv*, lii, pp.144–51 (25 Oct), 151–6 (28 Oct), 160–1 (5 Nov) and 170–6 (12 Nov 1915); *Okhrana*, 243, 345–d, pp.57 and 61 (2 and 10 Nov 1915); also *Den*, 28 Oct 1915, p.2.

10 *Krasnii Arkhiv*, lii, pp.181–3; *Okhrana*, 307a–1915, pp.173–6 (30 Nov 1915); also *Utro Rossii* and *Rech*, 1 and 2 1915, pp.1–2.

11 *Den*, 7, 10 and 17 Sep 1915, all p.2; and 5 Nov 1915, p.3.

12 Article 'Tragicheskoe Polozhenie', *RV*, 27 Sep 1915, p.2; also in Grave, *Burzhuazia*, p.65, and George Katkov, *Russia 1917: The February Revolution* (London, 1967), pp.178–9.

13 *Utro Rossii*, 18 Sep 1915, p.2.

14 *Den*, 3 and 24 Oct 1915, both p.2; *Okhrana*, 307a–1915, p.157 (2 Oct 1915); 27–1915, pp.102 (3 Nov 1915) and 171–6 (1 Dec 1915); *Krasnii Arkhiv*, lii, pp.170–7; Engelhardt, pp.620–6.

15 *Okhrana*, xvi, 27–57, 1915, pp.124–5; and 27–1915, 20–b (Don province), p.30; an open letter from Trubetskoi attacking Efremov's leadership was printed in many newspapers, including *Den*, 14 Dec 1915, pp.1–2.

16 Okhrana report of 16 Dec 1915 quoted in Grave, *Burzhuazia*, pp.15–18; TsGIA, 669 (Klyuzhev), 17, pp.45–7.

17 *Okhrana*, 27–1915, pp.94 (30 Oct 1915) and 249–50 (7 Nov); and xvi, 27–46, 1915, p.61 (28 Dec 1915).

18 Marye, pp.268–71; A.T. Vasilyev, *The Ochrana, the Russian Secret Police* (London, 1930), pp.153–4; *Alexandra*, p.231 (29 Nov 1915).

19 TsGIA, 1626 (Goremykin), i, 1897, pp.1–6; Rodzyanko, *Krushenie*, p.143; *Padenie*, vi, p.323 (Milyukov); TsGAOR, 155, 479, pp.2–3; *Okhrana*, 307a–1916, pp.57–60 (23 Feb 1916).

20 *Alexandra*, pp.251 and 256; *Nicholas*, p.128; *Den*, 29 Dec 1915, p.2; *Padenie*, i, pp.222–3 (Sturmer) and 333 (Naumov) and vi, pp.321–6 (Milyukov);

Rodzyanko, *Krushenie*, p.146; *Council*, pp.171 and 178.

21 *Krasnii Arkhiv*, lii, pp.187 and 191–3; *Okhrana*, 307a–1916, p.201 and xvi, 1916, 46b, pp.6 and 10 (28 Mar 1916); TsGIA, 1274, 1916, 17, p.4.

22 *Krasnii Arkhiv*, lii, p.184;*Okhrana*, 307a–1916, pp.1–3 (4 Feb 1916) and 12–14 (8 Feb); for the original drafts for the Resolution, see TsGAOR, 579 (Milyukov), item 383; RV, 6 Feb 1916, p.3.

23 *Alexandra*, p.225 (15 Nov 1915); *Nicholas*, p.144; Rodzyanko, *Krushenie*, pp.148–51; *Padenie*, vi, p.328 (Milyukov) and vii, p.130 (Rodzyanko); *Okhrana*, 307a–1916, p.15; *Duma*, iv, 17 (9 Feb 1916), 1220–5 and 1247–52; *The Times*, 24 Feb 1916 (n/s), p.8.

24 1907 Central Committee report on membership in TsGAOR, 523 (Kadet Party), iii, 14, pp.1–4; also Riha, *A Russian European*, p.197.

25 TsGAOR, 579 (Milyukov), iii, 61, pp.1–4; *Okhrana*, xiii, 27–57, p.12 (1 Feb 1912).

26 TsGAOR, 523 (Kadet Party), iii, 9, p.6, and TsGAOR, 125 (Kadet Fraction), i, 12, pp.5–6; Kadet electoral expenses reached 18,000 roubles in Kiev, 22,5000 in Riga and 24,5000 in Moscow: *Okhrana*, xiii, 27–57, p.42.

27 Okhrana report quoted in Dyakin, p.39.

28 *Okhrana*, xv, 27–1914, pp.5 (3 Jan 1914) & 10 (14 Jan); TsGAOR, 523 (Kadet Party), i, 31, pp.29–30, 81–3 and 90.

29 The Reval report of 12 Jan 1916 (*Okhrana*, 27–1915, p.250) is one of a number of replies to Police Department circular 1090 issued on 7 Nov 1915, requesting information on local Kadets.

30 *Okhrana*, 27–1915, pp.103–4 (17 Oct 1915); also Grave, *Burzhuazia*, p.310.

31 *Okhrana*, xvi, 27–1915, 30–b (Kaluga), p.5; 20–b (Don), p.17; 46 (Moscow), pp.103–6; 32–b (Kiev), pp.8–10; 35–b (Kostroma), p.3; and 68 (Samara), pp.33 and 40–1.

32 *Okhrana*, xvi, 27–1915, p.4 (17 Feb 1916); 27–46, 32–b (Kiev), pp.9–10.

33 The following section on the Sixth Congress is based on the official minutes kept by the Secretary of the Central Committee, A.A. Kornilov: TsGAOR, 523 (Kadet Party), iii, item 5, pp.1–147. More detail may be found in my article 'Milyukov and the Sixth Kadet Congress', *Slavonic and East European Review*, liii, 131 (Apr 1975), pp.210–29.

34 *Okhrana*, 27–1915, pp.124–5; 32–b (Kiev), pp.8–10; 69–b (Saratov), pp.3 and 230; and 27–1916, p.227.

35 TsGAOR, 523 (Kadet Party), iii, 10, pp.12–13 (5 Oct 1915); *Okhrana*, 307a–1916, p.67 (22 Feb 1916).

36 *Okhrana*, xvii, 27–1916, 46–b (Moscow), p.1 (10 Feb 1916).

37 TsGAOR, 523 (Kadet Party), iii, 9, pp.1–2.

38 *Ibid*, pp.7, 7, 9 and 317; also TsGAOR, 523 (Kadet Party), iii, 5, p.21.

39 The comprehensive police report on the Congress is in *Okhrana*, xvii, 27–1916, 46–b, pp.1–6; see selections in Grave, *Burzhuazia*, pp.73–5, and *K Istorii Klassovoi Borby v Rossii v gody imperialisticheskoi voiny* (Moscow, 1926), pp.310–13.

40 RV, 4 and 15 Jan 1916, pp.1 and 4; and 12 and 17 Mar, both p.2; also M.K. Lemke, *250 Dnei v Tsarskoi Stavke* (Petrograd, 1920), p.341.

41 *Rech*, 8 Feb 1916, p.1; *Duma*, iv, 21 (15 Feb 1916), 1673–97; *Okhrana*, 307a–3–1916, pp.33–4, 38, 44, 71, 75 and 201; Okhrana report of 29 February 1916 quoted in Grave, *Burzhuazia*, pp.75–81.

42 TsGAOR, 523 (Kadet Party), iii, 9, pp.11–19; TsGAOR, 579 (Milyukov),

item 371; *Padenie*, vi, pp.333–4 (Milyukov); *Duma*, iv, 32 (7 Mar 1916), 2837–88; Semennikov, *Monarkhia*, pp.119–20 and 163–4.

43 *Padenie*, ii, pp.125 and 135 (Kafafov); *Duma*, iv, 33, 3025–42 and 34, 3137–46 (8 and 10 Mar 1916); *Okhrana*, 307a–3–1916, pp.114 and 165–7.

44 Khvostov memorandum of 1 Mar 1916 in TsGAOR, 627 (Sturmer), item 40; TsGAOR, 523 (Kadet Party), iii, 9, pp.19–27; Grave, *Burzhuazia*, pp.86–94.

45 *Padenie*, v, p.164 (Sturmer); also conversation between Guchkov and Konovalov in Apr 1916 recorded in TsGAOR, 555 (Guchkov), 8, 1436, p.1.

46 RV, 13 Jan and 18 Feb 1916, both p.4; TsGAOR, 523 (Kadet Party), iii, 9, pp.37–41 and 47–58 (30 and 31 Mar 1916).

47 Miliukov, *Political Memoirs*, p.340; *Okhrana*, xiv, 27–1913, p.33 (20 Apr 1913); Okhrana reports for 29 Feb and 9 May 1916 quoted in Grave, *Burzhuazia*, pp.119–20 and 79–80; note also an open letter from Moscow industrialist S.A. Smirnov to Albert Thomas in RV, 4 May 1916, pp.4–5; and Rodzyanko's guarded remarks in 'Gosudarstvennaya Duma i Fevralskaya 1917 goda Revolyutsia' in S.A. Alexeyev (ed.), *Fevralskaya Revolyutsia*, 2nd edition (Moscow, 1926), pp.19–20.

48 Milyukov's diary of the trip is in *Krasnii Arkhiv*, liv/lv, pp.14–43; for a highly critical view, see Engelhardt, pp.632–60.

49 'Letter to the Editor' from Mandelshtam in RV, 28 Feb 1916, p.7; *Okhrana*, xvii, 27–46b (Moscow), pp.3–6 (28 Feb 1916).

50 TsGAOR, 523 (Kadet Party), iii, 9, pp.64–71 (26 Apr 1916), 72–8 (10–11 May) and 79 ff. (agenda).

51 Ibid., 5, pp.105 and 109; *Okhrana*, xvii, 27–1916, 46–b, pp.5–6; *Duma*, iv, 48 (16 May 1916), 4446; TsGAOR, 669 (Klyuzhev), 17, p.109.

52 *Den*, 4 Sep 1915, p.4; *Evreiskaya Zhizn* article included in an Okhrana report quoted in Grave, *Burzhuazia*, p.55; *Duma*, iv, 52 (7 June 1916), 4883–9; Louis Greenberg, *The Jews in Russia*, 2 vols (Newhaven, 1965), ii, p.120; TsGAOR, 669 (Klyuzhev), 17, p.102.

53 TsGAOR, 523 (Kadet Party), iii, 9, pp.1–2 (21 Feb 1916), 63 (31 Mar) and 73–9 (19 May).

54 RV, 20 May and 22 June 1916, both p.3; *Duma*, iv, 51, 52 and 53, pp.4797–81, 4889 and 4992–3; Okhrana report in TsGAOR, 627 (Sturmer), 44, pp.5–6.

55 TsGAOR, 627 (Sturmer), 42, pp.1–4; *Padenie*, v, pp.165–6 and 173–8 (Sturmer); *Council*, p.214.

56 Rodzyanko, *Krushenie*, pp.161–2; *Rech*, 6 June 1916, p.1; RV, 11 June 1916, p.4; *Alexandra*, p.362 (23 June 1916).

57 *Krasnii Arkhiv*, lviii, pp.5–23; *Duma*, iv, 60 (19 June 1916), 5792–9.

58 *Krasnii Arkhiv*, lvi, p.82; Miliukov, *Political Memoirs*, p.369; Klimovich report in TsGAOR, 627 (Sturmer), 44, pp.1–11; *Okhrana*, xvii, 46–b, pp. 6 (3 July 1916), 8–9 and 12–14 (15 Aug).

CHAPTER 5 THE 'STORM-SIGNAL OF REVOLUTION'

1 Engelhardt, pp.621–31; Miliukov, *Political Memoirs*, pp.362–3.

2 Paléologue, ii, pp.186, 268 and 286; Stone, pp.210–11 and 247–55.

3 Over the period April to December 1916, Nicholas made only one trip away from the Stavka, to Tsarskoe Selo and Kiev, 18–29 October, to see his

wife and mother; *Nicholas*, p.207 (11 June 1916).

4 Semennikov, *Monarkhia*, pp.259–66; Rodzyanko, *Krushenie*, pp.155 and 164–7; *Nicholas*, pp.219 and 221 (25 and 27 June 1916); *Padenie*, i, 224–5 and 240–2 (Sturmer) and 337–44 (Naumov); Engelhardt, pp.723–4.

5 Semennikov, *Monarkhia*, pp.12–14 and 258; Sazonov, p.307; *Padenie*, i, pp.244–5 and 282–6 (Sturmer) and vi, 343 (Milyukov); Paléologue, ii, pp.301–2; Buchanan, ii, pp.16–17; also Dyakin, p.219.

6 *Padenie*, i, pp.268–9 (Sturmer) and v, pp.448–9 (Alexander Khvostov).

7 Semennikov, *Monarkhia*, pp.139–40, 144–7, 150–1 and 153; *Krasnii Arkhiv*, lvi, p.132; Sturmer himself made the distinction between *diktator* and *rasporyaditel* in *Padenie*, i, p.242; Miliukov, *Political Memoirs*, p.361.

8 RV, 25 Mar 1916, p.5; *Duma: ukazatel* (St Petersburg, 1913), pp.19–24.

9 *The Times*, 12 July 1916 (n/s), p.9; RV, 3 June 1916, p.3; 27 July, p.1; 13 Aug, p.3; Engelhardt, p.723.

10 Miliukov, *Political Memoirs*, p.369; see also Chermensky, p.735.

11 Ibid., p.373; Okhrana reports of 30 Oct 1916 and 28 Jan 1917, quoted in Grave, *Burzhuazia*, pp.125 and 138; *Krasnii Arkhiv*, xvii, pp.6 and 25 (the distinction is between *oppositsionnost* and *revolyutsionnost*); RV, 8 and 12 Sep 1916, pp.3–4 and 1–2.

12 *Alexandra*, pp.394 and 409 (7 and 22 Sep 1916); *Nicholas*, pp.246 and 256–7 (14 Aug and 9 Sep 1916).

13 RV, 21 and 22 Sep 1916, pp.3 and 2; *Rech*, 21 Sep, p.1; *Padenie*, vi, p.342 (Milyukov); Engelhardt, pp.632–4.

14 *Okhrana*, xvii, 27–1916, 46, pp.11–12 (18 Sep 1916) and 19–20 (23 Sep); Semennikov, *Monarkhia*, p.160; Paléologue, iii, p.55.

15 *The Times* (Russian Supplement), 28 Oct 1916 (n/s), p.2; Florinsky, pp.175–7; I.P. Leiberov, 'O Revolyutsionnikh vystuplenyakh petrogradskogo proletariata', *Voprosi Istorii*, 1964:2, p.65; Bernard Pares, *The Fall of The Russian Monarchy* (New York, 1939), p.384.

16 General A.S. Lukomsky, *Memoirs of the Russian Revolution* (London, 1922), pp.40–5; Vasilii Gurko, *Memories and Impressions of War and Revolution in Russia 1914–1917* (London, 1918), pp.145–6, 158–62 and 191–202.

17 *Okhrana*, xvii, 46–b, pp.7–8 and 13–16; also TsGAOR, 579 (Milyukov), 698, p.7.

18 Semennikov, *Monarkhia*, p.160; Okhrana reports in Grave, *Burzhuazia*, pp.144–5, and Laverychev, p.150; Paléologue, iii, pp.73–5; Shlyapnikov, i, 238.

19 *Okhrana*, xviii, 27–1916, p.9; abridged versions of Milyukov's speech also in Grave, *Butzhuazia*, pp.142–3 and Riha, *A Russian European*, pp. 260–1; *Krasnii Arkhiv*, lvi, pp.82–3 (3 Oct 1916) and 87 (13 Oct).

20 *Okhrana*, xvii, 46–b, pp.7–8 (12 Oct 1916); Okhrana reports of 20 Oct quoted in Chermensky, p.756, and 30 Oct quoted in Grave, *Burzhuazia*, p.138.

21 *Okhrana*, xvii, 307a–1–1916, pp.78–9 (29 Sep 1916); Sturmer's report of 9 Oct 1916 to Nicholas quoted in Semennikov, *Monarkhia*, p.161.

22 Semennikov, *Monarkhia*, p.161; RV, 9 Oct 1916, p.4.

23 See booklet published by the Progressive Bloc, copies of which are in TsGAOR, 579 (Milyukov), item 382 and 605 (Rodzyanko), item 73; the whole booklet is reproduced in Shlyapnikov, ii, pp.99–107.

24 *Krasnii Arkhiv*, xvii, pp.5–6; Okhranna report of 20 Oct 1916 quoted in Grave, *Burzhuazia*, p.129; Sturmer's report of 31 Oct to Nicholas in Semennikov, *Monarkhia*, p.131; *Padenie*, v, p.72 (Sturmer).

25 Maklakov, 'On the Fall of Tsardon', p.90; *Krasnii Arkhiv*, lvi, pp.88–93 (20 Oct 1916), 99–102 (22 Oct) and 102–6 (24 Oct).

26 Okhrana report of 2 Nov 1916 quoted in Grave, *Burzhuazia*, pp.146–8; Riha, *A Russian European*, pp.261–2; TsGAOR, 579 (Milyukov), 1106, pp.1–4.

27 Paléologue, ii, pp.88–9; TsGAOR, 605 (Rodzyanko), 74, pp.1 and 2.

28 *Krasnii Arkhiv*, lvi, pp.110–14 (30 Oct 1916) and 114–17 (31 Oct); also Vladimir Gurko, pp.582–3 and Shulgin, pp.80–5.

29 *Okhrana*, xvii, 307a–1–1916, p.89 (8 Nov 1916); RV, 1 Nov 1916, p.2; *Padenie*, vi, pp.91–2 (Milyukov).

30 *Duma*, v, 1 (1 Nov 1916), 10–13 (Shidlovsky) and 35–48 (Milyukov); the original speech is in TsGAOR, 579 (Milyukov), item 60; see also Katkov, pp.190–5 and S.P. Melgunov, *Legenda o Separatnom Mire* (Paris, 1957), pp.279–318.

31 *Duma*, v, 1 (1 Nov 1916), 13–22 and 28–33 (Chkheidze and Kerensky) and 2 (3 Nov), 67–71 and 130–1 (Shulgin and Maklakov).

32 *Padenie*, i, pp.229 and 266 (Sturmer); Sturmer's report of 3 Nov to Nicholas in Semennikov, *Monarkhia*, pp.132–3; *Nicholas*, p.296.

33 *Padenie*, vi, pp.347–8; RV, 11 Nov 1916, p.3; *Okhrana*, xvii, 307a–1–1916, pp.89 (8 Nov 1916) and 157 (19 Nov).

34 Milyukov, *Istoria Vtoroi Russkoi Revolyutsii*, 3 vols (Sofia 1921–4), ii, p.277.

35 Examples of later Kadet hagiography might include Mandelshtam in *Rech*, 28 Mar 1917, p.2; A.V. Tyrkova-Williams, *From Liberty to Brest Litovsk* (London, 1919), p.3; I.I. Petrunkevich, *Iz Zapisok Obshchestvennogo Deyatelya: vospominania* (Berlin, 1934), p.355; and Milyukov himself in *Istoria*, i, p.34 and 'Fevralskie Dni' in Alexeyev (ed.), p.170.

36 *Nicholas*, pp.297, 298 and 299 (9 and 10 Nov and 4 Dec 1916); *Council*, p.243; *Alexandra*, p.441 (12 Nov 1916); Gilliard, pp.178–9; *Padenie*, ii, pp. 60–1 (Trepov).

37 *Krasnii Arkhiv*, lvi, pp.118–19; *Duma*, v, 6 (19 Nov 1916), 251–9; *Council*, pp.252–74; Vasilii Gurko, pp.180–2 and 189.

38 TsGAOR, 579 (Milyukov), 381, p.1 and 2184, pp.1–2; *Duma*, v, 6 (19 Nov 1916), 240–51; Rodzyanko, *Krushenie*, p.180; Kerensky, p.180.

39 Vasilii Gurko, p.189; *Duma*, v, 6 (19 Nov 1916), 229–318 *passim*; *Council*, pp.290–327.

40 TsGAOR, 627 (Sturmer), 15, pp.2–3; *Duma*, v, 4 (4 Nov 1916), 203–5; Semennikov, *Monarkhia*, p.135; *Rech*, 6 Nov 1916, p.1.

41 *Krasnii Arkhiv*, lvi, pp.117–20 and 126–31; *Okhrana*, xvii, 27–1916, 46, pp.28 (9 Nov 1916), 32–3 and 36–7 (14 Nov).

42 *Duma*, v, 10 (29 Nov 1916), 558 and 15 (13 Dec), 1051–72; *Okhrana*, xvii, 27–1916, 46, p.30; also Chermensky, pp.777–8 and 802.

43 Oznobishin, p.250; *Okhrana*, xvii, 307a–1–1916, pp.97 (10 Nov 1916), 161 (19 Nov) and 121 (7 Dec); and 343, 1916, pp.106–7 (11 Dec).

CHAPTER 6 ON THE EVE

1 *Okhrana*, xvii, 307a–1–1916, p.252 (28 Nov 1916); *Nicholas*, pp.306 and 307 (13 and 14 Dec 1916); also Engelhardt, p.728.

2 *Duma*, v, 18, 1179; Skobelev quoted in *Manchester Guardian*, 20 Jan 1917 (n/s),

p.7; *Council*, pp.446–8; Samuel Hoare, *The Fourth Seal: the end of a Russian Chapter* (London, 1930), p.106.

3 *Padenie*, vi, pp.350 and 357 (Milyukov); *Okhrana*, xvii, 27–1916, 46, pp.46, 48–9 and 53.

4 *Padenie*, v, pp.166–7 (Sturmer) and vi, pp.362–4 (Trepov); Shlyapnikov, ii, pp.8–9; Paléologue, iii, p.114; Hoare, p.113.

5 Copies of the appeals are in TsGAOR, 555 (Guchkov), item 59 and 579 (Milyukov), item 2857; *Council*, pp.436 and 439; Rodzyanko, *Krushenie*, p.203; Kerensky, pp.180–1; also Gleason, p.298.

6 *Duma*, v, 18 (16 Dec 1916), 1192–1201; RV, 14 Dec 1916, p.3; S.P. Mansyrev, 'Moi Vospominania' in Alexeyev (ed.), pp.260–1.

7 Prince Felix Yusupov, *Rasputin* (London, 1934), pp.73–232 *passim*; private diary of Nicholas in *Krasnii Arkhiv*, xx, pp.124 and 135.

8 Hoare, p.120; Vasilii Gurko, pp.227–9; *Padenie*, ii, pp.250–70 (Golitsyn) and 433–4 (Shcheglovitov) and vi, p.350 (Milyukov).

9 Hoare, p.123; Semennikov, *Monarkhia*, pp.427 and 435–6; *Padenie*, ii, pp.425–7 (Shcheglovitov); *Alexandra*, p.457 (15 Dec 1916).

10 Kurlov, pp.285–6; Shakhovskoi, p.197; Rodzyanko, *The Reign of Rasputin* (London, 1927), p.251.

11 RV, 4 and 5 Jan 1917, both p.2; *Council*, pp.451–7; Rodzyanko, 'Gosudarstvennaya Duma', p.35; *Padenie*, ii, pp.256–9 and 265 (Golitsyn) and v, pp.287–9 (Maklakov); A.A. Blok, *Poslednie Dni Imperatorskoi Vlasti* (Petrograd,1921), pp.16 and 46–8.

12 *Padenie*, vi, pp.278–9 (Guchkov); *Poslednia Novosti*, 8, 9 and 13 Sep 1936; L. Trotsky, *History of the Russian Revolution* (London, 1932), p.92; S.P. Melgunov, *Na Putyakh k Dvortsomu Perevorotu* (Paris, 1931), pp.143–93.

13 Rodzyanko, *Krushenie*, pp.205–7; Vasilii Gurko, pp.162–6; *Okhrana*, xvii, 27–1917, p.25 (8 Jan 1917); Engelhardt, p.726.

14 A copy of the Efremov declaration is in TsGAOR, 579 (Milyukov), item 453; *Okhrana*, xvii, 307a–1–1916, p.156 (19 Nov 1916) and 27–1917, pp.1–2 (6 Jan 1917).

15 RV, 16, 25 and 29 Nov 1916, pp.4, 5 and 5; *Okhrana*, xvii, 20–b, p.1 (16 Jan 1917) and 27–1916, 46, p.60 (19 Jan 1917); Mansyrev, 'Moi vospominanii', pp.257–61.

16 *Arkhiv Russkoi Revolyutsii*, vi, p.335; RV, 24, 26 and 27 Jan 1917, pp.4, 1–2 and 2; also Katkov, pp.219–23.

17 Rodzyanko, *Krushenie*, pp.205–7, 211–13 and 217–18.

18 *Okhrana*, xvii, 27–1917, pp.3–5 (7 Jan 1917), 23–4 and 61 (20 Jan); Shulgin, pp.119–21; RV, 11 Jan 1917, p.2.

19 Yusupov, pp.201–2; Shulgin, pp.119–21; Engelhardt, p.595.

20 *Okhrana*, xvii, 17, 20–b, p.3 (10 Jan 1917); TsGAOR, 111, v, 664, p. 52, quoted in Laverychev, p.169.

21 Hoare, pp.189–95; David Lloyd George, *War Memoirs*, 2 vols (London, 1938), i, p.941; Buchanan, ii, pp.52–4; Katkov, pp.223–5.

22 Lenin Library manuscript department, 260 (Ryabushinsky), item 26; Lloyd George, i, pp.945–6.

23 Milyukov, *Russia Today and Tomorrow* (New York, 1922), p.295; Paléologue, iii, p.188; see also Bloc conversations with General Castelnau covered in Okhrana report of 28 Jan 1917 in Grave, *Burzhuazia*, pp.121–2.

24 *Council*, pp.451–7; *Padenie*, ii, pp.256–9 (Golitsyn); Lloyd George, i,

pp.941–4 and 946; Semennikov, *Monarkhia*, pp.77–85; Lord Milner, 'Before Russia Went West', *National Review*, cv (Dec 1940), pp.659 and 661; Hoare, p.219.

25 Rodzyanko, *Krushenie*, p.216; *Padenie*, vi, pp.284–8 (Guchkov); RV, 2 Feb 1917, p.2; Blok, pp.31–6; Kerensky, p.183.

26 Grave, *Burzhuazia*, pp.181–2; note Milyukov's revisionist gloss in his *Political Memoirs*, pp.384–5; *Okhrana*, xvii, 46–b, pp.1–6 (4 Feb 1917).

27 *Okhrana*, xvii, 46–b, p.5; Laverychev, pp.165–6 and Chermensky, pp.856–8.

28 *Padenie*, vi, p.351 (Milyukov); *Council*, p.460; Blok, pp.39 and 48.

29 Rodzyanko, *Krushenie*, pp.219–20; *Duma*, v, 20 (15 Feb 1917), 1344; A.A. Shlyapnikov, *Semnadtsatii God*, 2 vols (Moscow, 1923), i, p.65.

30 *Duma*, v, 20, 1353–8; Kerensky, pp.186–7; *Council*, pp.464–5; *Padenie*, ii, pp.261–2 (Golitsyn); RV, 22 Feb 1917, p.3.

31 *Okhrana*, xvii, 27–1917, pp.26 (8 Jan 1917), 46 (17 Feb) and 58 (18 Feb); *Krasnii Arkhiv*, xx, p.35; *Duma*, v, 21 (17 Feb 1917) 1, 1499; also Dyakin, pp.315–17.

32 Miliukov, *Political Memoirs*, pp.383–4; Okhrana report of 19 Jan 1917 quoted in Laverychev, p.166; Maklakov, 'On the Fall of Tsardom', pp. 28–9; also Paléologue, iii, pp.167–8.

33 Okhrana report of 29 Jan 1917 quoted in Grave, *Burzhuazia*, pp.175–6; Engelhardt, pp.724–6 and 730; Shulgin, pp.141–2.

CHAPTER 7 THE RELUCTANT REVOLUTIONARIES

1 The best street-level eye-witness accounts of the February Revolution are Robert Wilton, *Russia's Agony* (London, 1918), Stinton Jones, *Russia in Revolution* (London, 1917) and especially Claude Anet, *La Révolution Russe*, 4 vols (Paris, 1919), vol.i.

2 Trotsky, p.139; Mansyrev, p.262; *Duma*, v, 23 (23 Feb 1917), 1593–7 and 1653–7; Kerensky, pp.188–9; *Council*, p.468.

3 *Duma*, v, 24 (24 Feb 1917), 1733–4; *Padenie*, ii, pp.253–4 (Golitsyn); *Council*, pp.466–7; in 'Gosudarstvennaya Duma', pp.37–8, Rodzyanko mistakenly dates the meeting on 25 Feb; Blok, pp.53–4.

4 *Rech* and RV, 25 Feb 1917, pp.2 and 3.

5 Perets, pp.18–19 and *Council*, p.476; Kerensky, p.190.

6 *Padenie*, i, pp.190–220 (Khabalov) and ii, pp.263–5 (Golitsyn).

7 This report by Okhrana agent 'Limonin' in *Byloe*, i (Jan 1918), pp.174–5 is the last to which I have found reference; Trotsky, pp.134–7; Sukhanov, p.25.

8 Miliukov, *Political Memoirs*, pp.387–8; Shulgin, pp.140 and 143–6; *Padenie*, ii, pp.263–4 (Golitsyn) and vi, p.100 (Protopopov); Shakhovskoi, p.199.

9 Rodzyanko, 'Gosudarstvennaya Duma', pp.38–9; Blok, pp.59–62.

10 Shulgin, pp.150 and 155; Kerensky, pp.190 and 193.

11 Milyukov, 'Fevralskie Dni', p.175; Shulgin, p.157; A.A. Bublikov, *Russkaya Revolyutsia* (New York, 1918), p.17; Kerensky, *The Catastrophe* (London, 1927), pp.12–13; *Poslednia Novosti*, 25 Mar 1924; Engelhardt, p.730.

12 *Izvestia*, 1, 27 Feb 1917; Chernov, pp.77–8; Shulgin, pp.162–4.

13 Rodzyanko, 'Gosudarstvennaya Duma', pp.40–1; 'Fevralskaya Revolyutsia 1917 goda', *Krasnii Arkhiv*, xxi, pp.6–7; *Padenie*, v, p.38 (Frederiks).

14 Shulgin, pp.158–9; Mansyrev, pp.264–7; *Volya Rossii*, 15 Mar 1921;

Shidlovsky, 'Vospominania' in Alexeyev (ed.), p.283; Miliukov, *Political Memoirs*, p.391.

15 Shulgin, p.162; *Izvestia*, 1, 27 Feb 1917; Bublikov, p.18.
16 Sukhanov, p.9; Rosenberg, p.52; *Izvestia*, 2, 28 February 1917.
17 Sukhanov, pp.15 and 39; Kerensky, pp.199, 201 and 232; Mansyrev, p.268.
18 Kerensky, pp.197–8; Rodzyanko, 'Gosudarstvennaya Duma', p.49; *Arkhiv Russkoi Revolyutsii*, iii, p.247; Shulgin, pp.178–9.
19 *Padenie*, ii, pp.266–8 (Golitsyn); Rodzyanko, 'Gosudarstvennaya Duma', p.38; Miliukov, *Political Memoirs*, p.388.
20 Ibid.; also Blok, p.74, and T. Hasegawa, 'Rodzianko and the Grand Dukes' Manifesto of 1 March 1917', *Canadian Slavonic Papers*, xviii, June 1976, 160–1.
21 *Arkhiv Russkoi Revolyutsii*, iii, pp.249–51; Rodzyanko, 'Gosudarstvennaya Duma', pp.39–40; *Krasnii Arkhiv*, xxi, pp.8–9 and 15–16; *Padenie*, ii, p.267 (Golitsyn); Shulgin, pp.164 and 178; Kerensky, p.198.
22 *Izvestia*, 1, 27 Feb 1917 and 3, 1 Mar 1917.
23 The best detailed account of the Tsar's predicament during the February Revolution is chapter 5 of Basily, pp.103–48; *Padenie*, v, p.38 (Frederiks); V.N. Voyeikov, *S Tsarem i Bez Tsarya* (Helsinki, 1936), p.261; *Arkhiv Russkoi Revolyutsii*, iii, p.249; *Krasnii Arkhiv*, xxi, pp.11–13.
24 Kerensky, p.201; also T. Hasegawa, 'The Problem of Power in the February Revolution of 1917 in Russia', *Canadian Slavonic Papers*, xiv, 4, pp.618–22.
25 Shulgin, pp.179 and 185; Rodzyanko, 'Gosudarstvennaya Duma', pp.40–1; Milyukov, 'Fevralskie Dni', p.176; *Izvestia*, 2, 28 Feb 1917.
26 *Izvestia*, 2, 28 Feb 1917; 3, 1 Mar and 4, 1 Mar; Perets, p.42; S. Mstislavsky, *Pyat Dnei: nachalo i konets Fevralskoi Revolyutsii* (Berlin, 1922), pp.33–44; Bublikov, pp.20 ff.
27 *Padenie*, v, p.300 (Ivanov); Basily, p.114.; Trotsky, p.104.
28 Hasegawa, 'Rodzianko', pp.161–4; Shidlovsky, 'Vospominania', pp.294–5; Sukhanov, p.110; Chernov, p.82; Shulgin, pp.214 and 239.
29 Katkov, pp.317–20; Hasegawa, 'Rodzianko', p.164; *Arkhiv Russkoi Revolyutsii*, iii, pp.255–6.
30 Lukomsky, pp.57–8; Krivoshein, pp.297; Basily, pp.115–17; Goulevitch, p.248.
31 Burdzhalov, i, p.310; Sukhanov, pp.116–26; Miliukov, *Political Memoirs*, pp.402–4; Hasegawa, 'Rodzianko', pp.157 and 165–6.
32 *Padenie*, vi, pp.262–3 (Guchkov); Shulgin, pp.237–43.
33 *Arkhiv Russkoi Revolyutsii*, iii, pp.255–62; Basily, pp.118–21.
34 *Russkaya Volya*, 7 Mar 1917; *Padenie*, vi, pp.263 and 275 (Guchkov); Shulgin, pp.281–2; Gilliard, pp.195–6 and 205–6.
35 Shulgin, pp.266–9; *Padenie*, vi, pp.263–5 (Guchkov); another, slightly different, account by Guchkov is in Basily, pp.127–8.
36 V.I Lenin, *Collected Works*, 4th edition (London, 1963–4), xxiii, p.310; Shulgin, pp.269–77 and 282–4; *Padenie*, vi, pp.265, 270–1 and 275–7 (Guchkov); Basily, pp.119–20 and 128–31; Nabokov, pp.49–50.
37 *Izvestia*, 6, 2 Mar 1917; Miliukov, *Political Memoirs*, p.407.
38 Sukhanov, pp.146 and 153; Miliukov, *Political Memoirs*, pp.407–8; Chernov, p.90.
39 Kerensky, pp.211 and 214–16; *Krasnii Arkhiv*, xxii, pp.15–16; *Arkhiv Russkoi*

Revolyutsii, iii, pp.266–8; Miliukov, *Political Memoirs*, pp.410–11.

40 Kerensky, ibid.; Miliukov, ibid.; *Padenie*, vi, pp.266–7; Shulgin, pp.284–303; Milyukov, 'Fevralskie Dni', p.187.
41 Ibid.
42 Shulgin, pp.303–7; Nabokov, pp.19–20 and 47–55.
43 *Izvestia*, 4, 1 Mar 1917; and 5, 2 Mar 1917.
44 *Arkhiv Russkoi Revolyutsii*, iii, pp.266–9; *Krasnii Arkhiv*, xxii, pp. 25–7; Miliukov, *Political Memoirs*, pp.396 and 407–8.
45 *Izvestia*, 7, 3 Mar 1917; Rosenberg, pp.50–1; Sukhanov, pp.53 and 116–57.
46 Miliukov, *Political Memoirs*, pp.375–6 and 396–400; Rodzyanko, 'Gosudarstvennaya Duma', p.48; Shidlovsky, 'Vospominania', p.287; Bublikov, pp.33–8; Nabokov, pp.44, 81–2 and 85.
47 Chernov, p.177; *Vestnik Partii Narodnoi Svobody*, 11 Mar 1917; Rodzyanko, 'Gosudarstvennaya Duma', pp.56–7.
48 Miliukov, *Political Memoirs*, p.400; Rodzyanko, 'Gosudarstvennaya Duma', pp.48 and 56–7; Nabokov, pp.48 and 55–6; Prince Pavel D. Dolgorukov, *Velikaya Razrukha* (Madrid, 1964), pp.13–14 and 18–20.
49 Gessen, pp.216–17; also Nabokov, pp.82–5, and Dolgorukov, pp.10–11.
50 Miliukov, *Political Memoirs*, pp.422 and 427; *Padenie*, vi, pp.267–8 (Guchkov); Nabokov, pp.85–9.
51 Bublikov, pp.30–1; Nabokov, p.44; Kerensky, pp.205–8; Shulgin, p.124.
52 Grigorii Aronson, *Rossia nakanune Revolyutsii* (New York, 1962), pp.109–43; Kerensky, pp.87–90 and 150–1; Milyukov, *Vospominania 1867–1917*, 2 vols (Paris, 1955–6), ii, pp.332–3; Katkov, pp.163–73; Nathan Smith, 'The Role of Russian Freemasonry in the February Revolution: another scrap of evidence', *Slavic Review*, xxvii, 4, pp.604–8.

CHAPTER 8 EPILOGUE
1 Rosenberg, *Liberals*, pp.6 and 31.
2 Bublikov, p.11.
3 Chernov, p.57; M.F. Hamm, 'Liberal Politics in Wartime Russia: an analysis of the Progressive Bloc', *Slavic Review*, xxxiii, 3, pp.467–8.
4 Cherniavsky, p.199; also *Okhrana*, 343, 1916, p.1067 (11 Dec 1916), and Engelhardt, p.729.
5 Moscow Okhrana report of 12 Oct 1916 quoted in Grave, *Burzhuazia*, p.142.
6 Chernov, pp.172–3; Milyukov, *Vtoraya Duma* (St Petersburg, 1907), p.28.
7 Chernov, pp.172 and 175; Vinaver, *Nedavnee*, p.135; also Tyrkova, *Na Putyakh*, pp.408–15.
8 Izgoyev *et al.*, *Vekhi*, p.125; Shulgin, p.147; also Oznobishin, pp.35–6, and Tyrkova, *Na Putyakh*, pp.311–12.

Select Bibliography

1 UNPUBLISHED ARCHIVAL MATERIAL
Central State Archive of the October Revolution (TsGAOR) in Moscow:
    funds 102 Department of Police
           115 Union of 17 October
           125 Constitutional Democratic Fraction
           523 Constitutional Democratic Party
           555 Guchkov, A.I.
           579 Milyukov, P.N.
           601 Nicholas II
           605 Rodzyanko, M.V.
           627 Sturmer, B.V.
           826 Dzhunkovsky, V.F.
Central State Historical Archive (TsGIA) in Leningrad:
    funds 669 Klyuzhev, I.S.
          1148 State Council
          1276 Council of Ministers
          1278 State Duma
          1571 Krivoshein, A.V.
          1626 Goremykin, I.L.
Lenin Library (manuscript department) in Moscow:
    funds 218 Engelhardt, B.A.
          260 Ryabushinsky, P.P.

2 PUBLISHED COLLECTIONS OF PRIMARY MATERIAL
Alexeyev, S.A., ed., *Fevralskaya Revolyutsia: revolyutsia i grazhdanskaya voina v opisaniakh belogvardeitsev*, 2nd edition (Moscow, 1926)
Cherniavsky, M., ed., *Prologue to Revolution* (New Jersey, 1967)
Gessen, I.V., ed., *Arkhiv Russkoi Revolyutsii*, 22 vols (Berlin, 1921–6)
Golder, F., ed., *Documents of Russian History 1914–1917* (London, 1927)
Grave, B.B., ed., *K Istorii Klassovoi Borby v Rossii v gody Imperialisticheskoi Voiny* (Moscow, 1926)
—— *Burzhuazia nakanune Fevralskoi Revolyutsii* (Moscow, 1927)
Kalinychev, F.I., ed., *Gosudarstvennaya Duma v Rossii; v dokumentakh i materialakh* (Moscow, 1957)
Krasnii Arkhiv, 106 vols (Moscow, 1923–41)
Pares, B., ed., *Letters of the Tsaritsa to the Tsar 1914–16* (London, 1923)
Semennikov, P.E., ed., *Monarkhia pered Krusheniem* (Moscow, 1927)
Shchegolev, P.E., ed., *Padenie Tsarskogo Rezhima*, 7 vols (Moscow, 1924–7)
Vulliamy, C.E., ed., *The Letters of the Tsar to the Tsaritsa 1914–1917* (London, 1929(

3 PUBLISHED RECORDS OF THE STATE DUMA AND STATE COUNCIL
State Duma: *Nakaz, Obzor Deyatelnosti komissii i otdelov, Prilozhenia, Proekty Zakonov odobrennie Gosudarstvennuyu Dumuyu, Stenograficheskie Otchyeti* and *Ukazatel* (Petrograd, 1914–17)
State Council: *Stenograficheskie Otchyeti* (Petrograd, 1914–17)

4 NEWSPAPERS AND JOURNALS
Birzhevia Vedomosti, Den, Golos Moskvy, Poslednia Novosti, Rech (and *Ezhegodnik Rech*), *Russkia Vedomosti* and *Utro Rossii*; and *Manchester Guardian* and *The Times*

5 PUBLICATIONS BY THE MODERATE PARTIES
Kadets: *Otchyet Partii Narodnoi Svobody; voennie sessii* (Petrograd, 1915)
—— *Vestnik Partii Narodnoi Svobody* (Petrograd, Mar–Apr 1917)
Octobrists: *Otchyet Tsentralnogo Komiteta Soyuza 17–ogo Oktyabrya o ego deyatelnosti 1913–1914 gg.* (Moscow, 1914)
Progressists: *Fraktsia Progressistov v Chetvertom Gosudarstvennom Dume* (St Petersburg, 1914)
—— *Zapiska Fraktsii Progressistov ob vozniknovlenii Progressivnogo Bloka* (Petrograd, 1915)
Progressive Bloc: a series of pamphlets was published in Petrograd in the course of 1916, comprising
Deklaratsia Progressivnogo Bloka
Vstrecha Progressivnogo Bloka s Protopopovym, 19 oktyabrya 1916 g.
Rech P.N. Milyukova 1 noyabrya 1916 g.
Rechi Shulgina i Maklakova 3 noyabrya 1916 g.

6 MEMOIRS AND OTHER PRIMARY TESTIMONY
Anet, Claude, *La Revolution Russe*, 4 vols (Paris, 1919)
Badayev, A.E., *The Bolsheviks in the Tsarist Duma* (London, 1932)
Bark, P.L., 'The Last Days of the Russian Monarchy', *Russian Review*, xvi, 3 (July 1957), 35–44
Basily, Nicolas de, *Memoirs: Diplomat of Imperial Russia 1903–1917* (Stanford, 1973)
Blok, A.A., *Poslednie Dni Imperatorskoi Vlasti* (Petrograd, 1921)
Bogdanovich, T., *Velikie Dni Revolyutsii: Vremennii Komitet 23 fevral po 12 mart 1917* (Petrograd, 1917)
Bublikov, A.A., *Russkaya Revolyutsia* (New York, 1918)
Buchanan, Sir George, *My Mission to Russia and other Diplomatic Memories*, 2 vols (London, 1923)
Buryshkin, P.A., *Moskva Kupecheskaya* (New York, 1954)
Chernov, V., *The Great Russian Revolution* (New York, 1936)
Dolgorukov, Prince Pavel D., *Velikaya Razrukha* (Madrid, 1964)
Francis, D.R., *Russia from the American Embassy 1916–18* (New York, 1921)
Gessen, I.V., *V Dvukh Vekakh: zhiznennii otchyet* (Berlin, 1937)
Gilliard, P., *Thirteen Years at the Russian Court* (London, 1921)
Guchkov, A.I., testimony in *Padenie*, vi, pp. 248–94
—— 'Iz vospominanii', *Poslednia Novosti*, Aug–Sep 1936
Gurko, Vasilii I., *Memories and Impressions of War and Revolution in Russia 1914–17* (London, 1918)
Gurko, Vladimir I., *Features and Figures of the Past: Government and Opinion in the*

reign of Nicholas II (London, 1958)

Hanbury-Williams, Sir John, *The Emperor Nicholas II as I Knew Him* (London, 1922)

Hoare, S., *The Fourth Seal: the end of a Russian Chapter* (London, 1930)

Izgoyev, A.S., *Rozhdennoe v Revolyutsionnoi Smute 1917–32* (Paris, 1933)

Jones, Stinton, *Russia in Revolution: being the experiences of an Englishman in Petrograd during the Upheaval* (London, 1917)

Kerensky, A.F., *The Catastrophe* (London, 1927)

—— 'Why the Russian Monarchy Fell', *Slavonic and East European Review*, viii, 24 (Mar 1930)

—— *The Crucifixion of Liberty* (London, 1934)

—— *Memoirs: Russia and History's Turning-Point* (London, 1966)

Kleinmichel, Countess, *Memories of a Shipwrecked World* (London, 1923)

Kokovtsov, V.N., *Out of My Past: Memoirs* (New York, 1935)

Kornilov, A.A., *Parlamentskii Blok* (Moscow, 1915)

Kryzhanovsky, S.E., *Vospominania* (Berlin, 1938)

Kurlov, P.G., *Konets Tsarisma* (Petrograd, 1923)

Lloyd George, D., *War Memoirs*, 2 vols (London, 1938)

Lockhart, R.H.B., *Memoirs of a British Agent* (London, 1932)

Lomonosov, Y.V., *Vospominania o martovskoi revolyutsii 1917* (Stockholm, 1921)

Lukomsky, General A.S., *Memoirs of the Russian Revolution* (London, 1922)

Lvov, Prince G.E., *Vserossiiskii Zemskii Soyuz* (Petrograd, 1917)

Maklakov, V.A., 'On the Fall of Tsardom', *Slavonic and East European Review*, xviii, 52 (July 1939), 73–92

—— *Iz Vospominanii* (New York, 1954)

Mansyrev, Prince S.P., 'Moi vospominania' in Alexeyev, pp. 256–81

Marye, G.T., *Nearing the End in Imperial Russia* (New York, 1930)

Meyendorff, Baron A., *The Background of the Russian Revolution* (London, 1929)

Milner, Lord A., 'Before Russia Went West', *National Review*, 115 (1940), 653–64

Milyukov, P.N., editorials in *Rech* and *Ezhegodnik Rech*, 1914–17

—— reports in *Otchyet Partii Narodnoi Svobody*, 1914–17

—— testimony in *Padenie*, vi, pp. 295–372

—— *Istoria Vtoroi Russkoi Revolyutsii*, 3 vols (Sofia, 1921–4)

—— *Russia Today and Tomorrow* (New York, 1922)

—— 'Fevralskie Dni' in Alexeyev, pp. 161–89

—— *Histoire de Russie*, 3 vols (Paris, 1933), vol. 3

—— *Vospominania 1859–1917*, 2 vols (New York, 1955–6)

—— *Political Memoirs 1905–1917*, ed. A.P. Mendel (Ann Arbor, 1967)

Mossolov, A.A., *At the Court of the Last Tsar* (London, 1935)

Mstislavskii, S.D., *Pyat Dnei: nachalo i konets Fevralskoi Revolyutsii* (Berlin, 1922)

Nabokov, V.D., *V.D. Nabokov and the Russian Provisional Government 1917*, ed. V.D. Medlin and S.L. Parsons (London, 1976)

Naumov, A.N., *Iz Utselevshikh: vospominania 1868–1917*, 2 vols (New York, 1955)

Nicolas II, *Journal Intime: 1914–18* (Paris, 1934)

Nolde, Baron B.E., *Dalekoe i Blizkoe* (Paris, 1930)

Oznobishin, A.A., *Vospominania chlena IV Gosudarstvennoi Dumi* (Paris, 1927)

Paléologue, G.M., *An Ambassador's Memoirs 1914–1917*, 3 vols (London, 1923–5)

Pares, B., *Day by Day with the Russian Army* (London, 1915)

—— *My Russian Memoirs* (London, 1931)
—— *The Fall of the Russian Monarchy* (New York, 1939)
Perets, Colonel G.G., *V Tsitadeli Russkoi Revolyutsii* (Petrograd, 1917)
Polner, T.J., and Lvov, G.E., *Russian Local Government and the Union of Zemstvos* (New York, 1930)
Protopopov, A., testimony in *Padenie*, ii, pp. 273–319; iv, pp. 3–115; and v, pp. 238–44
Rodichev, F.I., 'The Liberal Movement in Russia 1855–1917', *Slavonic and East European Review*, ii, nos 4 & 5 (June and Dec 1923)
Rodzyanko, M.V., 'Gosudarstvennaya Duma i Fevralskaya 1917 goda Revolyutsia' in Alexeyev, pp. 1–62
—— *Krushenie Imperii* (Leningrad, 1926)
—— *The Reign of Rasputin* (London, 1927)
Sazonov, S.D., *Fateful Years 1909–1916* (London, 1928)
Shakhovskoi, V.N., *Sic Transit Gloria Mundi 1893–1917* (Paris, 1952)
Shidlovsky, S.I., 'Vospominania' in Alexeyev, pp. 282–315
—— *Vospominania 1861–1922*, 2 vols (Berlin, 1923)
Shlyapnikov, A., *Kanun Semnadtsatogo Goda* (Moscow, 1920)
—— *Semnadtsatii God*, 2 vols (Moscow, 1923)
Shulgin, V.V., *Dni* (Belgrade, 1925)
Spiridovich, A.I., *Velikaya Voina i Fevralskaya Revolyutsia* (New York, 1962)
Struve, P.B., *Food Supply in Russia in the Great War* (New York, 1930)
Sukhanov, N.N., *The Russian Revolution 1917* (London, 1955)
Trotsky, L.D., *History of the Russian Revolution* (London, 1965)
Tyrkova-Williams, A.V., *From Liberty to Brest-Litovsk* (London, 1919)
—— 'Russian Liberalism', *Russian Review*, x, 1, 3–14
—— *Na Putyakh k Svobode* (New York, 1952)
—— 'The Cadet Party', *Russian Review*, xii, 3, 173–86
Vasiliev, A.T., *The Ochrana, the Russian Secret Police* (London, 1930)
Vinaver, M.M., *Nedavnee: vospominania i kharakteristiki* (Paris, 1926)
Voyeikov, V.N., *S Tsarem i Bez Tsarya* (Helsinki, 1936)
Wilton, R., *Russia's Agony* (London, 1918)
Yusupov, Prince Felix, *Rasputin* (London, 1934)

7 THESES, DISSERTATIONS AND OTHER UNPUBLISHED SECONDARY MATERIAL
Chermensky, E.D., 'Borba Klassov i Partii v chetvertom Gosudarstvennom Dume 1912–17 gg.' (unpublished PhD dissertation, Moscow, 1947)
Hutchinson, J.F., 'The Octobrists in Russian Politics 1905–1917' (unpublished PhD thesis, London, 1966)
McKean, R.B., 'Russia on the eve of the Great War' (unpublished PhD thesis, East Anglia, 1971)
Pearson, R., 'The Russian Moderate Parties in the Fourth State Duma, 1912–February 1917' (unpublished PhD thesis, Durham, 1973)
Piotrow, F.J., 'Paul Milyukov and the Constitutional-Democratic Party' (unpublished DPhil thesis, Oxford, 1962)

8 PUBLISHED SECONDARY MATERIAL
Aronson, G., *Rossia nakanune Revolyutsii* (New York, 1962)
Avrekh, A.Y., *Tsarism i Treteyunskaya Sistema* (Moscow, 1966)

Burdzhalov, E.N., *Vtoraya Russkaya Revolyutsia*, 2 vols (Moscow, 1967 & 1971)
Chermensky, E.D., 'Kadety nakanune fevralskoi burzhuazno-demokraticheskoi revolyutsii', *Istoricheskii Zhurnal*, 1941:3, 25–45
—— *Fevralskaya Burzhuazno-Demokraticheskaya Revolyutsia 1917 v Rossii* (Moscow, 1959)
—— 'IV Gosudarstvennaya Duma i sverzhenie samoderzhavia v Rossii', *Voprosi Istorii*, 1969:6, 63–79
Davies, D.A., 'V.A. Maklakov and the Westernizer tradition in Russia', in Timberlake, 78–89
Dyakin, V.S., *Russkaya Burzhuazia i Tsarism v gody pervoi mirovoi voiny, 1914–1917* (Leningrad,1967)
Eroshkin, N.P., *Istoria Gosudarstvennikh Uchrezhdenii Dorevolyutsionnoi Rossii* (Moscow, 1968)
Ferro, M., *The Russian Revolution of February 1917* (London, 1972)
Florinsky, M.T., *The End of the Russian Empire* (Newhaven, 1931)
Gleason, W.E., 'The All-Russian Union of Towns and the Politics of Urban Reform in Tsarist Russia', *Russian Review*, xxxv, 3, 290–302
Goldenweiser, A., 'Paul Milyukov, Historian and Statesman', *Russian Review*, xvi, 2, 3–14
Goulevitch, A., *Czarism and Revolution* (New York, 1962)
Greenberg, L., *The Jews in Russia: the struggle for emancipation*, 2 vols (Newhaven, 1965)
Gronsky, P., and Astrov, N., *War and the Russian Government* (Newhaven, 1929)
Grunt, A., 'Progressivnii Blok', *Voprosi Istorii*, 1945:3/4, 108–17
Haimson, L., 'The Problem of Social Stability in Urban Russia 1905–17', *Slavic Review*, xxiii, 4, 619–42 and xxiv, 1, 1–22 & 47–56
Hamm, M.F., 'Liberalism and the Jewish Question: the Progressive Bloc', *Russian Review*, xxxi, 2, 163–72
—— 'Liberal Politics in Wartime Russia: an analysis of the Progressive Bloc', *Slavic Review*, xxxiii, 3, 453–68
Hasegawa, T., 'The Problem of Power in the February Revolution of 1917 in Russia', *Canadian Slavonic Papers*, xiv, 4, 611–33
—— 'Rodzianko and the Grand Dukes' Manifesto of 1 March 1917', *Canadian Slavonic Papers*, xviii, 2, 154–67
Hosking, G.A., *The Russian Constitutional Experiment: Government and Duma 1907–14* (Cambridge, 1973)
Hutchinson, J.F., 'The February Revolution: myths and realities', *Canadian Slavic Studies*, i, 3, 482–9
Ioffe, H.Z., *Fevralskaya Revolyutsia 1917 goda v anglo-amerikanskoi burzhuaznoi istoriografii* (Moscow, 1970)
Karpovitch, M., 'Two Types of Russian Liberalism: Maklakov and Milyukov' in Simmons, E.J., ed., *Continuity and Change in Russian and Soviet Thought* (Cambridge, Mass., 1955)
Katkov, G., *Russia 1917: the February Revolution* (London, 1967)
Kayden, E., and Antsiferov, A., *The Cooperative Movement in Russia during the War* (Newhaven, 1929)
Kennan, G.F., 'The Breakdown of Tsarist Autocracy' in Pipes, pp. 1–15
Kochan, L., *Russia in Revolution 1890–1918* (London, 1966)
Krivoshein, K.A., *A.V. Krivoshein (1857–1921), ego znachenie v istorii Rossii nachala XX veka* (Paris, 1973)

Laue, T.H. von, 'The Chances for Liberal Constitutionalism', *Slavic Review*, xxiv, 1, 34–46
—— 'The Prospects of Liberal Democracy in Tsarist Russia', in Timberlake, pp. 164–81
Laverychev, V.Y., *Po Tu Storonu Barrikad: iz istorii borby moskovskoi burzhuazii s revolyutsei* (Moscow, 1967)
McKenzie, K.E., 'The Political Faith of Fedor Rodichev', in Timberlake, 42–61
Melgunov, S.P., *Na Putyakh k Dvortsomu Perevorotu* (Paris, 1931)
—— *Legenda o Separatnom Mire* (Paris, 1957)
—— *Martovskie Dni* (Paris, 1961)
Menashe, L., 'A Liberal with Spurs: Alexander Guchkov, a Russian Bourgeois in Politics', *Russian Review*, xxvi, 1, 38–53
Mosse, W.E., 'The February Regime: Prerequisites of Success', *Soviet Studies*, xix, 1, 100–8
Pearson, R., 'Milyukov and the Sixth Kadet Congress', *Slavonic and East European Review*, lii, 131, 210–29
Pipes, R., ed., *Revolutionary Russia* (London, 1968)
Rezanov, A.S., *Shturmovoi Signal P.N. Milyukova* (Paris, 1924)
Riha, T., 'Miliukov and the Progressive Bloc in 1915: a study in last-chance politics', *Journal of Modern History*, xxxii, Mar 1960, 16–24
—— 'Portrait of a Russian Newspaper (*Rech*)', *Slavic Review*, xxii, 4, 663–82
—— *A Russian European: Paul Miliukov in Russian Politics* (New York, 1969)
Rogger, H., 'Russia in 1914', *Journal of Contemporary History*, 1, 4, 95–119
Rosenberg, W.G., 'Kadets and the politics of ambivalence 1905–17', in Timberlake, 139–63
—— *Liberals in the Russian Revolution: the Constitutional Democratic Party 1917–1921* (Princeton, 1974)
Rozental, I.S., 'Russkii liberalism nakanune pervoi mirovoi voiny i taktiki Bolshevikov', *Istoria SSSR*, 1971: 6, 52–70
Schapiro, L.B., 'The Political Thought of the First Provisional Government', in Pipes, 97–113
Smith, N., 'The Role of Russian Freemasonry in the February Revolution: another scrap of evidence', *Slavic Review*, xxvii, 4, 604–8
Stavrou, T.G., ed., *Russia under the Last Tsar* (Minnesota, 1969)
Stone, N., *The Eastern Front 1914–1917* (London, 1975)
Timberlake, C.E., ed., *Essays on Russian Liberalism* (Missouri, 1972)
Treadgold, D.W., 'The Constitutional Democrats and the Russian Liberal Tradition', *Slavic Review*, x, 2, 85–94
Tyutyukin, S.V., ' "Oppositsia Ego Velichestva": partia kadetov v 1905–17 gg.' in Ivanov, L.M., ed., *V.I. Lenin o sotsialnoi strukture i politicheskom stroe kapitalisticheskoi Rossii* (Moscow, 1970), 193–229
Vernadsky, G., *Pavel Nikolaievich Milyukov* (Petrograd, 1917)
Zagorsky, S.O., *The State Control of Industry in Russia during the War* (Newhaven, 1928)
Zimmerman, J.E., 'The Kadets and the Duma 1905–7', in Timberlake, 119–38.

Index